TRANSITIONS FROM STATE SOCIALISM

Economic and Political Change in Hungary and China

YANQI TONG

ROWMAN & LITTLEFIELD PUBLISHERS, INC.
Lanham • Boulder • New York • Oxford

ROWMAN & LITTLEFIELD PUBLISHERS, INC.

Published in the United States of America
by Rowman & Littlefield Publishers, Inc.
4720 Boston Way, Lanham, Maryland 20706

12 Hid's Copse Road
Cummor Hill, Oxford OX2 9JJ, England

British Library Cataloguing in Publication Information Available

Library of Congress Cataloging-in-Publication Data

Tong, Yanqi, 1954–
    Transitions from state socialism : economic and political change in Hungary and
China / Yanqi Tong.
        p.   cm.
    Includes bibliographical references and index.
    ISBN 0-8476-8434-2 (cloth : alk. paper). —ISBN 0-8476-8435-0 (paper : alk. paper)
    1. Hungary—Politics and government—1945–1989. 2. Hungary—Politics and
government—1989– 3. Communism—Hungary. 4. Post-communism—Hungary.
5. Hungary—Economic policy—1945– 6. China—Politics and government—1976–
7. Communism—China. 8. China—Economic policy—1976– I. Title.
DB956.T64   1997
338.9438—dc21   97-25283

ISBN 0-8476-8434-2 (cloth : alk. paper)
ISBN 0-8476-8435-0 (pbk. : alk. paper)

Printed in the United States of America

♾™ The paper used in this publication meets the minimum requirements of American
National Standard for Information Sciences—Permanence of Paper for Printed Library
Materials, ANSI Z39.48–1984.

(2) AF   £4.49   C2

TRANSITIONS FROM STATE SOCIALISM

For my Parents

CONTENTS

FOREWORD

Yanqi Tong is one of a talented group of Chinese scholars who came to the United States for graduate training in the 1980s, and who are now teaching in American universities. I first became acquainted with Yanqi when, as a doctoral candidate in political science at Johns Hopkins University, she won a highly competitive fellowship to conduct her research at the Brookings Institution in Washington, where I was then a Senior Fellow. What impressed me about Yanqi was her ability to see the larger patterns in the political history of modern China, to place those patterns in comparative perspective, and, when necessary, to challenge conventional wisdom.

Transitions from State Socialism embodies all three of these characteristics. In broad brush strokes, it addresses one of the most central issues in contemporary Chinese history: the relationship between economic and political reform. It does so through a systematic comparison with another reforming communist country, Hungary, whose program of political and economic liberalization began in ways similar to China, but subsequently evolved in very different directions. To Yanqi, the puzzle is the sharp contrast between dramatic events of 1989: the steps toward a multiparty system in Hungary in May and the bloody massacre in Beijing in early June.

Yanqi's story of the interplay between political and economic reform in China and Hungary is a drama in several acts. In the first stage, the two countries moved in very similar directions, and for quite similar reasons. The Stalinist model of central planning, public ownership, and low levels of integration with the rest of the world produced economic stagnation in both countries, with relatively low rates of growth and poor-quality goods. This, in turn, undermined the implicit contract between the communist parties of China and Hungary and their own societies: that the communist parties' monopoly over political power would be tolerated because it would produce higher living standards for the Chinese and Hungarian people. This chronic economic stagnation was exacerbated by acute political crises: the Hungarian Uprising of 1956 and the Chinese Cultural Revolution of 1966-76.

Aware of the growing crisis of legitimacy, the communist parties of both countries launched programs of economic reform and political liberalization: Hungary in the late 1960s, China in the early 1980s. The outlines of the two reform programs were remarkably similar. The reformers in both countries significantly relaxed central planning, so as to allow market forces to play a greater role in allocating both consumer goods and the factors of production. They permitted more diverse forms of ownership, including both private ownership and foreign investment, in most sectors of the economy. Although the communist parties were not willing to construct democratic institutions in this initial stage of reform, they relaxed administrative restrictions over many aspects of political and social life and loosened ideological constraints over the discussion of many issues of public policy.

Within several years of their initiation, the Hungarian and Chinese reform programs had produced similar social and political consequences. Along with more rapid economic growth, economic reform created problems such as inflation, inequality, corruption, and uncertainty—all of which became grounds for social grievance. At the same time, political and ideological liberalization permitted the emergence of a popular opposition movement that could express those grievances more openly.

Equally important, both the communist regime and the popular opposition began to divide. The political leadership in China and Hungary split over the speed and extent of reform, whereas the two countries' opposition movements divided into moderates (who advocated peaceful and gradual change with the existing order) and radicals (who wanted a more revolutionary transformation of the system). Yanqi's analysis highlights the importance of the relationship among these various elements of elite and opposition in determining the eventual course of reform in Hungary and China.

Indeed, it was at this point that the paths taken by the two countries sharply diverged. In Hungary, a coalition emerged between the reformers in the leadership and the moderates in the opposition, which produced first an agreement on free elections and then, in 1990, a noncommunist government. In China, in contrast, the Tiananmen demonstrations produced not coalition but confrontation between the political leadership and the opposition. Radicals seized control of the antigovernment protests in Tiananmen Square, while conservatives seized control of the Party establishment. The result was the brutal crackdown on the demonstrators on 4 June 1989 and the repression of dissent thereafter.

But Yanqi's analysis does not stop with the dramatically contrasting events of 1989. She goes on to examine the further political and economic trends in Hungary and China since their evolutionary paths diverged. And it is here that her findings challenge much of the conventional wisdom about the implications of democracy and authoritarianism for countries in transition.

She argues, for example, that Hungary's strategy of political democratization and economic shock therapy has produced serious problems in that country. Radical economic reform—full privatization, thoroughgoing liberalization of prices, and complete integration into the international economy—contributed to a serious recession, high rates of inflation, and severe unemployment in Hungary in the early 1990s. At the same time, Hungary's commitment to democratization produced what Yanqi calls an "impotent state" that lacked the regulatory mechanisms to halt the recession or to guarantee social welfare during the transition. The result was the victory of the former Communist Party in the Hungarian elections of 1994.

On the other hand, the crackdown on dissent in post-Tiananmen China did not produce geographic fragmentation, widespread social unrest, or economic stagnation, as many initially predicted. Instead, China experienced spectacular economic growth under authoritarian rule throughout the 1990s. And yet, Yanqi is not blindly optimistic about China's future. She notes that China may yet disprove the Communist Party's assumption that it can create a market economy and a civil society without constructing democratic political institutions.

Transitions from State Socialism is thus an example of one of the most valuable approaches to the study of comparative communist systems: the structured, focused comparison of cases. Yanqi's comparison of China and Hungary shows that they experienced major similarities in the early stages of reform. She shows the importance of political coalitions between state and society in determining the further evolution of reform in the two countries. And finally, she shows that Hungary has grappled with severe economic and political problems despite the democratic breakthrough of 1989 and that China has experienced remarkable economic success despite the political repression since Tiananmen. In short, Yanqi challenges the conventional wisdom that, in economic and political affairs, all good things will necessarily go together.

Harry Harding, Dean
Elliott School of International Affairs
The George Washington University

ACKNOWLEDGMENTS

I would like to express my most sincere gratitude to Dr. Germaine A. Hoston for her insightful advice and inspirational support throughout the process of writing and revising this book. I am also greatly indebted to Dr. Harry Harding, who offered me invaluable comments and support while I was working on the manuscript. To Drs. Susan Woodward and Andrew Walder, who read my manuscript and provided thoughtful suggestions, I would like to express my appreciation.

Major revisions were completed while I was a research fellow at the Hoover Institute at Stanford University during 1993 and 1994, sponsored by a Title VIII grant. I would like to thank the Hoover Institute for the funding and other resources, without which the completion of this book would have been impossible.

I thank my publisher, Rowman & Littlefield, and especially Susan McEachern for her interest and confidence in the project. I am also grateful to my copy editor, Alice Colwell, for her most able and efficient work.

Sections of chapter 5 of this book were published in 1994 by *Comparative Politics* and in 1995 by *Communist and Post-Communist Studies*. I am grateful to these two journals for permission to adapt my previous articles.

Finally, I would like to thank my best friend, Xiahong Feng, for her unfailing support during those frustrating times of seemingly insurmountable difficulties in academic life.

CHAPTER 1

INTRODUCTION

Comparative Transitions

State socialism is in transition worldwide. Once a monopoly of communist parties who used the mechanism of a planned economy, state socialism is developing in various directions. Some countries, such as those in Eastern Europe and the former Soviet Union, have declared their intentions of moving toward a market economy and democracy. Others, like China, have announced that they would develop a market economy but preserve public ownership and a "people's democratic dictatorship." State socialist countries have followed a wide range of transition strategies, from shock therapy to gradualism and from pluralism to neoauthoritarianism. Despite their different goals and divergent approaches, they have all moved away from the traditional state socialist system, loudly or quietly, violently or peacefully, rapidly or slowly. At turns, outside observers have been excited, gratified, confused, disappointed, or shocked by this seemingly incomprehensible transition.

To enhance our understanding of this uncertain passage, we must begin with a definition of transition from state socialism. State socialism has traditionally been characterized by three basic features: a planned economy with public ownership of the principal means of production, a communist party monopoly of political power, and a communist ideology. The transition from state socialism is therefore a threefold process, involving transformation within these economic, political, and ideological dimensions. Although these three transitions do not necessarily occur simultaneously and may proceed at different speeds and to different degrees, they are closely intertwined.

The transition from state socialism starts when the system begins a sustained departure from traditional practice within any or all three of these spheres. Such a definition excludes the failed reform attempts by Hungary in 1956 and by Czechoslovakia in 1968 because these departures from the traditional system were not sustained. It also rejects the assumption that real transitions start only when the communist regime falls, that is, in Eastern Europe since 1989 and Russia sometime later. Instead, according to this definition, the transition process started in some communist regimes in the 1960s and 1970s, when they implemented market-oriented economic reforms that deviated from traditional state socialism. The dramatic developments in Eastern Europe, China, and the Soviet Union between 1989 and 1991 should be seen only as major milestones in a much longer process of transition, not necessarily as starting or ending points.

In a broader sense, the transition from state socialism is an ongoing process without a definite end. The middle term, however, may involve a number of different developments: in the political sphere, the installation of some form of democracy, preservation of some type of authoritarian rule, rotation in power of successive incompetent governments, or the emergence of revolutionary alternatives; in the economic sphere, the creation of a hybrid bureaucratic market system, the emergence of a corrupt market system, or the stagnation or partial collapse of the economy. These outcomes are determined to a large extent by initial conditions, reform strategies, the balance of the political forces activated during the transition process, as well as international influences.

Hungary and China were once at the forefront of this historical process with their programs of market-oriented economic reform and political liberalization. Hungary pioneered economic reform through the introduction of the market mechanism in 1968. Ten years later, China also devoted itself to comprehensive economic reforms that involved marketization and integration with the world economy. Although political reform was not a priority, both countries witnessed the concurrence of political liberalization and economic reform. For years, the economic and political development of Hungary and China was the most liberal among state socialist countries, and their reform programs were considered models for others.

Yet the two countries had very different political experiences in 1989. In the spring of that year, a massive protest movement in Beijing, initiated by university students and joined by hundreds of thousands of citizens, demanded further political reform. The government declared martial law and, in the face of continuing defiance from the citizens, ordered the army to open fire on demonstrators in Beijing's Tiananmen Square. As a result, an overall retrogression took place in the political sphere. In contrast to the subsequent collapse of the communist regimes in Eastern Europe, China seemed to drop from the forefront of reforming state socialist countries and to isolate itself from the worldwide wave of democratization.

As the world was first fascinated by the scope of the massive political protest and later shocked by the bloody massacre in Beijing, another drama was unfolding in Hungary. In May 1989 the Hungarian Socialist Workers' Party (HSWP) decided to establish a multiparty system. Later that year, in October, the HSWP voted to transform itself into the Hungarian Socialist Party, renouncing Leninist Marxism in favor of European democratic socialism. The Hungarian political venture was followed by the demolition of the Berlin Wall and a wave of dramatic political change in Eastern Europe, where the communist monopoly of power collapsed completely. The first free election of the Hungarian national assembly was held in March 1990. The Hungarian Socialist Party (the former HSWP) lost to the Democratic Forum (an anticommunist party with strong nationalist appeal and a measured approach to economic reform) and thereby became an opposition party.

Despite the euphoria about the apparent worldwide triumph of liberal democracy, the transition from state socialism has continued to present us with puzzles. Even before the shock waves produced by the Tiananmen crisis and the East European revolutions of 1989 had subsided, new tides began to surge. Since 1991, economic reform in China has resumed its momentum, and the economy has sustained an astonishing double-digit growth rate. For the first time, the nonstate sector accounted for more than half of the industrial output and nonagricultural employment in 1993. Moving decisively toward a market economy, China also announced a comprehensive set of financial, fiscal, and enterprise reforms to be implemented in 1994.

In contrast, economic reform in Hungary seemed to move much more slowly and painfully under a democratic political system than observers had expected. After 1990 Hungary experienced negative growth and was plagued by high rates of inflation and unemployment. In May 1994 the voters turned their backs on the incumbent Hungarian Democratic Forum and brought the former reform communists—the Hungarian Socialist Party—back to the center of the political stage.

A series of questions arises from this brief sketch of the reform experiences in Hungary and China. What are the mechanisms inherent in a state socialist system that promote or hinder its transformation? What are the relationships among economic, political, and ideological transitions? Why did some countries succeed in making democratic changes while others' reform programs culminated in political crisis? Can a market economy be successfully introduced without a genuine democracy? Will a transition to democracy necessarily lead to the creation of a market economy? Overall, what are the factors that determine the courses and outcomes of transitions from state socialism? Is there an optimal path of transition from state socialism?

In order to seek some answers to these questions, this book undertakes a comparative study of the transition from state socialism in China and Hungary. Why these two countries? To what extent are they comparable, given that they are so different in almost all cultural, geographical, and historical aspects? In fact, with regard to the issue of the transition from state socialism, China and Hungary are highly comparable. Not only were they both state socialist countries with similar political and economic systems, but both of them have also been on the road of transition from state socialism for a fairly long period. With ups and downs, these two countries have to a large extent kept their reforms alive and ahead of other state socialist countries. It is therefore possible to trace the transition processes in each country over a substantial period of time. Hungary and China have more in common with each other than with other state socialist countries where radical reform attempts were quickly aborted (like Czechoslovakia in 1968), where a weak state was unable to implement any meaningful reforms in the face of strong social opposition (like Poland until the fall of communist rule in 1989), or where economic reform was never seriously attempted (as in the former Soviet Union until 1992).

The similarities of the transitions in these two countries can be emphasized and explained in ways that would be missed in analyses that treat them separately. Their cultural, geographical, and social differences highlight their commonality all the more. Juxtaposing the Hungarian and Chinese experiences can teach us much about the mechanisms of transitions from state socialism and about the dynamics of the breakdown and reconstruction of political and economic institutions.

After their common beginning, the two countries diverged sharply. The drastically different political outcomes in Hungary and China in 1989 brought to the fore many of the characteristics of reforms peculiar to each; an analysis of those events is thus helpful in a comparison of the two countries. The timing, intensity, strategies, and policies of their transitions differed, as did international constraints. The contrast can be explained by a number of factors: conscious choices by the elite and counterelite, differences in the cultural and social contexts, and differences in the world-historical timing and sequence of the transitions. By examining these two extreme points on a spectrum from democratization to repression, we can develop hypotheses about the dilemmas and uncertainties of transition that may be applicable to a larger number of countries.

An Unsolved Question

The comparative study of China and Hungary revolves around the central question of the relationship between economic reform and political change. Economic reform in state socialism has several characteristics. First, it involves the introduction of market relations and elements of private ownership into a previously centrally planned and state-owned economy. Second, it shares the same objective as economic development: to increase wealth and productivity and raise the standard of living. Third, economic reform inevitably means the redistribution of resources, which is likely to generate social disorientation and instability. The outcome of economic reform may not be an efficient market economy but one of several hybrid, corrupt, confusing forms.

In turn, political change in a state socialist system involves a movement toward greater civil liberty and political rights, that is, liberalization and democratization. But again, the outcome may not always be a stable liberal democracy. It can be political instability and a collapse of order, or it can be bloody political repression. The relationships among all these variables of economic reform and political change present a rather complicated picture.

There are basically two groups of arguments on the interplay of these economic and political changes. One group embodies the liberal American belief that "all good things go together," suggesting that the development of the economy or of a market-oriented economy goes hand in hand with progressive political change.[1] The second school of thought suggests a negative relationship between the two, arguing that the economic problems and social tensions generated by economic reform may work against democratic forces and may foster the emergence of authoritarianism. Some also suggest that an authoritarian regime may be better suited for economic development than a democratic one.

Among the first, optimistic group, one argument emphasizes that market relations provide the individual freedom necessary for democracy. The basic assumption is that political freedom derives from economic freedom, and economic freedom is guaranteed only by a free market system. As Milton Friedman points out, "The great advantage of the market is that it permits wide diversity."[2] The development of the market can greatly reduce the range of issues that must be decided through political means, which tend to require substantial conformity. The intimate connection between economics and politics, this market school contends, is that democracy derives from the free operation of the market, whereas economic planning leads to totalitarianism.[3] According to this approach, therefore, the introduction of market relations in state socialist countries would enlarge the scope of individual freedom in the economic sphere and hence create the socioeconomic basis for the operation of democracy.

Another optimistic argument stresses the increasingly powerful demands for progressive political change brought about by socioeconomic development.[4] This proposition, advocated by the traditional modernization school, argues that socioeconomic development will create more diversified interests and bring more economic and technological resources to individuals and groups to be used in exerting their influence. Hence, political participation tends to increase with a person's level of socioeconomic resources.[5] As people are mobilized from their rural, traditional, relatively static settings into the dynamic industrial, literate, media-saturated urban environment, they have an increasing capacity to identify with others and to imagine themselves improving their social statuses and mastering their environments. This growing capacity for empathy, according to Daniel Lerner, leads to demands for political involvement and participation.[6] Therefore, the higher the level of socioeconomic development (as measured by wealth, industrialization, urbanization, and education), the more likely the rise of a democratic regime.

While the first two arguments emphasize the causal link from marketization or economic development to political democracy, the third subgroup of optimists portrays a causal link from politics to economics. They argue that political freedom and democracy are necessary conditions for successful economic development and reform. This line of argument was vigorously pursued by Western policymakers, prodemocracy activist groups, and radical intellectuals in state socialist societies, especially after the events of 1989. They believe in particular that without a political framework that permits civil rights and in which the government officials are accountable to voters, no economic development will be real or sustainable.[7] In addition, they assert that without a democratic political framework, communist regimes will always attempt to impose limits on economic reform once it threatens their monopoly of political power. So far, their arguments reflect a normative conviction rather than a generalization supported by empirical evidence. Earlier scholars, however, suggested that if democracy does not promote economic development, it is at least compatible with it.[8]

Since economic reform in state socialist countries involves the introduction of market mechanisms, the argument about the intimate relationship between the market and democracy is of crucial importance. Similarly, as economic reform may also raise the level of socioeconomic development, theories of traditional modernization could contribute to the explanation of the impact of economic development on the development of political participation and democracy in reforming state socialist countries. However, these approaches suffer from two major shortcomings when applied to reform in state socialism. First, they are unable to explain why or how a totalitarian system would choose to implement a market-oriented economic reform in the first place. Second, they fail to see the negative effects that economic development and reform can have on the political process. In short, such approaches are weak in analyzing both the dynamic and conflictual process of transition. Without taking into account the political conflict and dilemmas inherent in the reform of state socialist systems, any analysis of such reform would be incomplete and inaccurate.

The second group of arguments presents a much gloomier picture concerning the relationship between economic and political change in developing countries than does the first. One line of argument emphasizes the psychological gap between the expectations and the reality of development. It holds that economic development does not necessarily produce a fair distribution of wealth and that no economic growth can be sustained over a long period of time, regardless of the type of economic system. As a result, social grievances over income inequality and unfulfilled expectations may lead to political instability. According to Ted Gurr's model of "relative deprivation," economic development produces popular frustration and in turn results in collective political violence. The fundamental cause of popular frustration is an imbalance between what one gets and what one considers one's due. The greater the scope of deprivation relative to expectations, the more likely violent behavior becomes.[9] James Davies's "J-curve" model further elaborates the way in which unmet socioeconomic expectations are a source of frustration. According to this model, revolutions (the extreme form of political conflict) are most likely to occur when a prolonged period of objective economic and social development is followed by a short period of sharp reversal. The economic development in the former period would produce an expectation of continued growth to satisfy needs. When the actual development declines, the gap between what people want and what they get becomes intolerable and creates anxiety and frustration.[10]

The models of relative deprivation and the J-curve suggest that unfulfilled societal expectations are an important source of political conflict. These explanations fit well with the experience of reforming state socialist countries. Economic reform is likely to generate high expectations but is unlikely to satisfy these expectations either immediately or for a long period. Looking at the recent experiences of Eastern Europe and Latin America, Adam Przeworski asserts that the efforts to introduce market mechanisms into a planned economy necessarily lead to a temporary deterioration in aggregate consumption, because of factors such as inflation and unemployment. This "valley of transition" is socially costly and politically risky,[11] as people will be more likely to feel deprivation. Such transition will increase instability and erode social support for reform and may result in the abandonment of democracy, reform, or both.

In addition to the unfulfilled socioeconomic expectations, unfulfilled political expectations also serve as potential sources of conflicts. Noting that "the opposition of the urban intelligentsia to the government is a pervasive characteristic . . . of almost every type of modernizing society," Samuel Huntington has warned that reform could well raise political expectations and thus exacerbate political discontent among the urban intelligentsia:

> The student, in particular, becomes exposed to the modern world and to the advanced nations of the West. In his mind two great gaps exist, one between the principles of modernity—equality, justice, community, economic well-being—and their realization in his own society, and a second between the actual conditions which exist in the advanced nations of the world and those prevailing in his own society. . . . The student thus becomes ashamed of and alienated from his own society; he becomes filled with the desire to reconstruct it completely to bring it into the front rank of nations. Divorced from his family and from traditional norms and behavior patterns, the student identifies all the more completely with the abstract standards and principles of modernity.[12]

Such alienation and relative political deprivation are common characteristics in reforming state socialist societies. Limited political liberalization loosens the rigid ideological control over the society. People exposed to Western liberal ideas, especially intellectuals, become more and more alienated from the existing political situation and are impatient for rapid change. The unsatisfied political expectations are even more likely than economic disappointment to generate radical tendencies and produce political conflict, and sometimes crisis, between the intellectuals and the regime.

The second set of pessimistic arguments posits that the contradiction between economic development and existing political institutions will result in the maintenance or restoration of authoritarian rule. Using the experiences of modernization in Third World countries, Huntington produced a theory of political decay that stresses the negative relationship between economic development and political liberalization. His principal thesis is that the increasing social mobilization and political participation brought about by modernization often exceed the capacities of political institutions of the given society, creating political instability and disorder. Instead of a trend toward democracy as predicted by the traditional modernization school, there is an "erosion of democracy" and a tendency toward autocratic military and one-party regimes. Not only does social and economic modernization produce political instability, Huntington further argues, but the degree of instability is also related positively to the rate of modernization.[13]

The theory of bureaucratic authoritarianism reiterates this negative relationship between economic development and democratic change. In response to the proliferation of military regimes in the relatively well-developed economies in Latin America, the theory of bureaucratic authoritarianism raised the hypothesis that "in late-developing nations, more advanced levels of industrialization may coincide with the collapse of democracy and an increase in inequality."[14] According to this argument, at certain stages of industrialization in late-developing countries, popular democracy that breeds strikes, demonstrations, and disorder may become intolerable to the industrial elites (technocrats and the army). These elites will then restore authoritarian rule in order to continue industrialization.

Not only may economic development or reform create political instability in a regime, but the process of political liberalization may itself produce violent conflict that reduces the chance for democracy. In their attempt to explain the uncertainty of the transition from authoritarian regimes toward "something else," Guillermo O'Donnell and Philippe Schmitter have offered some insights into the political aspect of the process. They believe that the attainment of political democracy is preceded without exception by a significant liberalization, which is also likely to generate violence, frequent protests, strikes, and demonstrations. If these events become widespread and recurrent, the prospects for political democracy are drastically reduced.[15]

Based on a similar line of reasoning is the argument that the political order provided by an authoritarian regime would be more conducive to economic development. The emphasis on political order in the process of economic reform, known as "neoauthoritarianism," has been popular in China. The advocates of neoauthoritarianism, citing the experiences of Taiwan, South Korea, and Singapore, argue that economic reform will inevitably cause pain and therefore provoke opposition; it is necessary to have an authoritarian system to overcome that opposition. Only political stability, presumably achieved through political control, could provide the necessary environment for successful economic reform.[16]

In short, this second group of theories suggests that the interaction of economic development and reform and democratic change is not a linear process and not entirely positive. It first cautions that socioeconomic modernization, political liberalization, and economic reform may not generate steady development in the short term. Therefore, the heightened economic and political expectations may lead to intense frustration and consequently to violent conflicts. Second, the gap between rapid social mobilization and the limited institutional accommodation tends to produce political instability. Finally, at certain stages, economic reform or economic development may bring about consequences that are politically intolerable to the regime and may therefore result in, or require, authoritarian rule rather than democracy.

The theories in the second group seem to explain the sources of political conflict in a dynamic economic process. Yet scholars return time and again to the theories in the optimistic group, either to support them or attack them, suggesting their continued vitality. The relationship between politics and economics remains an unsolved question and continues to pose challenges to our conventional knowledge and wisdom. This book will test to what extent these theories are applicable to the study of transitions from state socialism and to what extent the experiences of these transitions can contribute to the solutions to this question.

A Relational Approach

The transition from state socialism involves a comprehensive phenomenon that requires a comprehensive approach. This book attempts to develop a general comparative framework in which the conflicts, dilemmas, crises, and outcomes of transition might be located. In this book I adopt a relational approach to study the interactions of two sets of actors (the political leadership and the society) in three processes (ideological, economic, and political transitions) over a sequence of four phases.

The study of politics can be divided into two major approaches: society-centered and state-centered. Until very recently the latter dominated the study of state socialist systems. Totalitarianism, which emphasizes the omnipotent role of the party-state in exercising total control over the political, social, and economic lives of society, was the most influential model. Although this model has been losing ground since the 1960s, the state-dominant structure of state socialist systems continues to inspire scholarly interest in the state and the actors within it. For example, the recently popular model of fragmented authoritarianism argues that authority below the very peak of the political system is fragmented and disjointed, and the central leaders must "bargain" with subordinate units in order to adopt and carry out their policies, which are often dramatically reshaped in the process of implementation.[17]

The emergence of the Solidarity movement in Poland in the 1970s brought a shift to society-centered approaches in the study of state socialism.[18] The 1989 Tiananmen protest movement in China and the collapse of the communist regimes in Eastern Europe subsequently generated tremendous academic interest in the development of civil society in state socialist systems. Students of communism discovered that a civil society, characterized by a network of independent social organizations, was a key factor in bringing down the communist regimes in Eastern Europe and would effectively challenge the remaining authoritarian systems elsewhere in the world.[19] The strength of this approach lies in its ability to explain and describe dynamic changes within state socialist systems. It portrays the civil society as exerting pressure on the regime to change. However, a society-centered approach cannot fully explain how societal autonomy could develop under state socialism in the first place or why civil society is larger and more effective in some state socialist countries than in others.

The transition from state socialism is in some respects the process of shifting from a stage of prevalent state dominance to a stage of more societal autonomy, or from totalitarianism to pluralism. The approaches adopted to study this transition therefore reflect the same shift, that is, from statist approaches to society-centered ones. But as the state remains an important actor in the transition, particularly in formulating and implementing the reform policies, and as the newly acquired societal autonomy has not been fully institutionalized, we should adopt a "transitional" approach that focuses on both state and society and on their relations with each other. Although such a relational approach is arguably preferable for all stages, it is especially applicable during this transition period.

The relational approach assumes that politics arises at the meeting point between state and society. It is particularly interested in the objectives and resources that states and societal actors bring to their interactions with one another.[20] The relational approach does not assume, however, that the relationship between state and society is zero-sum with regard to either power or objectives. That the state is strong does not necessarily imply that the society is weak; conversely, a weak society may be governed by a weak state and not necessarily by a strong one.[21] The state and society may share a wide range of objectives, laying the groundwork for a cooperative relationship. Only if they perceive each other's objectives as incompatible are they likely to develop a confrontational relationship.

Moreover, a relational approach assumes that the power and interests of state and society are determined at least in part through their mutual interaction.[22] The policies of the state can empower certain social groups by granting them more access to resources that the state controls. The state's decisions on social, economic, and political matters will create new interests among the sectors of society affected by those decisions. Conversely, unwritten social contracts between the state and its various societal constituencies may help define the objectives of the state, constrain its power, or increase its resources.

By adopting a relational approach, then, this book focuses on the interactions between different groups of actors from the state and society at various stages of reform. Of particular importance is the formation of different coalitions among actors of the state and society, which shape the courses and the outcomes of transitions from state socialism.

Two Sets of Actors

The first set of actors comprises various factions within the state. In a state socialist system, the Party leadership plays a dominant role in the political process of the state. Yet the Party leadership is not a single and monistic unit; it contains a broad spectrum of factions with different interests, perceptions, and objectives. Moreover, the composition and strength of those factions can change in the course of reform. This book adopts a threefold division among conservatives, moderates, and reformers within the Party leadership.

The conservatives are those who are staunchly committed to communist orthodoxy and who believe that they have a mission to eliminate all traces of capitalist pathologies from the country's life. They acknowledge the problems of socialism but prefer "perfecting" rather than reforming the system. Moderates consist of those who advocate a limited reform program. On the one hand, they realize that the system needs reform; on the other, they do not want the reform programs to endanger the existing regime. They are potential allies for either conservatives or reformers. The reformers are willing to institute far more fundamental reforms, ranging from market-oriented economic reform to political liberalization and even democratization. They are the driving force behind the transition from state socialism. But this does not mean that the reformers do not share some of the basic values of an authoritarian regime, such as the concern with surviving in office and a disposition to use repression.

This first set of actors shares several characteristics. First, neither reformers nor conservatives alone are likely to pursue or obstruct reform successfully. They have to create informal coalitions with the moderates or seek support from various social sectors, which opens a variety of possibilities for the course of transition. For example, in preparation for economic reform in Hungary, Janos Kadar struck a compromise with the population, rallied intellectuals to design the reform program, and managed to neutralize the Soviet objection to his reform program. Deng Xiaoping also formed a broad reform coalition and forced the resignation of Hua Guofeng, then chairman of the Party, who preferred to "perfect" the system.

Second, the composition of the factions varies over time. There is no fixed membership for each group. As the objectives of the transition become broader, and the oldest generation of conservatives falls out of contention, some previous moderates may object to further changes and join the ranks of conservatives, and previous reformers may split into new moderates and advocates of more radical reforms. In this respect the formation of factions is more likely to be issue-specific and less likely to be based purely on personal connections. For example, Kadar, the patron of reform in Hungary, had become an obstacle to further reform in the late 1980s. Deng Liqun, whom many considered the staunchest conservative in China, was in fact a member of the reformist coalition against Hua Guofeng in 1978.

Finally, at critical moments the divisions among these factions within the leadership are likely to send ambiguous signals to both allies and opponents in society. The typical case is the 1989 Tiananmen protest movement. Aware that there was opposition to political repression within the leadership, the protesters at times acted under the illusion that the conservative force was vulnerable, and the movement would prevail if only they could persist a little longer.

The second set of actors includes the intellectuals, rural peasants and urban workers, political opposition groups, and social and economic organizations. These societal actors are thus considerably more diverse than the political leadership of the state. Reform programs at various stages will promote or hurt the collective interests of each sector of society by creating new resources or redistributing old ones. Reform can also create new sectors that did not exist before, such as entrepreneurs. The gains and losses of these groups will affect their interactions with the state.

The intellectual circles have a strong interest in the freedom of acquiring and disseminating alternative sources of information. They are natural allies of the reformers in initiating programs that break away from traditional state socialist systems. The radical elements of the intellectual sectors are also most likely to form opposition groups to criticize and challenge a repressive regime.

Peasants and workers constitute the majority of the population. They are concerned more with concrete socioeconomic conditions than with new ideas. Their material gains and losses under reform will evolve into support and resistance to the regime and its policies, the balance of which will help determine the stability of the transition and the survival of the regime. For example, given more freedom and opportunities to enrich themselves, the Chinese peasants are the beneficiaries, and therefore the supporters, of reform. On the contrary, workers in general are the beneficiaries of the traditional planned economy, under which they enjoyed guaranteed employment, health care, housing, and pensions. They will feel threatened by reform measures that intend to dismantle the old system, and they will support the regime only so far as the welfare system remains relatively intact.

The effectiveness of these actors in promoting their demands depends on their economic resources, their numbers, and their ability to organize. The emerging social and economic organizations, such as various intellectual salons, cultural clubs, professional associations, and private enterprises, exemplify the new wealth and autonomy that certain segments of society have gained during the transition. These organizations are gradually developing their own sphere of operation and may play an important role in shaping the future course of transition.

The opposition, by directly challenging the regime, represents the most radical tendencies of the parts of society that prefer fundamental change. It is these groups that are the most likely to exert pressure for democracy and, if they are well organized, may negotiate with the regime for such a change. They are also the most likely to propel the system into crisis if they are able to mobilize all the dissatisfied social sectors on their side in a massive upsurge. There are both radical and moderate currents within the opposition: The moderates prefer a peaceful and gradual change and are more willing to cooperate with the reformers in the leadership to push for progress, whereas the radicals ask for a more revolutionary transformation and often hold uncompromising positions when dealing with the state. As in any political spectrum, the group that holds the fundamental values tends to believe in their own moral superiority, and the moderates have to justify their compromise as a tactical move.

Three Transitions

As noted, transitions from state socialism have three dimensions: economic, political, and ideological. The notion of economic transition has a straightforward meaning, usually summarized by the two terms "marketization" and "privatization." There is little disagreement about marketization, which involves the introduction of market mechanisms into the operation of the economic system. According to a detailed definition given by Ed Hewett, a market-oriented economic reform should include the simultaneous change of the price system to reflect more freely the shifts in supply and demand; the reform of the financial system to increase the authority of the banks over competing applications for funds; the restructuring of the labor system to enable enterprises to compete more freely for labor; the development of the legal system to define clearly the rights and obligations of enterprises and to regulate monopolies, unfair competition, price gouging, and so on, as well as the transformation of the role of the Party to allow enterprises to operate without Party interference.[23]

"Privatization," however, is an overly simplified term for the second aspect of the economic transition from state socialism. As state ownership is the mainstay and the microeconomic basis for the entire planned economy, which in turn is the major source of rigidity and inefficiency, changes in the form of ownership are inevitable. Yet the reform experiences in state socialist systems have demonstrated that the costs and consequences of privatization are controversial. Rather than "privatization," therefore, I use the term "diversification," which implies a much broader range of alternatives to state ownership, such as collective ownership, government contracting, and foreign investment.

Political transition is generally defined as a continuing process of "liberalization" and "democratization." The transition usually begins with liberalization, which, according to O'Donnell and Schmitter, is "the process of making effective certain rights that protect both individuals and social groups from arbitrary or illegal acts committed by the state or third parties."[24] They define democratization as a process in which the rules and procedures of a democratic system are applied to political institutions previously governed by other principles, expanded to include persons not previously enjoying such rights and obligations, or extended to cover issues not previously subject to citizen participation.

Although the attainment of political democracy is preceded without exception by a significant, if unsteady, liberalization, liberalization can exist without democratization. Political liberalization is a process of decompression, which may unleash tremendous political energy. If political liberalization generates widespread violence, frequent protests, and recurrent strikes, the prospects for political democracy are drastically reduced. An authoritarian regime may be willing to permit liberalization but not democratization, for the former does not impose an immediate threat to its power. Likewise, reformers within the leadership are more willing to support democratization, whereas the moderates seek to draw the line at liberalization.

Compared with the economic and political transitions, the ideological transition has a less clear sense of direction and purpose. Ideology is a set of values and norms that provides a basis for judgment and a guide to social behavior. Under state socialism, orthodox Marxist ideology provided a justification for the political and economic systems. For the reforms to commence, this justification has to be deconstructed. The transition from orthodox Marxist ideology can therefore be characterized as "ideological liberalization," for lack of a better term. It starts with a breaking away from orthodox communist ideology—a rejection of the concepts of class struggle and dictatorship of the proletariat and of all the related paradigms within which the intellectual and artistic life of the system must operate. However, it is not at all clear what its replacement would be. Although many people in the West would prefer to see liberalism replace communism, it is more likely that some deep-rooted cultural nationalism may fill in the void left by Marxist ideology.[25] Of all three transitions, ideological change can occur earliest and fastest, and it is therefore often the case that ideological transition leads the other two. The reformist elite initiates ideological liberalization to redefine official ideology to justify the reform programs. The sudden inflow of alternative information, however, changes people's perceptions much more rapidly than any changes in the political and economic structures, which possess more inertia. It was the collapse of faith in communism and romanticized expectations of capitalism that mobilized the masses to challenge and finally bring down the communist regimes in Eastern Europe and the former Soviet Union.

But other aspects of the ideological transition seem to be among the last to be accomplished. Moral values, which were usually associated with communist ideology, are likely to further deteriorate during the chaotic and unstable processes of political and economic transition. The absence of a value system that can provide norms for social behavior will impede the other two transitions, because democratic and market institutions require an appropriate cultural foundation if they are to function properly. Right after the 1989 revolutions in Eastern Europe, Ralf Dahrendorf pointed out that the construction of a democratic constitution and market institutions would take several months to a couple of years but that the growth of civility and a sense of citizenship would probably require several generations.[26] He might have underestimated the complexities that come with economic and political transitions, but he did pinpoint the immense difficulties involved with a successful ideological transition.

All three transitions are dynamic processes. All involve psychological and institutional adjustments, which may be very costly in both economic and human terms. A transition that causes minimum human suffering, economic disruption, and social instability requires a farsighted strategy, prudent policies, and capable authorities to carry them out. The price of change is high, and whether the eventual change will be worth the price cannot be known in advance.

Four Phases

The analytical framework of this book therefore traces the interactions between two sets of actors from state and society through three transition processes. For the convenience of analysis, their interactions are examined over a sequence of four stages, although in reality these four phases overlap with no clear demarcation among them.

Phase One

Phase one is the commencement. The reformers within the leadership formed a coalition with the moderates, overpowered the conservatives, mobilized social support, and initiated reforms. Although economic reform was the priority on the reform agenda, the implementation of a market-oriented economic reform was impossible within a rigid ideological and political environment and required a certain degree of ideological and political liberalization. Therefore, in both Hungary and China, ideological controls were loosened to formulate more flexible economic reform policy, administrative controls were reduced to encourage a livelier economy, and political controls over society were relaxed to mobilize various sectors of the society to participate more actively in the operation of the economy.

Ideological and political liberalization not only made economic reform conceptually and operationally possible but also rallied broad social support for the reform coalition. This strengthened the position of the reform coalition in its struggle with the conservatives. Yet various social forces did not play a crucial role in the commencement stage because the political system was still highly authoritarian, offering little room for societal initiatives. It was more a matter of elite choice.

There were serious limits to this preliminary political reform. The unique position of the reformers in state socialist countries determined the nature of political change. They had to operate within a constrained environment and adopt a centrist approach in pursuing their reforms. Committing themselves to reforms on the one hand and to the Party leadership on the other, reformist leaderships in both China and Hungary were constantly conducting a two-front struggle: They had to fight the orthodox left to encourage innovation and at the same time had to contest the deviations of the right to maintain their legitimacy. In particular, the reformist coalition did not hesitate to suppress any challenges to the Party leadership.

Phase Two

In the second phase, the ongoing ideological and political liberalization and economic reform increased the autonomy of the society. By departing from traditional conceptions of economic structure, economic reform continuously required redefinition of the notion of socialism, which in turn reinforced the process of ideological opening. Economic reform in Hungary and China diversified the structure of ownership by allowing the nonstate sector to prosper, changed the labor system by granting job mobility, and pluralized the sources of the supply of goods and services. All these measures enlarged the range of individual freedom in economic life. It was on this basis that various social groups started to gain autonomy, wealth, and access to political resources.

However, economic reform also engendered social grievances over the inflation, inequality, and corruption that had developed in the course of structural transition. The psychological and institutional adjustment to a market system took much longer than people had first imagined. As the state tried to extricate itself from its previous paternalistic function, the society continued to hold it accountable for many things it had been responsible for in the past. The implicit social contract, under which the state was fully responsible for the socioeconomic welfare of the population, later became the most serious problem in economic transition.

Phase Three

Societal pressures for political reform emerged in the third phase. The introduction of new ideas and values and the creation of new political resources by economic reform generated new political preferences and mobilized various groups in society. Together these factors stimulated increasing societal demands for further political reform.

There were several types of societal challenge to the political establishment. One was a passive challenge, which was mainly the withdrawal of moral support for the regime. It resulted from the spiritual vacuum left by the abandonment of orthodox communism without the adoption of an alternative ideology. It was also exacerbated by the socioeconomic grievances caused by economic reform. The typical expression of the passive challenge in Hungary and China was pervasive mass alienation, characterized by a crisis of faith and the widespread corruption.

The second challenge was produced by the emergence of a civil society during the transition processes. Ideological and political liberalization left space for the development of independent civil organizations, while economic reform provided a financial basis. In itself, this incipient civil society did not reject the validity of Marxist ideology or challenge the legitimacy of one-party rule; therefore, it did not threaten the survival of the political system. But by creating a set of institutions and behavior that could not be explained by established doctrine or effectively regulated by the existing political system, the development of civil society exerted pressures for change in the previous political framework and the operating principles of the political system. In the late 1980s, a civil society was emerging in Hungary and China, especially with the proliferation of private enterprises.

The third challenge generally took the form of organized protest movements. It raised direct political demands to the regime, ranging from removal of certain officials to the development of democratic procedures. This active challenge was made possible by ideological and political liberalization that allowed the introduction of democratic ideas and tolerated greater dissent. It was also supported by a more economically autonomous social base. The organized protest movement produced the most visible challenge to the political establishment. In Hungary the opposition groups enjoyed a semilegal status, while in China such challenge came mainly from student demonstrations.

Phase Four

Phase four involved the adaptation of the political leadership to these new societal challenges. In both Hungary and China, political leadership made certain ideological and institutional adaptations, accepting the notion of pluralism and making the legislature and mass organizations more responsive.

In the fourth phase, various groups within the political leadership and society had to set up rules to govern the new political game. In particular they needed to learn how to negotiate and ultimately form coalitions with one another. Both the political leadership and the society were fragmented by the different economic interests and political orientations that developed during the reform process. The interaction between the strategies of the emerging societal protest movements and the policies proposed by factions within the political leadership in the fourth phase determined the directions and extent of political change, whether democratization, repression, or instability.

In a discussion of the general process of transition to democracy, Adam Przeworski has suggested that the various possible outcomes of political transition are the result of different coalitions among factions within the regime and the opposition. According to Przeworski, when reformers within the regime ally with their hard-line colleagues, and moderates in the opposition ally with radicals, the authoritarian regime usually survives. But when reformers within the regime form an alliance with moderates in the opposition, the outcome is likely to be democracy, as long as reformers can neutralize the hard-liners, and moderate opposition can control the radicals. Other coalitions lead to other outcomes. For example, if reformers join the alliance of moderates and radicals in the opposition, they are accepting democracy without guarantees of their own survival. If the moderates join the alliance with reformers and hard-liners, there will be liberalization without democratization.[27]

All these strategic choices are determined primarily by the perceptions and calculations of the more flexible actors on both sides, that is, the reformers within the regime and the moderates within the opposition. A key factor is whether a coalition emerges between the reformist factions in the party leadership and the more responsible and moderate elements of the political opposition. The formation of such a coalition linking reformers in both state and society may create a political context that facilitates the emergence and adoption of a wide variety of economic and political initiatives. As we already know, the Hungarians opted for this choice and the Chinese did not.

Beyond Phase Four

The Tiananmen massacre in China and democratization in Hungary are the landmarks in the middle range of the long transition away from state socialism. Hungary made a break with its previous political system by introducing democratic pluralism. The temporary alliance between the reform communists and moderates in opposition disappeared when the communists were defeated in the 1990 election. However, economic transition did not produce visible progress and became more painful. The Hungarian experience demonstrated that a democratic political system is no guarantee of the success of economic reform.

China has continued along the neoconservative path of transition, transforming itself into a developmental authoritarian system. Despite continuing disagreement over the pace of economic reform, reformers and conservatives continued their alliance to prevent Western-style democratic reform. Events in China have proved, at least for the time being, that the democratization of the political system and the privatization of the economic system are not prerequisites for rapid marketization and economic development.

Thus the economic reform programs in China and Hungary remain quite comparable, although the two countries' political systems are now dramatically different. This raises two questions for the future: Will those political differences affect the countries' abilities to implement and sustain painful economic reform? And will economic reform eventually lead to the reconvergence of their political systems? The transition from state socialism is far from complete.

Intervening Factors

Several intervening factors affect the different strategies and choices made by the protest movement and the political leadership in each country: the rates and timing of economic, political, and ideological change during the reform process; the political culture of each country; the political learning of the state and societal elites; and the international environment.

Although the pace and timing of economic, political, and ideological transitions reflect the choices made by the leadership in the early stages of transition, they in turn greatly affect their later decisions. In general, the faster the rate of change, the greater the social disorientation and the greater the chance of a mobilization of political grievances. The protest movement that results is in turn likelier to adopt radical strategies that the existing political establishment cannot accommodate, and the Party leadership will be more inclined to use repression. As all three transitions generate negative outcomes at one point or another—economic reform produces a "transition valley," ideological liberalization leads to a spiritual vacuum, political liberalization grants freedom without proper rules—the sequence of these transitions may be of particular importance. It is desirable to avoid a situation in which the low points all come together at the same time.

Political culture shapes the political orientations of the masses as well as the elite. At the elite level, it affects the strategies and choices of both the protest movement and the political leadership. Democracy begins to emerge when a relatively small circle of elites decides to accept the existence of political diversity and to solve their conflicts peacefully through democratic procedures.[28] These political elites have to accept the proposition that democratic institutions are relatively effective for the fulfillment of their objectives. If compromise and reconciliation with political adversaries, the essence of modern democratic politics, are completely outside the conceptual framework of both the leadership and opposition, there is less chance that they will adopt democratic solutions to their conflict.

At the mass level, political culture plays an important role in the transition to and maintenance of democracy because democracy requires of its citizens a distinctive set of political values and orientations: moderation, tolerance, civility, efficacy, knowledge, and participation. The political culture that is particularly appropriate for democratic political systems is a civic culture of pluralism, consensus, and diversity, with a particular mix of parochial, subject, and participant orientations in the population.[29] Authoritarian political cultures stand in contrast to this democratic ideal. For example, the Confucian culture tends to emphasize loyalty to the collectivity over freedom for the individual, to stress order over conflict, to favor paternalistic and personal political authority, and therefore to neglect institutional constraints on the exercise of power.[30]

The practice of state socialism also bred its own brand of political culture. With the strong state control over their individual lives, the population developed a pronounced feeling of "us" versus "them" in their attitudes toward the regime and a widespread irresponsibility toward public affairs and public property. Yet they also regarded the state as the caretaker that should be responsible for everything, even when the state wanted to withdraw from its previous intervention in economic affairs. These distinctive features of a state socialist political culture constrain the transition from state socialism.

The absence of a civic culture, however, does not preclude the possibility of a transition to democracy. Another crucial intervening factor is the process of political learning of the elites inside and outside the regime. The concept of political learning holds that "beliefs are not fixed immutably in childhood and that they can be affected by political events."[31] Political elites learn lessons about what works and what does not. They learn from past errors and from the success and failure of their counterparts abroad. They also learn from interactions with other political elites and from the development of new political ideas. During this political learning process, old beliefs are discredited and new values are established. This change of values needs not be universal, but a "critical mass" of learners, both incumbents and oppositionists, must develop before the risky game of building democracy can begin.[32] A word of caution here: this process can be double-edged. The poor performance of new democracies may persuade elites in other countries not to follow suit.

Although the transition from state socialism is primarily a domestic affair, it cannot be isolated from the international environment. State socialism was a worldwide movement. In Hungary the communist regime was created and later consolidated with the help of the Soviet Union, so the Soviet Union became part of the Hungarian political establishment. Before the collapse of the Soviet empire in 1989, the Soviet Union in effect constantly set the parameters for economic and political reform in East European countries. The possibility of Soviet intervention was not only a threat but also a reality in some countries. This factor was a crucial consideration in the domestic bargaining process among reformers, conservatives, and opposition in Hungary.

The international environment can also be part of the context for change. What happens in one country may be inspired by or inspire changes in other countries, as was evident in the eventful year of 1989. Some people argue that the Tiananmen massacre in China taught the communist elite in Eastern Europe to avoid such a bloody result. China was unfortunate, they believe, for if Chinese people had waged their protest after the collapse of communism in Eastern Europe, they might have had a much better chance of success. A recent counterargument suggests that what is happening in Eastern Europe and the former Soviet Union should make the Chinese feel lucky that the Tiananmen incident occurred prior to the events in Eastern Europe, for China could have experienced much worse chaos and disaster had the protest movement prevailed. Both arguments imply that the political learning process of the elites can be strongly affected by international experience.

NOTES

1. For a discussion of American liberalism, see Robert A. Packenham, *Liberal America and the Third World: Political Development Ideas in Foreign Aid and Social Science* (Princeton, N.J.: Princeton University Press, 1973).

2. Milton Friedman, *Capitalism and Freedom* (Chicago: University of Chicago Press, 1962), p. 15.

3. Friedrich A. Hayek, *The Road to Serfdom* (Chicago: University of Chicago Press, 1944); and George Stigler, *The Citizen and the State: Essays on Regulation* (Chicago: University of Chicago Press, 1975).

4. Seymour M. Lipset, "Some Social Requisites of Democracy," *American Political Science Review* 53 (1959): 75.

5. Robert Dahl, *Preface to Democratic Theory* (Chicago: University of Chicago Press, 1956); Sidney Verba, Norman H. Nie, and Jae-on Kim, *Participation and Political Equality* (Cambridge: Cambridge University Press, 1978), pp. 57-59, 292-93.

6. Daniel Lerner, *The Passing of Traditional Society* (New York: The Free Press, 1958).

7. Various pieces of this argument appear throughout the journals published by pro-democracy activist groups, such as *Zhongguo Zhi Chun* and *Beijing Zhi Chun*.

8. William McCord argued in the 1960s that political development should be parallel to social and economic development and strongly objected the notion that "freedom" should be sacrificed for the sake of "bread." *The Springtime of Freedom: Evolution of Developing Societies* (New York: Oxford University Press, 1965).

9. Ted Robert Gurr, *Why Men Rebel* (Princeton, N. J.: Princeton University Press, 1970).

10. James C. Davies, "Toward a Theory of Revolution," *American Sociological Review* 27:1 (1962): 5-18.

11. Adam Przeworski, *Democracy and the Market: Political and Economic Reforms in Eastern Europe and Latin America* (Cambridge: Cambridge University Press, 1991), pp. 136-37.

12. Samuel P. Huntington, *Political Order in Changing Societies* (New Haven: Yale University Press, 1968), pp. 369-73.

13. Ibid.

14. David Collier, ed., *The New Authoritarianism in Latin America* (Princeton, N.J.: Princeton University Press, 1979), pp. 1-31.

15. Guillermo O'Donnell and Philippe C. Schmitter, *Transitions from Authoritarian Rule: Prospects for Democracy: Tentative Conclusions About Uncertain Democracies* (Baltimore: The Johns Hopkins University Press, 1986).

16. There were some heated discussions on "neoauthoritarianism" in late 1988 and early 1989. See, for example, "Guanyu xinquanwei zhuyi de taolun" [Discussions on neoauthoritarianism], *Xinhua Wenzhai* 4 (1989): 1-9. It is also believed that the think-tanks of the former Party secretary Zhao Ziyang advocated this model.

17. Kenneth Lieberthal, ed., *Bureaucracy, Politics, and Decision Making in Post-Mao China* (Berkeley: University of California Press, 1992).

18. Andrew Arato, "Civil Society against the State: Poland 1980-1981," *Telos*, no. 47 (Spring 1981): 23-47; and "Empire vs. Civil Society," *Telos*, no. 50 (Winter 1981-82): 19-48.

19. For example, Frederick Starr, "Soviet Union: A Civil Society," *Foreign Policy* 70 (Spring 1988): 26-41; Lawrence Sullivan, "The Emergence of Civil Society in China, Spring 1989," in *The Chinese People's Movement: Perspectives on Spring 1989*, ed. Tony Saich (New York: M. E. Sharpe, 1990), pp. 126-44; Vladimir Tismaneanu, ed., *In Search of Civil Society: Independent Peace Movements in the Soviet Bloc* (New York: Routledge, 1990); Chandran Kukathus, David Lowell, and William Maley, eds., *The Transition from Socialism: State and Civil Society in the USSR* (Melbourne: Longman Cheshire, 1991); Thomas Gold, "Party-State Versus Society in China," in *Building a Nation-State: China after Forty Years*, ed. Joyce Kallgren (Berkeley: Institute of East Asian Studies, University of California, 1990), pp. 125-51; and Martin Whyte, "Urban China: A Civil Society in the Making?" in *State and Society in China: The Consequences of Reform*, ed. Arthur Lewis Rosenbaum (Boulder, Colo.: Westview Press, 1992), pp. 103-20.

20. Theda Skocpol, "Bringing the State Back In: Strategies of Analysis in Current Research," in *Bringing the State Back In*, eds. Peter Evans, Dietrich Rueschemeyer, and Theda Skocpol (Cambridge: Cambridge University Press, 1985), pp. 3-37.

21. Alfred Stepan, "State Power and the Strength of Civil Society in the Southern Cone of Latin America," in *Bringing the State Back In*, pp. 317-43.

22. Ibid.

23. Ed A. Hewett, *Reforming the Soviet Economy: Equality Versus Efficiency* (Washington D.C.: The Brookings Institution, 1988), pp. 14-16.

24. O'Donnell and Schmitter, *Tentative Conclusions about Uncertain Democracies*, pp. 10-11.

25. Samuel Huntington, "The Clash of Civilizations?" *Foreign Affairs* 72, no. 3 (Summer 1993): 22-49.

26. Ralf Dahrendorf, *Reflections on the Revolution in Europe* (New York: Random House, 1990), pp. 105-7.

27. Przeworski, *Democracy and the Market*, pp. 66-79.

28. Dankwart Rustow, "Transitions of Democracy: Toward a Dynamic Model," *Comparative Politics* 2, no. 3 (April 1970): 355; and Robert Dahl, *Polyarchy: Participation and Opposition* (New Haven: Yale University Press, 1971), p. 36.

29. Gabriel Almond and Sidney Verba, *The Civic Culture* (Princeton, N.J.: Princeton University Press, 1963), pp. 13-14.

30. Lucian Pye, *Asian Power and Politics: The Cultural Dimensions of Authority* (Cambridge, Mass.: Belknap Press, 1985), pp. 326-41.

31. Ibid., p. 274.

32. Nancy Bermeo, "Democracy and the Lessons of Dictatorship," *Comparative Politics* 24, no. 2 (April 1992): 273-91.

CHAPTER 2

HUNGARY AND CHINA UNDER STATE SOCIALISM

The Legacies

Historical Settings

The different historical settings of China and Hungary provided different contexts for the operation of their economic and political systems under state socialism as well as for the courses and outcomes of their subsequent reforms. By "historical" I mean the traditions, culture, patterns of behavior, and revolutionary experiences that developed from the past.

Hungary is a small European country with a population of about 10 million. Since their settlement in the Danube valley in the ninth century, Hungarians had seen their land devastated by the Mongols, occupied by the Turks, and dominated by the Austrians. Although in 1867 Hungary was granted an equal partnership in a dual monarchy of the Austro-Hungarian Empire, it was not until after World War I that Hungary gained its independence as a sovereign country. It allied itself with the Germans during World War II and was taken over by the Russian Red Army at the end of the war. Hungary thus fell into the Soviet sphere of influence in the postwar world order.

Despite the difference between its linguistic system and that of the rest of Europe, Hungary has always considered itself to be an organic part of the West. At the end of the tenth century, the Hungarian chieftain Vajk ordered all his subjects to convert to Roman Catholicism. Roman Catholicism brought Hungary into the mainstream of Western European nations, and this orientation toward Western European has persisted for the past 1,000 years.[1]

Although the church became completely dependent on the party-state when the Communist Party assumed power, it remained a major institution in Hungarian society. Today the majority of the population is still Catholic.[2]

Following Western tradition, Hungary also had some experience with a semiparliamentary democracy between the two world wars. Several parties (such as the Party of Unity, National Liberals, Independent Smallholders, and the Peasant Union) competed for parliamentary seats and were able to articulate the interests of various sectors of society. During that period parliaments were elected, albeit dominated by a "government party"—the Party of Unity—and based on a highly restrictive franchise and with open balloting in rural areas.[3]

By contrast, China is a huge Asian country with 1.2 billion people, about one-fourth of the world's population, and with a civilization some 5,000 years old. China was a closed, self-reliant, and secular central kingdom. The premodern Chinese political order was characterized by the paramount importance assigned to an official political philosophy, Confucianism, which served as a principal instrument of governance. This official ideology emphasized unity, order, and collective moral values over individual initiative.

China's defeat by Great Britain in the First Opium War in 1840 led to a century of humiliation for the once-proud civilization. Foreign powers carved out areas of influence where they enjoyed economic and political privileges in China. After the downfall of the Qing dynasty in 1911, China fell into chaos, foreign invasion, and civil war. All these experiences left China with a deep suspicion of foreign powers as well as a desire to resume its former great power status. In 1949 the communists waged a peasant revolution and established the People's Republic of China (PRC).

One of the most important contrasts in the revolutionary experiences of Hungary and China is that the two parties took different paths to power. The Communist Party had not been a powerful political force in Hungarian history. The short-lived 1919 communist regime, with its contempt for the peasantry and its spirit of internationalism, had produced a negative reaction from a population that perceived socialism as alien and hostile to the Hungarian national identity.[4] After that, the Hungarian Communist Party worked either underground or in exile in the Soviet Union. At the end of World War II, the Communist Party had a membership of just 3,000. Only after merging with the Social Democratic Party and assuming the new name of the Hungarian Workers' Party (HWP) did the communists gain control of the country in the 1949 election, an outcome that was guaranteed by Soviet occupation forces.

In contrast to the Hungarian party, the Chinese Communist Party (CCP) came to power by means of prolonged armed struggle and enjoyed popular support. Mao Zedong had sinicized Marxism quite successfully in the early years of the CCP through his struggle with Soviet-trained Party leaders. Integrating Marxism with revolutionary practice in China, Mao developed a strategy of mobilizing the peasantry and building rural bases to surround and capture the cities. During the revolutionary period, with its own armed forces, its rural base areas, and its established governments in those areas, the CCP became a well-developed indigenous force in China, achieving national victory through its own efforts.

These different revolutionary experiences greatly affected the pattern of the party-society relationship, the power structure within the communist leadership, and the political style of the elite during the period of state socialism. First, during the long revolutionary struggle for national power, the Chinese communists developed much deeper social roots than their Hungarian counterparts. As an indigenous force, the Party enjoyed broad mass support and developed efficient organizational methods for mass mobilization. In Hungary, although the Communist Party had been active before its ascendancy to national power, it was unable to gain real strength in terms of social support and organizations.

Second, as the Soviet Union provided the power base for the Communist Party, it became part of the political establishment in Hungary. Major policy decisions had to be made according to the potential reaction from the Soviet Union. In contrast, the communists in China achieved victory by rejecting the Soviet instructions, and the CCP always maintained independence in most of its decision making. After China's split with the Soviet Union in the early 1960s, no international power exercised much influence over its domestic policies. In Hungary the presence of the Soviet troops and the prospect of Soviet intervention ensured adherence to an orthodox political line. In China, however, an indigenous old guard acted as protectors of orthodoxy.

Third, as the result of the years spent developing rural bases and waging a peasant revolution, the operation of the political system in China was less institutionalized than in Hungary. The CCP came to power with the conviction that mobilization and struggle were the essence of politics. Military virtues—enthusiasm, heroism, sacrifice, and engaging in collective effort—acquired great value. Politics was not simply a matter of peaceful political competition or routine administration but an effort to mobilize human resources in a crisis situation. The "mass line" was a fundamental CCP principle that emphasized sustaining the people's support by providing them with service and developing popular checks on the powers wielded by bureaucracy and intellectuals. As we will see later, the propensity to mass movements profoundly affected the political and economic development of the People's Republic.

Without a broad base of support, the Hungarian communists had to rely more on bureaucratic control. They also seemed to be more comfortable with compromise and negotiation, a tradition that can be detected as far back as 1919. As Ivan Volgyes has pointed out, many observers failed to grasp that the 1919 communist regime was the product of negotiation, not of violent revolution. When the Karolyi government resigned in March 1919, and no one was willing to take over the war-torn country, the Communist Party formed a coalition government with the Social Democratic Party to fill the vacuum.[5] Again in 1949, it was the merger with the Social Democratic Party that gave the communists control of the country. These experiences may indicate a predisposition of the Hungarian communists to a peaceful management of politics.

Communist Ideology

Communist ideology refers to the body of doctrine that the Communist Party teaches all citizens, from schoolchildren to the higher Party leadership. This canon comprises not so much the original writings of Karl Marx, Frederick Engels, or V. I. Lenin but rather the official interpretations of their works by Party theorists. These exegeses were developed in part to rationalize policies at specific moments in time and in part to reflect popularly accepted interpretations of doctrine that had emerged as the result of political socialization.[6]

The major tenets of communist ideology, such as historical materialism, dialectic materialism, and mode of production, can be very confusing and dry. But the message behind them was clear and simple: Socialism and communism were the inevitable results of objective historical laws and were bound to be superior to capitalism. The main assumption was that socialism offered more favorable conditions for the development of production forces. Because the Party had mastered the law of historical development and knew what was good for the people better than the people themselves knew, it was the agent destined to lead the people down the historical road to communism. The most essential role of ideology was to serve as the basis of legitimacy for the ruling party.

In his famous article "What Is To Be Done?" Lenin forcefully argued that the theory of socialism only grows out of the philosophic, historical, and economic theories elaborated by educated representatives of the propertied classes, that is, by intellectuals. The Party should be responsible for the transmission of this revolutionary consciousness to the working masses, Lenin insisted, otherwise the workers would accept bourgeois ideology instead.[7] The emphasis on the decisive role of the vanguard elite automatically diminished the importance of democracy, with its stress on participation from below. Societal demands were addressed not through mechanisms of representation but by the Party leaders; the masses would have to rely on their wisdom. As Daniel Bell noted,

> While dogmas such as dialectical materialism, historical materialism, the superiority of collective property, and the nature of scientific communism remain on a formal level, the doctrinal core, the central fact is not any specific theoretical formulation *but the basic demand for belief in the Party itself.* . . . It is not the creed but the insistence on the infallibility of the interpreters that becomes the necessary mechanism of social control. Thus, the crucial feature of Soviet ideology . . . is the idea . . . that Party direction is essential in all fields of work.[8]

The finely elaborated set of doctrines had several additional functions in the state socialist system. It served as a means of communication to transmit information within the polity. The specific language, concepts, and paradigms developed over time provided citizens of these countries with a conceptual lens through which to view the world and acted as a vehicle for guiding intellectual and artistic life. Moreover, this set of established ideological preferences determined what policies were required and desirable and what policies were prohibited. It also identified a set of values for society and provided standard social norms and guidelines for all aspects of life—political, social, and economic.[9] The values most emphasized were discipline, self-sacrifice, and subordination of the individual to the collective.

After the communists came to power, they launched extensive drives to inculcate the population with socialist values and communist ideology. Political education was mandatory. Party members were required to take courses in Party history, as well as Soviet Party history and Russian versions of Marxism-Leninism. Depending on their importance, Party and state posts required completion of courses that lasted from several months to four years.[10]

The Party used all propaganda instruments, from schools and the mass media to the workplace and entertainment, to promote political socialization. It successfully limited access to alternative sources of information through strict censorship. Universities required courses on Marxism and Party history. Newspapers carried articles explaining Party policies and headlines declaring the success of production drives. Radio stations broadcast interviews with workers who had invented new methods of production and factory managers who surpassed monthly production quotas. Literature, theater, the cinema, and even music existed only as the didactic agents of the Party line and socialist realism. Their task was to illustrate the values of socialist society and to contrast them with capitalist decadence. They set forth the positive and negative models toward which people were to orient themselves.[11]

In comparison with that of other state socialist countries, however, Hungarian political socialization seemed relatively ineffective.[12] Except for the Stalinist period under Matyas Rakosi from 1949 to 1953, as long as people repeated what the Party wanted them to say or did what the Party wanted them to do, the Party did not much care what people truly believed.[13] The Party was either unable or unwilling to wage more thorough political socialization campaigns.

The same was not true in China. The strong ideological orientation in traditional China continued into the communist period, with Marxism, Leninism, and Mao Zedong Thought replacing Confucianism. The central ideology in the political system was sustained during the Mao period, when repeated campaigns purged those who deviated ideologically. The emphasis on the role of official ideology plus the strong ability of the Party to mobilize mass movements made the socialization of revolutionary values far more thorough in China than in other state socialist societies.

An extreme case of such a highly indoctrinated polity can be found in China during the Cultural Revolution, during which the symbols of ideological commitment and conformity were virtually omnipresent. Quotations from Marx, Lenin, and Mao were indiscriminately used throughout the pages of written documents, from the covers of cookbooks to applications for wedding certificates. Until the fall of Lin Biao in 1971, every Chinese was expected to carry a pocket-sized copy of quotations from Mao's works and to consult it frequently for answers to the problems of daily life.

The emphasis on ideological purity and orientation toward mass movements may have proved effective in China's revolutionary struggles but was counterproductive in economic and political development after the revolution. With his stress on "redness" rather than "expertise," as Harry Harding has noted, Mao "retarded what, given the history of other communist states, would have been the normal evolution of the Chinese political system. He delayed the progress toward pragmatism, the routinization of charisma, the relaxation of totalitarian controls, and the emergence of a better-educated, technocratic elite that occurred in most other socialist countries in the post-Stalin era."[14]

The Economic System

The economic systems in Hungary and China under state socialism were basically patterned after the Soviet model. This model favors a developmental strategy of forced industrialization (primarily through the expropriation tal strategy of forced industrialization (primarily through the expropriation of peasantry), the concentration of economic resources in the hands of the state (through nationalization and collectivization of the principal means of production), and a central planning system to mobilize and allocate these resources.

With the exception of Yugoslavia, all the state socialist countries established after World War II adopted this model for their economic systems. Both Hungary and China thus undertook a fundamental transformation of the pattern of ownership in their economies. The means of production in agriculture, industry, banking, and commerce were transferred from private hands to public or collective ownership. At the end of 1949, all Hungarian enterprises with more than ten workers were nationalized.[15] In China, private industry and commerce were transferred to the state or to worker collectives in 1956. China's agricultural land and capital, which had been distributed to the peasants during the land reform after 1949, were amalgamated first into "mutual aid teams," then into cooperatives in 1956, and then into "people's communes" in 1958. The initial collectivization of agriculture in Hungary was not as successful and had to be repeated between 1959 and 1961.

After the collectivization of agriculture and the nationalization of industry, both the Hungarian and Chinese economies were governed, as in the Soviet Union, by a system of mandatory central planning. In such a system, output targets, input quotas, and financial indicators measuring the efficiency of production were set by a hierarchical structure from a central planning agency down to the individual enterprise. Although the process was always incomplete and imperfect, and in reality planners and managers did bargain over the plan indicators, the central planning system regulated the distribution of goods, allocation of investment, and utilization of labor more tightly than in any earlier period in history.[16]

The First Five-Year Plans in Hungary and China followed Soviet priorities, emphasizing the development of heavy industry rather than the growth of the agricultural or consumer goods sectors. The Soviet model intended to achieve a high rate of investment that would rapidly build up an autarchic production structure. The investment rate averaged 24 percent in the 1950s in both countries.[17]

Apart from the common features of Soviet-type economic planning, the two economies also bore some differences. First, China's level of economic development was lower than that of Hungary. For example, at the beginning of reform in both countries, China maintained a large agricultural sector, employing more than 70 percent of its labor force, while employment in the Hungarian agricultural sector accounted for only about a quarter.[18]

than Hungary. China's economic isolation was imposed in part by external constraints. The Korean War (1950-1953) foreclosed China's ability to acquire technology and aid from the West. For several years, the Soviet Union was China's only significant source for financial credit, advanced equipment, and technical advice. The Sino-Soviet split in the late 1950s ended that dependence and further restricted China's interaction with other socialist countries.

But China's closed-door policy was also self-imposed. It stemmed from the suspicion of foreign influence and the principle of self-reliance that had developed in the revolutionary years in Yanan, when the CCP and its army had to produce all goods needed for their subsistence. Thus, after the late 1950s, economic relations with foreign countries were limited essentially to trade for cash. China did not accept foreign investment and after the repayment of the last Soviet credits in the mid-1960s refused any further foreign loans except for short-term letters of credit. Despite a short-lived drive to make the Hungarian economy self-sufficient in the early 1950s, the Hungarian economy in contrast remained relatively open, depending heavily on foreign trade. It conducted most of its trade within the Soviet bloc but also had trade relations with the West.

The third difference involved the degree of bureaucratization of the economy. Over the years Hungary had closely followed the Soviet path and consolidated its central planning system. China instead emphasized "redness" over "expertise" and the "mass line" over technological inno-vations. Mao Zedong strongly believed in the ability of mass movements to accomplish monumental tasks and never liked the faceless bureaucratic machine created by the planning system. In 1958 he launched a radical drive for industrialization known as the Great Leap Forward. It was a supreme attempt to ignore technological and physical constraints, substituting for capital goods China's most plentiful resource, labor power, in the same way the CCP had successfully substituted committed soldiers for modern weapons during the guerrilla and civil war days. Workers were called upon to work shift after shift with little rest; machines were driven without stopping for maintenance and repairs. Farmers were urged to build furnaces to melt iron in their backyards in order to raise iron production. The Great Leap Forward ended in economic crisis with a dramatic decline in production output, widespread shortage of consumer goods, and a serious famine. During the Cultural Revolution from 1966 to 1976, although the Party had abandoned the methods of mass mobilization to achieve industrial-ization, it continued to stress ideological purity over technical competence. Politics commanded economic development; the ongoing political campaigns took priority over economic productivity. Workers had to participate in political studies during working hours, and any attempt to tighten discipline was denounced as capitalist management.

Fourth, related to this low level of bureaucratization, the organization of the economy in the two countries differed. In Hungary, as in the Soviet Union, industries were organized along functional lines: Enterprises were grouped by industry under the direct supervision of ministries. The Chinese economy, in contrast, was arranged according to territorial principles more than industrial functions. As many scholars have pointed out, this produced a fragmented central planning system and ownership structure and granted greater autonomy to local governments.[19]

As a whole, both the Hungarian and the Chinese economies embodied the basic traits of a Soviet-style economic system, establishing public ownership of the principal means of production and central planning. But China's economic system also possessed at various times populist and radical orientations that sometimes landed China in economic disaster, as in the Great Leap Forward, and always engendered technological incompetence. Yet China's shortcomings under central planning may have turned out to be advantages during reform, for the low level of industrialization may have provided a felicitous environment for rapid growth; its inward-oriented development strategy meant China had no foreign debt; and the cellular structure of the economy gave local governments greater incentive to reform. In comparison, the Hungarian economy was relatively open to the world system and relied more on bureaucratic management than revolutionary impulse. The more open trade relations in turn created a huge foreign debt, and a bureaucratized economy increased the costs of structural adjustment.

The Political System

The political system of state socialist countries consists of two major civilian organizational hierarchies, the party and the state, plus a variety of mass organizations that also links these hierarchies and the citizenry. The Hungarian Socialist Worker's Party and the Chinese Communist Party were modeled on the Communist Party of the Soviet Union. The organizational hierarchy was formed through a series of indirect elections from the primary units (a village, a factory, or a residential street) through different administrative levels (with different names in different countries) up to the Central Committee and the Politburo, which in practice is the highest and most important policy-making body in the country. Although Party secretaries at every level were officially elected by the Party membership, they were in fact appointed by higher Party authorities.

According to their constitutions, the National Assembly in Hungary and the National People's Congress in China were the highest organs of state, with the power to legislate and to elect and recall major executive officials. But in practice these congresses assembled in short meetings to study Party directives and unanimously pass any resolution presented to them by Party leaders. Since the function of the legislature tended to be ceremonial, the elections of the delegates were of no importance and served primarily as rewards for loyal followers. Elections, although they were regularly held, were noncompetitive, with one candidate nominated for each position. Deputies were designated by the authorities and were elected by a ceremonial vote. Grateful to the Party for their appointment, deputies were responsive to the authorities. This sense of loyalty reinforced the rubber-stamp function of the legislature.

The Communist Youth League and the trade unions were among the most important mass organizations in state socialist societies. Under the monistic leadership of the Party, they served to relay Party policies to much broader social strata, mobilize political support for the Party, and represent the specific interests of their respective constituencies, as interpreted by the Party.

The Patriotic People's Front was another key organization in Hungary. Its tasks were to organize elections to the National Assembly, raise public consciousness of certain problems (e.g., environmental protection), and to mobilize individual and group action in support of Party policies. A rough parallel in China can be found in the Chinese People's Political Consultative Conference and eight "democratic parties."[20] They functioned more as mass organizations than political parties because they had no opportunity to share national leadership, nor did they desire to do so.

The basic characteristic of the political system in state socialist societies was the monopoly of power by the Communist Party. As already noted, this was legitimized in terms of the Party's representing the genuine interest of the people and ensured by the elimination of autonomous social organizations and other political forces. Marxism-Leninism as applied in these societies did not recognize any political power centers other than the Communist Party, which claimed to be the sole liberator of human society. Since the Communist Party knew best and represented the will of the people, there was no need for independent organizations to voice other societal interests. The one-party system, taking charge of the political, economic, cultural, and social affairs of the country, precluded the need for autonomous political or social organizations.

The Party dominated policy-making in all institutions and all aspects of life. The Party's own organizations paralleled and supervised ministries, enterprises, government institutions, and mass organizations at all levels and were the sole decision-making bodies. Government agencies served virtually as administrative arms of the Party committees. The Party also controlled appointments to important government posts, as well as to the leading positions in the mass organizations. To ensure the effective implementation of Party policies, the same officials often held leadership positions in the Party and government at all levels.

Despite these similarities, the political systems of Hungary and China also developed significant differences after the communist takeover. The Hungarian communists gained control of the country in the 1949 election under Soviet supervision. Without a solid popular base, the political system established under the leadership of Party secretary Matyas Rakosi from 1949 to 1953 operated as a reign of terror. Political life was dominated by a personality cult and ceaseless purges. Several thousand upper- and mid-level Party functionaries were executed or imprisoned in the Rakosi years, and more than 350,000 members of HWP were purged.[21] Between 1952 and 1955, the authorities investigated over one million individuals for political motivations; about 10 percent of Hungarian society was in some way subject to police action.[22] This overt repression alienated a large part of the population from the communist regime.

When Stalin died in 1953, Rakosi lost his powerful backing in Moscow, and Hungary experienced a brief period of relaxation. Imre Nagy assumed the position of the premier and started a mild reform known as the New Course, which halted collectivization of agriculture and redirected investment away from heavy industry. Nagy, however, was forced to resign in 1955 when Georgi Malenkov, who had acted as his protector in Moscow, was defeated in the power struggle in the Kremlin.

In October 1956 a popular uprising exploded as diverse nationalistic elements joined in calling for the withdrawal of Soviet troops, de-Stalinization, and the reinstitution of a pluralistic political system in Hungary. Soviet tanks moved into the streets of Budapest and suppressed the revolt. The Soviet Union selected Janos Kadar as the Party secretary of the country. Once again, the government owed its power to the Soviet Union. The 1956 incident, although lasting only thirteen days, shook the country profoundly. Nagy, who had been selected as premier again during the uprising, was arrested and executed along with his associates. The whole country was politically suppressed.

The Chinese communists came to power in 1949 with much more self-confidence. The establishment of a new political system therefore depended less on police action and more on mass mobilization and the prestige the CCP had accumulated during its struggle against the Nationalist regime. In the early 1950s, it led a rather successful military campaign against the United States in the Korean War, boosting the national pride of a country that had been humiliated by foreign powers for the past hundred years. The collectivization of agriculture and nationalization of industry went smoothly, with relatively little violence, thanks to the tremendous organizing skills the Party had developed during the revolution.

Despite its enormous popularity, the CCP was just as intolerant of criticism as were other communist parties. Political life in China was characterized by a series of political campaigns to purge those inside the Party who disagreed with Mao and those who criticized the Party from outside. In 1957 the Party launched the large-scale Anti-Rightist movement to eliminate those who had criticized the Party leadership. About 550,000 people were labeled rightists and sent to labor camps.

In the early 1960s China openly split with the Soviet Union, embarking on a even more radical revolutionary course. In 1966 Mao launched the Cultural Revolution to rid the CCP of capitalist roaders. He called for dictatorship of the proletariat within the superstructure, especially in education, mass media, and the arts. This was the most devastating period in the PRC's history. Revolution spread from schools to factories, farms to government institutions. Mao deliberately encouraged his personality cult to mobilize the masses. The masses formed their own organizations and engaged in endless infighting over which of them represented Mao's genuine revolutionary line. Party committees at all levels ceased to function and were replaced with revolutionary committees, which consisted of representatives from revolutionary mass organizations, cadres, and the army. During the entire Cultural Revolution, China was dominated by radical policies that emphasized revolution over construction and ideological purity over economic performance.

In summary, both Hungary and China shared the basic features of a Leninist political system, centered on the Communist Party dictatorship. Yet while political life in Hungary was characterized by routinized institutional control and police action, China's was dominated by a charismatic leader and waves of political campaigns. For example, the political purges in the Rakosi period were mainly secret police actions in true Stalinist style, whereas Chinese purges took the form of mass movements. The reliance on the secret police required a bureaucratic establishment, while the mobilization of the masses relied primarily on ideological inspiration. Both countries had experienced political crisis. But the 1956 crisis in Hungary was caused by strong anticommunist sentiments, while the Cultural Revolution was launched by the paramount leader in the name of communism. International constraints also differed between the two. Hungary was under the strong influence of the Soviet Union: the fates of Rakosi, Nagy, and Kadar demonstrate that the policies and power struggles in Moscow had a direct impact on politics in Budapest. China, long a maverick, was fairly independent of the Soviet Union in its political pursuits.

The Decision to Reform

The theory of totalitarianism posits that state socialism is unable to initiate reform by itself, nor is the system reformable. The main argument is that the Communist Party will never give up its monopoly of economic, social, and political lives. It will not allow, not to mention launch, any changes that will undermine its power. Although challenged by the reforms in some state socialist countries since the 1960s, this theory continued to hold ground by predicting at each stage of reform that the Communist Party would never undertake thorough reform measures or would collapse.

The reform experiences in Hungary and China, however, indicate a path different from that predicted by the theory of totalitarianism. It leads to neither a monolithic polity nor total collapse, but to partial collapse, partial reformation, innovation, and transformation. To be sure, reform policies were seriously restricted by the ideological and political considerations of the Party elite. But these elites had a range of political views, and they were learning and adjusting. The whole system has been undergoing an evolutionary rather than revolutionary change. To understand this dynamic, we must first start with the decision to reform.

Economic Difficulties

Both Hungary and China had some notable economic accomplishments to their credit. People were guaranteed food, housing, employment, health care, and a minimal but equal standard of living. The average growth rate in Hungary from 1950 to 1967 was an impressive 6.1 percent.[23] Despite the depression and famine occasioned by the Great Leap Forward and the political instability created by the Cultural Revolution, China had, in the aggregate, achieved respectable rates of growth between 1952 and 1975, averaging 11.5 percent in industry, 3.1 percent in agriculture, and 8.2 percent overall.[24] At the same time, however, the two economies also encountered serious problems that finally led to the initiation of reform.

The motivation behind economic reform was widespread dissatisfaction with economic performance. Hungarian economist Tamas Bauer has suggested that there were two types of dissatisfaction. The first was "operational dissatisfaction." Those who participated in economic decision-making as managers in enterprises or officials in the state administration were dissatisfied with the irrationalities in the operation of the system. The second type was "performance dissatisfaction." Politicians and citizens in general were increasingly disappointed with the performance of the economy. These two types of dissatisfaction interacted in bringing about changes in the economic mechanism.[25]

The chronic economic difficulties that Hungary and China faced before the reform were largely the result of the inefficiencies inherent in a Soviet-style centrally planned economy. The inefficiency of the planning system was reflected in the high investment rate needed to sustain growth. For example, Hungary reported an investment rate of 24 percent of gross national product (GNP) in the 1950s; a more realistic estimation was 37 percent.[26] In China the investment rate during the First Five-Year Plan (1953-1957) was 24 percent of national income. This climbed to 33 percent during the Fourth Five-Year Plan (1971-1975) and peaked at 36.5 percent in 1978.[27] This was a very high rate by any international standard and particularly so for a developing country. Inefficiency was also exhibited in the low returns to investment. A huge quantity of investment was frozen in a large number of projects that brought no return. In 1955, for example, unfinished investments amounted to 92 percent of the annual expenditure on investments in Hungary.[28]

Another symptom of inefficiency was the pileup of unusable inventories, due to irrational prices, a lack of contact between producer and consumer, and a pervasive emphasis on quantity rather than quality of output. The Hungarian planning office reported that "significant quantities have been placed 'in stock' of industrial products (and raw materials, semifinished products, manufactured goods and imported articles) for which there is no demand on either domestic or foreign markets." In 1960 the office estimated that "the proportion of superfluous stocks to total stocks has reached as much as 20 to 60 percent." In 1961-1963 these inventories rose by 33 percent.[29]

One major cause of inefficiency was the rigidity of the economic structure. Any change had to go through a multistage approval process. As two Chinese economists put it, enterprises "had to seek approval for doing everything, big and small, from the higher departments which were divorced from the frontline of production, had no responsibility for the results of the operations of the enterprises and often gave impractical and disconnected mandatory directives."[30] Lack of enterprise-level flexibility in financial matters also led to obvious irrationalities in investment allocation and undermined worker and managerial initiatives.

Another long-term problem for centrally planned economies concerned technology. Central planning stifled innovation. In Hungary the low standard of technology and the indifference of companies to improve it led to noncompetitiveness in the world market. In some cases as much as 60 percent of output was rejected for export. In one worst case, a line of television sets had to be repaired an average of three times during their warranty period.[31] In the early 1960s, unable to produce goods that were competitive abroad, Hungary could not export enough to cover the payments for its imports and suffered from a serious economic disequilibrium. The most conspicuous sign was its mounting indebtedness to non-Comecon countries. Debts rose from 1,600 million forints in 1959 to 4,100 million in 1963, which had to be offset by further borrowing and the rescheduling of exiting credits.[32]

The problem of technology was even worse in China, which was cut off not only from access to advanced Western technology but also from Soviet sources. In the late 1970s, Chinese technology lagged ten to twenty years behind the levels of industrialized countries overall, with a gap of thirty to forty years in some fields. The Chinese themselves estimated that fully 60 percent of the technology employed in their industry in 1980 was completely obsolete and that much of the rest was in dire need of upgrading.[33]

Popular dissatisfaction with the economic system was deepest with regard to living standards. The high investment rate restricted the growth of consumption. As a result, the standard of living did not improve as rapidly as the countries' national incomes. Urban residents faced serious shortages of housing, services, and consumer goods, despite their inferior quality. Such dissatisfaction was intensified by unfavorable comparisons with the economic performances of the industrialized and newly industrialized countries. The consumption gap between the East and the West was obvious, and in the 1960s Hungarians, allowed to travel to the West, could observe the gap for themselves. The contrast was particularly shocking for China, as it had been closed to the outside world for so long. While China was busy engaging in the political campaigns of the Cultural Revolution, its neighbors, Japan, Taiwan, Singapore, South Korea, and Hong Kong, all scored incredible economic achievements. Once the crisis of the Cultural Revolution was over, Chinese leaders found that China had been left far behind.

Both countries had been trying to correct the defects within their economic systems ever since they had established them. For example, during the New Course (1953-1956) and in the early 1960s, partial economic reform was introduced in Hungary. Despite the recollectivization of agriculture during the period of 1959-1962, the private plot was henceforth declared a "vital" and "organic" part of cooperative farming.[34] In 1965 the obligatory agriculture targets outlined in the economic plan were abolished, and supply quotas disappeared in 1966.[35] In China, during the mass movements such as the Great Leap Forward and the Cultural Revolution, Mao had attempted to introduce more egalitarian and populist elements into the Soviet economic model. In the early 1960s, China adopted certain liberal economic policies to decentralize administrative decision-making power down to the local government. In each case, these efforts were merely negated in yet another round of recentralization.[36] Mere tinkering with the existing system did not solve the economic problems of either China or Hungary. More fundamental systemic reform came to be viewed as necessary.

However, if the problems with the planned economy were systemic, then the dissatisfaction with economic performance and an unfavorable comparison with the capitalist industrialized countries should have appeared in all state socialist economies. What were the factors that led some countries to draft a program of far-reaching reforms and prevented others from doing so? The explanation for the emergence of the reform programs must be sought in the political realm. In China and Hungary, the consensus for reform was reached after acute political crises and subsequent changes in political leadership.

The Ascendancy of Reformist Leadership

Large-scale political crisis serves as a catalyst for reform in two ways. First, it often results in a change of leadership, which opens the possibility for the new leaders to disassociate themselves from past practices and to initiate changes. Second, it creates pressure on the leadership to address the causes of political crisis in order to prevent new ones. Most often the case is that the incoming leadership opts to take a more pragmatic approach so as to improve the standard of living of the population and appease the society traumatized by the crisis.

In Hungary Janos Kadar appeared on the political stage after the 1956 incident as an extremely unpopular leader because of his role in the suppression of the uprising and the execution of its leaders. Since he was himself a victim of the Rakosi dictatorship, Kadar had no intention of returning to a totalitarian system.[37] Some evidence even suggests that as early as December 1956 Kadar intended to undertake the same economic reform program as the short-lived Nagy government. Yet he was unable to do so because he needed to consolidate his political power, which would be incompatible with the decentralization necessary for economic reform. Furthermore, he was operating under tight Soviet supervision.

Kadar therefore took a centrist line, engaging in what he called a "two-front" struggle. On the one hand, he denounced the Stalinist rule of the Rakosi regime and waged a battle against the dogmatism of the conservatives. On the other hand, he declared loyalty to the Soviet Union and the course of socialism and relentlessly attacked the "revisionists."

Kadar gradually purged the dogmatists from the leadership and filled their positions with supporters of the moderate line. For example, in 1960 he dismissed the minister of agriculture, Imre Dogei, from his post and from the Central Committee for having pursued "sectarian and pseudoleftist activities."[38] Two years later Dogei was expelled from the Party. At the August 1962 Central Committee plenum, five members of the Rakosi clique (Rakosi, Erno Gero, Istvan Kovacs, Gyula Alpai, and Vilmos Olti) and fourteen former security police officers were expelled. Karoly Kiss, former chairman of the Central Control Committee, was removed from the Politburo for not acknowledging unacceptable the practices of the committee prior to 1956. Kadar also used the occasion to get rid of more recent hard-line opponents, expelling six Party members for factional activities. Gyorgy Marosan, a member of the Politburo, was relieved of all his Party offices in October 1962 for attempting to rally dogmatic opposition to Kadar.

The Eighth HSWP Congress in November 1962 marked the consolidation of Kadar's leadership, with the confirmation in office of loyal supporters. The congress emphasized that the main danger in political life was dogmatism rather than revisionism. By the end of 1962, the Party had acquired a coherent and unified leadership, characterized by a pragmatic approach, willing to embrace change.

All these changes were tolerated, if not encouraged, by Soviet leader Nikita Khrushchev. After Khrushchev's ouster in 1964, Kadar lost no time in securing the sanction of his successor. He and Leonid Brezhnev met seven times during the latter's first year in office. The relatively more conservative inclination of Brezhnev encouraged dogmatist pressure from inside Hungary. Yet Kadar overrode the opposition.[39] How he managed to secure endorsement from the conservative Brezhnev remains unclear. It seems that the emphasis on economic restructuring rather than political change made the Hungarian reform less threatening to the Soviet Union.

Kadar was not the architect of a detailed reform program, but he provided the essential political defense for it. He acted as a shield behind which economic experts were left relatively free to debate, elaborate, and evaluate, without political interference, the relative merits of different approaches to various aspects of reform. The reform initiative in Hungary centered on Rezso Nyers, elected Central Committee secretary and placed in charge of economic affairs in 1962. Nyers's intention from the start was for reform to be comprehensive and consistent, and this intention was effectively translated into official policy.

The first moves toward economic reform were underway behind the scenes in 1963, as Nyers established his own informal advisory body as a brain trust on economic issues. In a general effort to create a favorable climate of opinion, Nyers undertook a campaign to publicize and defend the principle of reform and published some notable books criticizing the Stalinist economic system.[40] The December plenum of 1964 approved the basic concept of reform and authorized Nyers to set up a series of expert committees to produce the basic guidelines. In May 1966 the Central

Committee gave its formal approval to the reform proposal and scheduled implementation for 1 January 1968. That the Central Committee endorsed the final reform plan by only a narrow margin indicates the strength of the opposition within the Party and the difficulties Kadar had overcome to launch a comprehensive reform program.[41]

The nature of China's political crisis, the Cultural Revolution, was very different from that of Hungary. However, it, too, demoralized the entire population and resulted in a change of leadership. The political spectrum after the Cultural Revolution consisted of remnant revolutionary Maoists, restorationists, and reformers.[42] The revolutionary Maoists, who advocated radical political and economic policies, had lost most of their power after the purge of the radical leaders of the Cultural Revolution. The restorationists, headed by the chairman of the Party, Hua Guofeng, favored a policy of restoring and improving the traditional system of central planning. Hua had risen to power during the Cultural Revolution and continued to endorse most of Mao's past policies. Hua's reluctance to denounce the political purges of the Cultural Revolution, especially the suppression of the 1976 Tiananmen incident, a popular movement against the radical policies of the Cultural Revolution, made him extremely unpopular and gradually cost him political support.

The reformers, Deng Xiaoping as their head, advocated a deeper reform of the economic system. Twice purged during the Cultural Revolution, Deng was keenly aware of the urgency of reform: "Some serious problems which appeared in the past may arise again if the defects in our present systems are not eliminated. Only when these defects are resolutely removed through planned, systematic, and thorough reforms will the people trust our leadership, our Party and socialism."[43] Deng was reappointed vice-chairman of the Party, vice-premier, and chief of staff of the People's Liberation Army in 1977. Yet he had to establish a power base and mobilize support against Hua Guofeng in order to pursue his reform program.

Unlike Kadar, Deng emerged after the Cultural Revolution as a popular leader renowned for his pragmatic approach. Maintaining connections with many power holders in the Party and the army, Deng clearly possessed personal and political assets unmatched by Hua in a society that places great weight on the seniority and personal quality of its leaders. Deng assigned his supporter, Hu Yaobang, to be the head of the powerful Organization Department of the Central Committee. Hu subsequently pushed for the massive rehabilitation of cadres victimized during the Cultural Revolution. The return of these veterans to the political stage undoubtedly strengthened Deng's power base. Deng Xiaoping also mobilized support from vocal sectors of the broader population, mainly the intellectuals, to create popular pressure for a more explicit repudiation of the Cultural Revolution and a more rapid and thoroughgoing rehabilitation of its victims. Thus, the balance of power gradually shifted in favor of Deng's coalition.

The Third Plenum of the Eleventh Central Committee held in December 1978 explicitly endorsed several key elements of Deng's program, namely, the shift of the focus of the Party's work from class struggle to economic modernization, the ideological stand of "seeking truth from facts," and the promotion of a system of "democracy and legality." However, because the preparation period for reform in China was shorter than in Hungary (one year compared to more than ten years), the program was more a vague desire than a carefully designed plan. The subsequent decade of reform was characterized as "groping for stones while crossing the river" (*mozhe shitou guohe*).

Deng's power was finally consolidated when Hua Guofeng was forced to resign as premier in 1980 and as chairman of the Party in 1981. He was replaced as premier by Zhao Ziyang, a highly pragmatic and experienced provincial official, and as the chairman (later general secretary) by Hu Yaobang. Deng also engineered the resignation of six veteran vice-premiers: Chen Yun, Li Xiannian, Xu Xiangqian, Wang Zhen, Wang Renzhong, and himself. By so doing, Deng removed some of the likely opponents to reform, such as Li Xiannian, and strengthened Zhao Ziyang's control over the State Council.

The initiation of reform in both countries clearly presented parallel trajectories: from a serious political crisis to a change of leadership, to the weakening of the conservatives and the strengthening of the reformers. The successful establishment of a reform coalition within the communist leadership proved that the time was ripe for change.

It should be noted that neither regime undertook serious political restructuring when it first pursued economic reform. Although it may be inaccurate to assert that they believed that they could restructure the economic systems without making any political changes, it was true that neither leadership seriously committed itself to the democratization of its society. In Hungary it was well understood that political reform could not exceed Soviet tolerance, as Soviet intervention in 1956 had left a painful imprint on the country's history. In China, in the minds of the leaders who had been its victims, the memory of the Cultural Revolution raised the specter of a chaotic mass involvement in politics. However, a more relaxed political environment was an indispensable part of economic reform and the effort to restore legitimacy. These steps toward greater political liberalization are discussed in the next chapter.

NOTES

1. Andrew Felkay, *Hungary and the USSR, 1956-1988* (New York: Greenwood Press, 1989), p. 8; and Leslie Laszlo, "Religion and Nationality in Hungary," in *Religion and Nationalism in Soviet and East European Politics*, ed. Pedro Ramet (Durham: Duke University Press, 1989), pp. 286-98.

2. Peter Toma, *Socialist Authority: The Hungarian Experience* (New York: Praeger, 1988).

3. There were stringent educational and residency requirements for the franchise: six years of education and at least six years of residency in one place. Voting age was set at twenty-four for men and at thirty for women, except for those who possessed high-school degrees, had businesses of their own, or were mothers of at least three children. Andrew C. Janos, *The Politics of Backwardness in Hungary: 1825-1945* (Princeton, N.J.: Princeton University Press, 1982), p. 212.

4. Ibid., p. 199.

5. Ivan Volgyes and Mary Volgyes, *Czechoslovakia, Hungary, Poland: Crossroads of Change* (New York: Thomas Nelson, 1970), pp. 149-50.

6. The popular textbooks for Marxism in China, for example, included Ai Siqi, ed., *Bianzheng weiwuzhuyi Lishi weiwuzhuyi* [Dialectical materialism, historical materialism], (Beijing: People's Press, 1961); Yu Guangyuan, and Su Xing, eds., *Zhengzhi Jingjixue* [Political economics], (Beijing: People's Press, 1977); Editing Group for "Fundamentals of Political Economics," *Zhengzhi Jingjixue Jichuzhishi* [Fundamentals of political economics], (Shanghai: Shanghai People's Press, 1974); and Editing Group of the Department of Political Education, Shanghai Normal University, *Shehui fazhanshi* [History of social development], (Shanghai: Shanghai People's Press, 1974).

7. V. I. Lenin, "What Is To Be Done?" in *The Lenin Anthology*, ed. Robert C. Tucker (New York: W. W. Norton, 1975), pp. 24-25.

8. Daniel Bell, "Ideology and Soviet Politics," *Slavic Review* 24, no. 4 (December 1965): 602, emphasis in original.

9. For discussions of the function of ideology, see Franz Schurmann, *Ideology and Organization in Communist China* (Berkeley: University of California Press, 1968), pp. 1-104; and John Bryan Starr, *Ideology and Culture: An Introduction to the Dialectic of Contemporary Chinese Politics* (New York: Harper & Row, 1973).

10. Bennett Kovrig, *Communism in Hungary: From Kun to Kadar* (Stanford, Calif.: Hoover Institute Press, 1979), p. 260.

11. Ivan Volgyes, "Hungary: From Mobilization to Depoliticization," in *Political Socialization in Eastern Europe: A Comparative Framework*, ed. Ivan Volgyes (New York: Praeger, 1975), pp. 92-131; and Schurmann, *Ideology and Organization in Communist China*, pp. 58-72.

12. Volgyes, "Political Socialization in Eastern Europe: A Conceptual Framework," tables on pp. 14, 16, and 27, in Volgyes, *Political Socialization in Eastern Europe*.

13. Ibid.

14. Harry Harding, *China's Second Revolution: Reform After Mao* (Washington, D.C.: The Brookings Institution, 1987), p. 28

15. Peter A. Toma and Ivan Volgyes, *Politics in Hungary* (San Francisco: W. H. Freeman, 1977), p. 11.

16. For a more detailed description of the state socialist economy, see Janos Kornai, *The Socialist System: The Political Economy of Communism* (Princeton, N.J.: Princeton University Press, 1992).

17. Gyorgy Ranki, "The Introduction and Evolution of Planning in Hungary," in *Market Reforms in Socialist Societies: Comparing China and Hungary*, ed. Peter Van Ness (Boulder: Lynne Rienner, 1989), p. 40; and Harding, *China's Second Revolution*, p. 16.

18. Jeffrey Sachs and Wing Thye Woo, "Structural Factors in the Economic Reforms of China, Eastern Europe, and the Former Soviet Union," *Economic Policy* 18, no. 1 (1994): 102-45; and Patrick de Fontenay, et al., *Hungary: An Economic Survey* (Washington, D.C.: International Monetary Fund, 1982).

19. Barry Naughton, "Reforming a Planned Economy: Is China Unique?" in *From Reform to Growth: China and Other Countries in Transition in Asia and Central and Eastern Europe*, eds. Chung H. Lee and Helmut Reisen (Paris: OECD, 1994), pp. 49-74; Yingyi Qian and Chenggang Xu, "Why China's Economic Reforms Differ: The M-Form Hierarchy and Entry Expansion of the Non-State Sector," *Economics of Transformation* 1, no.2 (1993): 135-70; and Minxin Pei, "Microfoundations of State-socialism and Patterns of Economic Transformation," *Communist and Post-Communist Studies* 29, no. 2 (1996): 131-45.

20. They are: the Revolutionary Committee of Guomindang, Democratic League, Chinese Democratic Construction Association, Association for Promoting Democracy, Chinese Peasants' and workers' Democratic Party, Chinese *Zhigong* [public devotion] Party, *Jiusan* [September Third] Study Society, and Alliance for Taiwan Democratic Autonomy.

21. Kovrig, *Communism in Hungary*, p. 247.

22. George Schopflin, "Hungarian People's Republic," in *Marxist Governments: A World Survey, vol.2*, ed. Bogdan Szajkowski (London: Macmillan, 1981), p. 390.

23. Hungarian Central Statistical Office, *Statistical Yearbook 1968* (Budapest: Statistical Publishing Company).

24. State Statistical Bureau of China, *Statistical Yearbook of China, 1984*, p. 24.

25. Tamas Bauer, "Perfecting or Reforming the Economic Mechanism?" *Eastern Euro-pean Economics* 26, no. 2 (Winter 1987-88): 5-34.

26. William F. Robinson, *The Pattern of Reform in Hungary: A Political, Economic and Cultural Analysis* (New York: Praeger, 1973), p. 4.

27. Dwight H. Perkins, "The Prospects for China's Economic Reforms," in *Modernizing China: Post-Mao Reform and Development*, eds. A. Doak Barnett and Ralph N. Clough (Boulder, Colo.: Westview Press, 1986), p. 40.

28. Nigel Swain, *Hungary: The Rise and Fall of Feasible Socialism* (London: Verso, 1992), p. 74.

29. Ivan Berend, *The Hungarian Economic Reforms: 1953-1988* (Cambridge: Cambridge University Press, 1990), p. 122.

30. Liu Guoguang and Wang Ruisun, "Restructuring of the Economy," in *China's Socialist Modernization*, ed. Yu Guangyuan (Beijing: Foreign Languages Press, 1984), p. 89.

31. Berend, *The Hungarian Economic Reforms*, p. 125.

32. Ibid., p. 114.

33. *Far Eastern Economic Review*, 31 January 1985, p. 50.

34. Robinson, *The Pattern of Reform in Hungary*, p. 114.

35. Ivan Volgyes, "Dynamic Change: Rural Transformation, 1945-1975," in *The Moder-nization of Agriculture: Rural Transformation in Hungary, 1848-1975*, ed. Joseph Held (New York: Columbia University Press, 1980), pp. 351-508.

36. Wu Jinglian, "Choice of Strategy in China's Economic Reform," paper prepared for the American Economic Association annual meeting, Chicago, December 1987.

37. Janos Kadar was arrested in 1951 for treason and espionage. Kovrig, *Communism in Hungary*, p. 245.

38. Ibid., p. 351.

39. Ibid., p. 364.

40. Judy Batt, *Economic Reform and Political Change in Eastern Europe: A Comparison of the Czechoslovak and Hungarian Experiences* (New York: Macmillan, 1988), pp. 126-32.

41. Kovrig, *Communism in Hungary*, p. 364.

42. For a detailed discussion of the shift of political balance after the Cultural Revolution, see Harding, *China's Second Revolution*, pp. 40-69.

43. Deng Xiaoping, "On the Reform of the System of Party and State Leadership," *Selected Works of Deng Xiaoping* (Beijing: Foreign Languages Press, 1984), p. 316.

CHAPTER 3

PRELIMINARY IDEOLOGICAL AND POLITICAL LIBERALIZATION

A far-reaching economic reform program in a state socialist system cannot be isolated from ideological and political structures. The implementation of economic reform calls for a certain political flexibility to allow intellectual innovation and popular participation. Creating such a flexible political environment—whether intended to offset the conservative opposition to policy changes, stimulate new ideas, or mobilize public support for the reform—required preliminary ideological and political liberalization in both China and Hungary. The ideological liberalization increased doctrinal flexibility, which made fundamental economic change conceptually possible, gave the leadership a freer hand to pursue policy alternatives, and promoted the cooperation of the intellectual community with the reformist leadership. The political liberalization relaxed the government's control and encouraged a reconciliation between the state and the society after a political crisis. It was this initial political reform that set the stage for the ensuing market-oriented economic reform.

Yet these preliminary reforms were just that: preliminary. Political and ideological liberalization was never intended to lead to democratization, and the notion of the Party's leadership was never left open to challenge. The process of political reform thus followed a middle course between the attempt to preserve the old system and the demand for more fundamental changes.

Ideological Liberalization

A More Pragmatic Approach to Marxism

The economic system in state socialist countries emerged as a result of the revolutionary establishment of a new state that embarked upon construction of an economic system according to a preconceived ideological design. Therefore, any systemic change to this orthodox model presented ideological difficulties. In a polity where ideology was highly valued, economic reform that in some fundamental aspect contradicted previously accepted doctrine required ideological liberalization. This was accomplished in both Hungary and China by adopting a more pragmatic approach to Marxism. The basic character of this approach was not to abandon Marxism, which remained vital to the legitimacy of the Party, but to acknowledge that Marxism needed to be "developed" according to "changing reality." In so doing, the reformist leadership widened the range of acceptable interpretations of Marxism so that the official ideology itself could justify the reform. This pragmatic approach also gradually reduced the role of ideology in many aspects of life, so that Marxism became less relevant to the operation of the system.

In the early 1960s, having gradually recovered from the shock of the 1956 crisis, Hungary entered a more or less relaxed period during which the grip of Marxist ideology over society was loosened, and the groundwork for economic reform was laid. The relaxation of ideological restraints involved no single dramatic event but was a gradual and enduring process. In March 1962 Erik Molnar, the president of the Hungarian Historical Society, launched an attack on dogmatism in *Magyar Nemzet* (Hungarian nation), the political daily of the Patriotic People's Front (PPF). He argued that reality underwent constant change. For this reason, one could not accept ready-made theories of Marxism; such theories reflected a past reality and merely provided a general outline of future development. The attitude that everything of importance had already been resolved and that one need not pay constant attention to concrete and newly emerging problems, Molnar asserted, reflected an intellectual laziness that could "kill the living soul of Marxism." This article symbolized the beginning of the reform movement in Hungary.[1]

The somewhat relaxed ideological environment encouraged economists to call for a overhaul of the economic system. In 1963 *Kozgazdasagi Szemle* (Economic review) published an article by Tibor Liska, "Critique and Conception," advocating a regulated market economy. He argued for the first time that production relations were also of a market character in a socialist society and that a socialist economy had to be developed under the guidance of the world market.[2] To some scholars, this message was so blatantly opposed to the official economic policy and ideological course that they thought the real question was how and why it had been published at all. It was more likely the result of prompting from a higher level after long deliberation than an editorial whim to create a stir.[3]

The Agitprop Department of the Central Committee of the HSWP organized an ideological conference in December 1963. At the beginning of the conference, conservatives waged an offensive, accusing the reformers of "unpolitical behavior," "neglect of partisanship," and "kow-towing" to bourgeois economics.[4] Although in a much more indirect and milder form, some even revived the argument of the late 1950s that equated those who wanted reforms with the enemies of the socialist order. However, the orthodox ideological stance did not hold up. Many economists stood up for the reform initiatives. In his closing remarks, Rezso Nyers, a member of the Politburo at the time, not only rejected a petrified ideological line but also announced the start of concrete work on the development of the economic mechanism.[5] This conference marked the last serious conservative attempt to obstruct Hungarian economic reform on ideological and political grounds instead of discussing the subject on its merits. After that, both public and official opinion recognized the need to consider comprehensive economic reform.

In 1964 the Central Committee of the HSWP decided to investigate officially and in greater detail the possibility of far-reaching economic change. Nyers, who was commissioned to direct this effort, quickly established a series of committees consisting of approximately 150 Party workers, economists, and engineers, who considered the problem in depth over the following eleven months.[6] Committee members were told to think in a manner unconstrained by any ideological parameters. The reform program that this group produced, known as the New Economic Mechanism, indeed reflected a departure from the traditional state socialist economic system in two fundamental aspects. The first was the transformation of the centralized system of mandatory physical planning to a new system designed to link planning with market forces through indirect market instruments. Under this concept, firms would have more freedom to decide on investment and employment, and profits were to become the measure of success. The second change was the liberalization of prices so that they could reflect more truly the production costs and the market equilibrium between supply and demand.

In its resolution on economic reform in May 1966, the HSWP leadership took the stance that the specific features of a given socialist economy at a given period in time could not be considered eternal because they were subject to the laws of change and development.[7] With this simple but highly significant statement, the regime made it clear that the reform was not only in line with genuine Marxism-Leninism but also, and more important, an experiment subject to ongoing review, criticism, and revision.

This pragmatic approach challenged the applicability of orthodox Marxism to contemporary Hungary. In one article, for example, Lajos Maroti claimed that although Marxism-Leninism basically determined the character of the socialist system, the details of the operation of that system involved a great many alternatives. The far-sightedness of Marx in his time could not be unambiguously applied to the concrete conditions of a concrete country a hundred years later. There were no ready-made formulas for the further growth of socialist democracy, the author argued; "all this had to be 'invented' by ourselves."[8]

As noted in the previous chapter, China had a long history of using an official philosophy (such as Confucianism) or a national ideology (such as Marxism) to regulate social behavior. The grip of ideology tightened in the Cultural Revolution and lingered into post-Cultural Revolution period. In February 1977, five months after the death of Mao Zedong, *Renmin Ribao* (People's daily), *Hongqi* (Red flag), and *Jiefangjun Bao* (Liberation army daily), the three most influential Party propaganda organs, published a joint editorial that declared the determination of the current leadership (Hua Guofeng and his associates) to continue the basic line of the Maoist era: "Whatever policies Chairman Mao devised we will resolutely support, and whatever directives Chairman Mao laid down we will forever observe." This line was later referred to as the "two whatevers." The policies and directives of Mao that were to be supported and observed involved a rigid ideological line that emphasized on class struggle, the dictatorship of the proletariat, and continuous revolution, as elaborated in the political report of the Eleventh Party Congress of August 1977. Mao's theory of continuing the revolution under the dictatorship of the proletariat was applauded as "the most important achievement of Marxism in our time" and remained paramount in China. The following passage expresses the core of this ideological line:

> The socialist society covers a historical period of considerable length and in this period classes, class contradictions and class struggle, the struggle between the socialist road and the capitalist road and the danger of capitalist restoration invariably continue to exist, and there is the threat of subversion and aggression by imperialism and social imperialism. Therefore, in this historical period, it is imperative for the proletariat to persist in its struggle against the bourgeoisie and in its dictatorship over the latter and it is imperative to persist in continuing the revolution under this dictatorship.[9]

This statement preserved the ideological rigidity that had developed during the Cultural Revolution and left no room for exploring liberal strategies for economic development.

In order to seek freedom from ideological constraints in policy matters, the reformist group within the leadership, headed by Deng Xiaoping, took cautious but firm steps to demystify Marxism-Leninism and Mao's thought, especially the latter. The first few internally circulated speeches of Deng Xiaoping after his return to power in 1977 were concerned with how to understand Mao's thought completely and accurately. Mao himself, Deng argued, had said that "Marx, Engels, Lenin, and Stalin had all made mistakes—otherwise why did they correct their own manuscripts time and again? The reason they made these revisions was that some of the views they originally expressed were not entirely correct, perfect or accurate."[10]

The first public attack on dogmatism, widely believed to have been authorized by the reformist camp, came in a special commentary entitled "Practice Is the Sole Criterion for Testing Truth," published on 11 May 1978, in *Guangming Ribao* (Brightness daily). With lengthy citations from Marx, Lenin, and Mao, the article argued the simple proposition that Marxism-Leninism and Mao's thought had to be tested in practice, as the great leaders themselves had declared. As a philosophical doctrine, this may not appear particularly sophisticated or exciting, but in the context of the times it had serious implications. It was directly opposed to Hua's "two whatevers," and it was the first time that the infallibility of orthodox ideology had been questioned. Following this article, the reformist leaders deliberately provoked a nationwide debate over the "criterion of truth," known as "the emancipation of the mind" movement, so as to establish a consensus on the propositions that Mao was not a god, Mao had made mistakes, Mao himself had admitted his mistakes, and his policies therefore might not have been correct.[11]

This stance incurred stubborn resistance. In November 1978 Hu Sheng, a high-ranking propaganda specialist, made a speech in which he reproached the provincial party secretaries for making public their views concerning the issue of the "criterion of truth" when the Central Committee had not yet taken a clear stand.[12] Wang Dongxing, a member of the Politburo and a supporter of the Cultural Revolution, insisted that Chairman Mao's words and policies should be followed to the letter.[13] *Hongqi*, the theoretical organ of the Party, remained mute on this question for some time, which was rightly interpreted as siding with the conservative opposition. Not until late 1979 did it publish a self-criticism apologizing for its long silence.[14] It also subsequently admitted that the emancipation of the mind movement had met with strong resistance from within the Party.[15]

An official, if mild, endorsement of the emancipation of the mind movement was finally made in the communiqué of the Third Plenum of the Eleventh Central Committee in December 1978. Compared with the political report of the Eleventh Party Congress, the communiqué was a critical turning point. It announced a shift in the emphasis of the Party's work to socialist modernization, with the statement that "the large-scale turbulent class struggles of a mass character have in the main come to an end." This explicitly reversed the basic ideological line of Mao's era.[16] It also declared for the first time in Party history that "it is necessary to act firmly in line with economic laws, [and] attach importance to the role of the law of value."[17] This indicated that the CCP had begun to accept that there were objective laws beyond its will that governed economic development. Together with the call for the whole Party to concentrate on advancing agriculture, the Third Plenum signaled the start of the profound economic reforms that dominated the following decade in China.

As a follow-up to the Third Plenum, a theoretical conference (*lilun wuxuhui*) convened between 8 January and 3 April 1979, with 300-500 participants. The meeting was apparently called by Hu Yaobang, who was in charge of the Organization Department of the Central Committee, to criticize the "two whatevers." Because of the excitement produced by the Third Plenum, the conference became an opportunity for freer intellectual discussion and policy debate. Topics included the evaluation of Mao and the Cultural Revolution, the roles of leader and the masses, and the elimination of lifetime tenure for officials.[18] The sharp criticism of Mao and past policies aroused further apprehension among conservatives, leading to the imposition of limitations on political reform, discussed later in this chapter.

On 7 December 1984, *Renmin Ribao* published a commentary entitled "Theory and Reality," which used language strikingly similar to that used in Hungary thirteen years before. The article asserted that Marx had died a hundred years ago, the situation had changed since then, and some of his arguments might not be entirely correct. Indeed, the commentator argued that the works of Marx and Lenin, written in their times, could not resolve contemporary problems. This article provoked controversy both inside and outside China. What overseas observers saw as a call to abandon Marxism alarmed conservative Party leaders. *Renmin Ribao* issued a correction the following day, saying that it had meant that "we cannot expect the works of Marx and Lenin to solve *all* contemporary problems."[19]

This incident reflected the persistence and inflexibility of ideology in China. The debate on the applicability of Marxism to contemporary China was not raised again in public, or at least caught little public attention. It appeared that the reformists were convinced that it was more effective to reduce the role of ideology quietly, as it had done since the initiation of ideological liberalization, than to debate the applicability of Marxism head on.

The strategy of the reformist leadership can be illustrated by the interview with a member of Party general secretary Zhao Ziyang's staff by a Hong Kong magazine in 1986. On ideological matters, he commented, "We don't have much time, we have to do the most effective and beneficial tasks within a short time, we have no time to engage in ideological disputes." Asked about the official adherence to the cardinal principle of socialism, he replied, "I have a very simple logic: Socialism must be good, then whatever good things I have done must be socialism. Why bother to tangle with ideology?"[20] Using this guideline, China experimented with and adopted various economic policies, from foreign investment to contracting systems, virtually on the basis of practical merits rather than on ideological grounds.

In China the reduction of the role of ideology was evident in the less frequent use of heavily loaded ideological terms such as "Chairman Mao," "Mao Zedong Thought," "Marxism-Leninism," "class," "class struggle," and "the dictatorship of the proletariat" in official documents. For example, the phrase "Chairman Mao" appeared about once in every three sentences (29.7 percent) and "class/class struggle" in almost one out of five sentences (18.5 percent) in the political report of the Eleventh Party Congress in 1977. In the communiqué of the Third Plenum of the Eleventh Central Committee in 1978, in contrast, "Chairman Mao" appeared in only 13.3 percent of the sentences and "class/class struggle" barely made one out of every forty sentences (2.2 percent). In the political report of the Twelfth Party Congress in 1982, the frequency of usage dropped further to 1.2 percent and 1.6 percent, respectively. After 1984 the use of "Chairman Mao," "Mao Zedong Thought," and "Marxism-Leninism-Mao Zedong Thought" dropped to zero in major Party documents. The same trend can be found in the occurrence of the term "dictatorship" in Party documents which fell sharply after 1978 and dropped to zero in the resolution on economic reform in 1984.

Quotations from Marx, Engels, and Mao that once peppered official documents similarly began to disappear. Displays of their writings in Chinese bookstores made way for other books in the social sciences and popular entertainment. Orville Schell noted that the multivolume sets of selected works of the various "great leaders" of the Communist movement "could be seen spread out unimaginatively in window displays, quickly yellowing in the sun, their pale, artless bindings covered with a telltale film of grit and dust. So hard was it to sell these Party-sponsored collections of dogma that one would sometimes encounter huge piles of them stacked like surplus building materials in back storage areas of these stores."[21]

Chinese newspapers, the major propaganda instrument of the Party, also became less ideologically oriented. In 1964, before the Cultural Revolution, 61 percent of China's newspapers were directly related to Party propaganda work. In 1975, before the reform, this ratio had risen to 84 percent. By 1985 it had been reduced to 17 percent. At the same time, the proportion of newspapers with a specialized focus, such as market information, consumer reports, and entertainment news, rose from 10 percent in 1978 to 66 percent in 1985.[22] This change in ratio was due to the increase in the number of specialized publications rather than a reduction in the number of propaganda journals.

Alternative Sources of Information and Emerging Intellectual Freedom

The pragmatic approach to Marxist ideology permitted greater access to alternative concepts, methodologies, and information and therefore created a relatively open intellectual atmosphere in both Hungary and China. One characteristic of emerging intellectual freedom was the development of a more liberal attitude toward other, mainly Western, approaches to the social sciences, which had earlier been condemned as "bourgeois" and hence hostile to the interests of a socialist society. Scholarly exchange with the West was encouraged, along with more independent research in economics, sociology, and, to a lesser degree, political science. In the cultural sphere, there was greater tolerance of a wider range of literature and artistic expression. The Party leadership seemed to have realized that Marxism alone, especially class analysis, had been unable to provide an accurate account of a complex postrevolutionary society. A hitherto monotonous and narrow intellectual life began to diversify and expand.

The "Ideological Guidelines" of 1965 welcomed the new freedom of Hungarian scientists to study "bourgeois" research methods in an effort to apply them to Hungarian circumstances wherever appropriate.[23] Western theories were introduced, although with some criticism, to Hungarian audiences.[24] Meetings with Western scholars and experts, such as the round table conferences of American and Hungarian economists and of Italian and Hungarian economists, were held regularly every two or three years. After 1966 an academic journal, *Acta Oeconomica*, was published in English to foster the exchange of research ideas with a foreign audience.

Marxism and Leninism remained the general guideposts to the future, but scholars employed more sophisticated methodologies, more accurate data collection, and more detailed analyses of the present in their research. William Robinson observed that almost all sectors of Hungarian society enthusiastically endorsed the wide-scale utilization of Western academic disciplines and the application of Western research methods. The influence of the West was obvious not only in the sources cited in academic studies but also in the type of fieldwork researchers undertook, the terminology they used, the concepts they applied, and the conclusions they drew.[25]

Western theories, first economic, sociological, and philosophical, later political, were introduced in China as well. Bored with narrowly delimited discourse and thirsty for different perspectives, people found Western ideas and approaches quite refreshing. According to one report, at Beijing University seventy to eighty students signed up for an elective course on the economics of capitalism, while only seven to eight students opted for a course on Marxist economics.[26] Jean-Paul Sartre fit well with the increasingly popular philosophy of individualism. Sigmund Freud was fascinating since he explained human behavior in terms of libido instead of class origins. Even Alvin Toffler's *Third Wave* swept the nation because he did not discriminate between capitalism and socialism but said both were part of an industrial wave of human history, and because he fostered the dream that the Chinese had missed the second wave but could catch up with the third.[27] One graduate student from Beijing University explained, "It was not a matter of [whether these thinkers' views were] right or wrong but was a matter of another way of looking at things when people were bored with Marxism."[28]

Among college students cybernetics became one of the most fashionable theories in the social sciences. Others were systems engineering, dissipation (as in thermodynamics), and mutation (as in biology). There was a drastic change in the political language that officials, intellectuals and even ordinary people used. "System," "information," and "feedback" became the most popular terms in publications, replacing such terms as "class" and "revolution."[29]

There was a seeming similarity behind the interest of Hungarian and Chinese social scientists in studying these more "scientific" methodologies. On the one hand, it reflected a desire to explore non-Marxist approaches. On the other, it was a tactical device for avoiding conservative attacks. In Hungary the enthusiasm for econometrics and empirical research, such as surveys on income distribution and social mobility, in part reflected the conviction that mathematical equations and coefficients were less susceptible to criticism grounded in orthodox doctrine.[30] A young researcher at a major institute for the Central Committee in China frankly explained that the introduction of cybernetics, mathematics, and systems engineering into policy-making was an attempt to bypass the conservative leaders who did not tolerate open challenges to Marxism but knew nothing about science.[31]

Another important aspect of the growing intellectual freedom was the characterization of some of the social sciences as "science," indicating that they were governed by some objective laws and that a certain freedom of thought should be allowed in these fields. The first discipline to receive such sanction was economics—a crucial development because the emergence and success of economic reform depended on the cooperation of a community of economists, free to innovate, with the reformist leadership.

In Hungary the establishment of economics as a science occurred very early, almost immediately after the death of Stalin. Although open debate and publication of explicitly reformist economic literature in Hungary was virtually halted after the summer of 1957, the increasingly repressive ideological atmosphere of the late 1950s did not disrupt the development of economics as a scientific discipline. By the early 1960s, as a result of political liberalization, the discipline was finally freed from the more crass forms of direct ideological interference. Hungarian economists produced some quality research, such as Janos Kornai's *Anti-Equilibrium* (1971) and later *Economics of Shortage* (1980), which pinpointed the "soft budget constraint" as the cause of an economics of shortage in socialism and became a major contribution to the study of socialist economy.[32]

Research in political science unfolded in Hungary after the early 1970s. At first publications were rarely issued under the rubric of political science but under the headings of "political sociology," "state science," "scientific socialism," "international economic relations," or the "history of politics." According to Sandor Szorcsik, political science research initially concentrated on political institutions, public administration, the council system, parliament, and legislation; subsequently, other issues, such as the structure of interests and the institutional forms of democracy, came into prominence. The analysis of the economic and ideological factors of political power and the characteristics of political activities was emphasized later. Increasing stress was laid upon substantial problems of social democracy, political consciousness, and political culture.[33]

In November 1978 *Renmin Ribao* introduced the hitherto unorthodox notion that the "laws" of the social sciences, like those of the natural sciences, were "independent of the desires or standpoint of any individual or class."[34] The field of economics became relatively free and full of lively debates. The existence of more than three or four different groups of opinions and schemes on any theoretical or practical economic problem came to be considered perfectly normal. Details of discussions of several major principles of socialism are examined in chapter 4. Economic research institutes affliated with each of the central government's economic ministries, commissions, and departments were either rehabilitated or expanded. After 1978 there was a proliferation of economic research institutes in the local (provincial and municipal) government economic departments as well as the local academies of social sciences.

The political recognition of the necessity that economics be treated as a science independent of political values was quite rapidly followed by a similar recognition of the need for the study of scciety. The acceleration of social change, the complex character of progress, and the rise in social problems all resulted in a considerably higher demand for scientific research. Accordingly, the role of ideology in sociology, psychology, and even political science was reduced and greater intellectual freedom permitted. In Hungary a Sociological Research Group was created in 1963, and a similar body for social-psychological research was founded in 1965. China set up the Institute of Sociology under the Chinese Academy of Social Sciences (CASS) in 1979. People in this newly established field were mobilized to investigate the results of reform policies and to explore alternatives. In conjunction with some major universities, research institutes conducted many large-scale investigations using statistical sampling, attitudinal surveys, case studies, and follow-up surveys.[35]

The Chinese Political Science Association (CPSA) was founded in December 1980, and the Institute of Political Science was established within the Chinese Academy of Social Sciences a year later. A political science major was created at Beijing University after 1983. *Zhengzhixue Yanjiu* (Political science studies), a journal for political science launched in 1985 and published bimonthly since 1986, symbolized the start of a more active role for China's political scientists in the political reform process. However, the sensitivity of political issues and the lack of qualified researchers crippled the development of political science in both countries. As Samuel P. Huntington has argued, "It is impossible to have political scientists in the absence of political participation and political science has only developed with the expansion of political participation."[36]

As part of the "open-door" program and as a sign of the relaxed intellectual atmosphere, China conducted a comprehensive scholarly exchange with the West. For the first time, Western scholars were invited as guest professors to introduce Western social science theories into Chinese universities, which meant that these courses would be taught without the Marxist critique that a Chinese professor might feel obliged to provide. China also sent a large number of students and scholars to study in Western countries, mainly the United States. According to Leo Orleans, from 1979 through 1987, about 56,000 Chinese students and scholars came to the United States, of whom about 19,000 returned to China.[37] By 1989 the estimated figure of Chinese students and scholars in America had risen to 40,000.

The cultural sphere in both countries also enjoyed more freedom of expression. In 1966 the Central Committee of the HSWP issued a policy that permitted works that were "ideologically debatable and more or less in opposition to Marxism or socialist realism, as long as they [possessed] humanistic value and [were] not politically hostile." The secretary responsible for cultural affairs, Gyorgy Aczel, acknowledged that the imposition of Marxism had led to the overpoliticization of culture. Marxism did not have a monopoly of ideology and culture, according to Aczel, but only a hegemonic position.[38] This nuanced shift of terminologies indicated a more tolerant position on ideological matters. In a report to the Central Committee, the Ministry of Interior expounded the principle that people liable to ideological "errors" or those who harbor "hostile" ideologies should be countered not by the police but by the ideology of Marxism-Leninism itself.[39] This guideline was reflected in the "three-t" policy: Marxist works were supported (*tamogatott*), anti-Marxist works were prohibited (*tiltott*), and those in between were tolerated (*turt*).[40] Permitting this third category, which was vaguely defined and subjected to somewhat unpredictable limitations, allowed the arts and sciences to flourish in Hungary in the late 1960s. Sociographic investigations were allowed to describe dismal conditions in remote villages. Writers were allowed to show their concern for the cultural survival of the neighboring Magyar minorities. Even certain types of political satire were permitted on stage and screen.[41]

In China the Party promised to end the use of "campaigns" as a method of literary censorship. Writers would no longer arbitrarily be tagged as counterrevolutionary or antisocialist, or punished for "incorrect thought." The slogan "Literature Must Serve Politics" was abandoned in the summer of 1980 after a lengthy debate and replaced by a carefully wrought compromise: "Literature Must Serve the People and Serve Socialism." The revised slogan implied the existence of a newly acceptable apolitical area between support of and opposition to Party policy.[42]

Literati and artists either involved themselves in politics by exposing the negative side of past political life or detached themselves from politics by pursuing purely artistic expression. Typical of the first trend was reportage such as *Ren Yao Zhijian* (Between men and demons), which exposed the abuse of power in local government, and a much broader trend titled *shanghen* (scar) literature. The latter was represented by the school of so-called *menglong shi* (misty poetry) and the *xingxing* (star) school of visual art. In either case orthodox ideology was losing its hold. In the beginning, because society was used to strict control over the mass media and to literary works that praised only superhuman proletarian heroes, the new works aroused considerable public debate and caused the authorities a certain amount of anxiety.[43] Despite periodic criticism and attacks, these heterodox trends gradually became normal aspects of cultural life.

The increasing intellectual freedom facilitated the development of strategies for economic and political reform. But intellectual life was by no means free from restrictions; it was crippled by official and self-appointed censors. Time and again, conservatives tried to tighten controls on intellectual life. Nevertheless, the regime's willingness to hold open consultations also encouraged intellectuals, especially economists and sociologists, to work with the regime and provide advice. Together, these reforms created greater ideological freedom to pursue policy alternatives and promoted the cooperation of the intellectual community with the reformist leadership, which prepared the way for the ensuing economic reform.

Relaxation of Coercive Political Control

During the Stalin era, the notions of class struggle and the dictatorship of the proletariat were officially considered the essence of Marxism-Leninism and were widely employed by the communist parties in power to analyze and control their societies. The arbitrariness of these concepts victimized many high-ranking Party leaders as well as ordinary citizens during the Rakosi period in Hungary (1949-1956) and the Cultural Revolution in China (1966-1976). These ideas also conflicted with economic development; they not only turned the workplace into a battleground for class struggle (as occurred in China during the Cultural Revolution) but also excluded certain sectors of society, such as intellectuals and experts, who often were labeled as bourgeois, from using their knowledge and expertise to promote economic development. When the Party shifted its emphasis to economic reform and sought the active participation of society in its efforts, it had to reach a reconciliation with society by relaxing coercive political control. A critical step was to modify the notion of class struggle.

The notion of class struggle had both policy implications as well as social consequences. The concept prescribed the range of acceptable policy by providing a narrow definition of anything "proletarian." Any behavior or idea that deviated from the official line was labeled as "bourgeois" and "counterrevolutionary" and therefore subject to the dictatorship of the proletariat. When the entire society was immersed in class struggle, not only the Party apparatus but also most social units and individuals were mobilized to monitor the deviant behavior of others. To encourage people to watch one other, the Party offered rewards to informers, although some of them did seem to have been motivated by a genuine belief in the purity of revolution. The application of class labels categorized a section of society as an enemy subject to dictatorship. It also created a class-conscious society in which family members and relatives of the "class enemies" were discriminated against and deprived of opportunities for upward mobility, such as higher education and better employment.

The moderation of the notion of class struggle in Hungary was best reflected in Kadar's "alliance policy," formulated after the 1956 incident and sanctioned in 1962 by the Eighth Congress of the HSWP. It reversed the previous view of the Rakosi period from "Those who are not with us are against us" to "Those who are not against us are with us." The main purpose of the policy was to form, at least in spirit, an alliance of Party and non-Party people who could work toward common goals. All were encouraged, without regard to family background, past activity, or personal philosophy, to participate in Hungary's socialist construction. This proclamation had a positive effect on the population at large by eliminating mistrust, suspicion, and indifference.[44] It became the key element in the New Economic Mechanism, which required the exploitation of expertise, leadership skills, and talent from all corners of society.

Gyorgy Aczel, the HSWP secretary for ideology, related the following anecdote regarding the attenuation of the notion of class struggle: In 1958 a number of theorists spent three days arguing whether the Leninist slogan "Get the support of the poor peasants and fight the kulaks" was still valid. They were not able to decide and asked Janos Kadar to join them and listen to the discussion. Kadar came, listened, and then asked, "When did Lenin say 'get the support of the *former* poor peasants, and fight the *former* kulaks'?"[45] Standard class labels, he implied, were obsolete.

In the "Guiding Principles for the Congress by the Central Committee of the HSWP" issued in 1963, the party took a stand against "the false thesis of the permanent and absolute intensification of the class struggle." The Party "appeals also to those strata that formerly did not sympathize with our objectives, or were opposed to them, to support socialist construction."[46] The "Guiding Principles" stated that "the bulk of the members of the former exploiting classes, and even more their descendants, have adapted themselves to our new social order. Our socialist state and our laws ensure full civic rights to all law-abiding citizens, regardless of whether or not they formerly belonged to the exploiting classes."[47]

The regime denounced "the doctrine of the constant sharpening of the class struggle, the principle that the enemy must first of all be sought within the party," and "the view that there can be hardly any talk of errors since it was primarily undermining by the enemy that had to be taken into account."[48] As part of the "alliance policy" program, a general amnesty was announced, the number of forced labor camps was considerably reduced, the systems of internal exile and security internment without trial were eliminated, admission to university was no longer based on class origins, the jamming of Western radio broadcasts was stopped, and increasing numbers of Hungarians were allowed to travel to the West.[49] It was estimated that the number of Hungarians who visited nonsocialist countries quadrupled, going from 35,000 in 1960 to 143,000 in 1967.[50]

Paul Lendvai, a Hungarian who had gone into exile after 1956, returned to Hungary in 1964 and observed that the ability to travel to the West had reduced the popular distrust of the government. Wherever he looked, he could see a relaxation of tension between people and the Party. One of his childhood friends did not regret his decision to stay in Hungary after 1956, saying, "I couldn't care less about communism. I'm totally disinterested in politics. . . . What counts with me is the fact that I haven't had to rewrite my autobiography since 1958, that I can get on with my work in peace and—most important of all—we're able to earn some cash."[51]

Through political liberalization as represented by Kadar's "alliance policy," the Party struck a compromise with society. It turned a population hostile after the 1956 incident into cooperative, or at least indifferent, partners. By abolishing discriminatory measures against professionals and intellectuals, the liberalization also created opportunities for citizens to work with the regime to pursue reform programs.

In China, when the Third Plenum of the Eleventh Central Committee announced in 1978 the ending of "the large-scale turbulent class struggle of a mass character," the relief within the society was tremendous. The notion of class struggle was modified, redefined, and deemphasized. Usage of the term in Party documents was sharply reduced. The concept of "continuing the revolution under the dictatorship of the proletariat" was officially denounced.[52] In the "Resolution of Historical Problems" of 1981, the phrase "dictatorship of the proletariat" was quietly changed to "dictatorship of the proletariat/people's democratic dictatorship." Soon thereafter it became just the "people's democratic dictatorship," a term that had been used in the late 1940s and early 1950s and was less harsh and more inclusive than the one it replaced. The official stand on class struggle in the 1982 political report of the 12th Party Congress—"Although not a principal contradiction, class struggle will exist for a long time to come and may grow acute"—was modified in the "Resolution on Spiritual Civilization" of 1986 to read: "Although [it] exists, class struggle is no longer a principal contradiction."

The idea that class struggle was the key link was vanishing from all spheres: economic, political, and intellectual. Economists criticized leftist slogans such as "Profit first is a capitalist principle," "The superstructure determines the economic base," and "Commodity exchange produces capitalists," which had virtually subordinated economic development to class struggle. These attacks on leftism primarily served one purpose, that is, to remove the notion of class struggle from the economic sphere so that the economy could perform without too much political interference. The theme of the equality of all before the truth, regardless of their class status, appeared time and again in newspapers and academic journals. Intellectuals, once labeled as "bourgeois specialists" who needed to be reformed, were eventually categorized as part of the working class.[53] Discussions about the establishment and perfection of a legal system to replace arbitrary class struggle occupied a large portion of academic attention. The equality of all before the law was officially announced, indicating that citizens would be entitled to fair trials and no one would enjoy privileges above the law.[54] Despite the continuing declaration of the existence of class struggle in all subsequent Party documents, it was fair to say that after the beginning of the political liberalization, the notion of class struggle faded from public life and revived only when there was a need for strengthening political and ideological control.

Soon after the Third Plenum of the Eleventh Central Committee of the CCP, the Central Committee adopted a decision to remove class designations.[55] According to a report in *Hongqi*, about 2.78 million people were relieved of the labels "landlord" and "rich peasant" and 700,000 freed from the label "capitalist."[56] All those who were politically persecuted during the Cultural Revolution were rehabilitated, and all the rightists were cleared of blame for wrongdoings. Since their families and relatives had been victims of discrimination as well, the number of those who benefited from the decision to do away with class labels was multiplied severalfold. After the moderation of the notion of class struggle, class origins were no longer important in the recruitment of college students, Party members, or government employees. Once a blank that had to be filled in on almost every form, "family origin" simply disappeared from personal records. Furthermore, although "bourgeois" continued to carry negative connotations in official vocabulary, it did quite the opposite in unofficial usage.

The direct consequence of the moderation of the methods of class struggle in China was the depoliticization of society. As class struggle dropped out of the leadership's attention, there were fewer incentives for people to inform on their neighbors than to find some way to make money; the system of monitoring deviant ideas and behavior gradually dissolved. People were less and less intimidated by the label of "class enemy." Although heretical ideas could not appear in official newspapers, and political opponents continued to be imprisoned or expelled from the Party, outsiders were often stunned at how freely people criticized the Party and its leaders in the street and in their homes in ways absolutely unimaginable a few years before.

Another direct consequence of the loosening of the notion of class struggle was the creation of a cooperative relationship between the establishment and society. As a county Party secretary put it, "Before the reform, when we used the notion of class struggle to analyze people, we saw class enemies everywhere. Now that we use the notion of economic reform to analyze people, we see experts everywhere."[57] The new policy rallied popular support and social resources for economic reform.

As in Hungary, the relaxation of political controls in China involved lifting the ban on listening to foreign radio stations such as the Voice of America and BBC, the violation of which just a few years earlier could have resulted in prison sentences of several years. A growing number of Chinese were allowed to travel and study abroad. From 1983 to 1988, according to a news report, about 300,000 people went abroad for personal purposes. Since only about half of those who obtained passports also obtained foreign visas, the number of people the Chinese government granted permission to leave was double that figure.[58]

The easing of political control marked a preliminary departure from the totalistic system. It loosened the coercive binding that confined people to the official structure and created possibilities for future change. While ideological liberalization stimulated the conception of economic reform, the relaxation of political control fostered the social environment that would allow reform to be put into practice.

The Limits to Political Reform

Although ideological liberalization and the relaxation of political control constituted the beginnings of political reform in Hungary and China, there were serious restrictions to the process. Political reform is dynamic: the sudden inflow of alternative information can change people's perceptions much faster than can changes in the more inert political and economic structures. Political decompression in China and Hungary tended to generate political energy and to raise questions about the absolute power of the Communist Party. In response, the Party reiterated that its leadership was to be regarded as an immovable cornerstone.

In Hungary the Party never hesitated to set the limits to political reform. In a speech given in 1969, Bela Biszhu, a member of the Politburo, declared that Party leadership was not open to challenge:

> We supported ideological and scientific research aimed at achieving a deeper, truer, knowledge of reality, and thus helping to promote the construction of socialism and the further development of its achievements. But we most resolutely oppose attempts, disguised as "ideological" or "scientific" that aim by organizational means to become political forces and ultimately to make the power of the working class, the people's power, open to question.[59]

The power of the working class, according to Biszhu, was located in its representatives, the Party leadership. Although never explicitly specified, four aspects of Hungarian life were beyond attack: the Party leadership, Marxism, socialism, and the alliance with the Soviet Union.

From the very beginning, the Chinese Communist Party, too, made it clear that its leadership was unquestionable. When the theoretical conference immediately after the Third Plenum of the Eleventh Central Committee produced sharp criticisms of Mao and past Party policies, more conservative members of the leadership complained that some people were trying to eliminate Party leadership and were going too far in their calls for political reform. Persuaded by their argument, Deng Xiaoping announced in his concluding remarks to the meeting on 30 March 1979, that challenges to the Party leadership, the socialist system, the dictatorship of the proletariat, and Marxism-Leninism-Mao Zedong Thought were not to be allowed.[60] These later became known as the four cardinal principles. They were included in the constitution of the People's Republic of China in 1982, and the principle of the leadership of the Communist Party was declared the most important of the four.

These cardinal principles, Hungarian and Chinese, remained vague. On the one hand, they did delineate, as an ultimate boundary, the proposition that the Party leadership was not subject to challenge. However, since the basic principles were never clearly defined, there was still plenty of room for interpretation. In fact, their contents, such as socialism, had changed over the years, from public ownership and central planning to mixed ownership and a market economy.

Whenever the Party perceived a threat to its leadership, it launched counterattacks against its critics in an effort to consolidate its control. In Hungary these efforts took the form of personnel purges and individual harassment. For example, Andras Hegedus, the director of the Sociological Study Group, was officially reprimanded in the 1968 communiqué of the Central Committee of the HSWP secretariat for his rightist views; he was later removed from his position for criticizing the 1968 Soviet invasion of Czechoslovakia.[61] In 1973 the secretariat launched an investigation of three dissenting intellectuals: Hegedus, Janos Kis, and Mihaly Vajda. The investigation team reported that these scholars had "overstepped the boundaries of our ideological public life" by attempting to present a different version of Marxism. All three were expelled from the Party.[62] In October 1974 the police detained sociographer Gyorgy Konrad, sociologist Ivan Szelenyi, and poet Tamas Szentjoby on charges of antisocialist agitation. They were accused of illegally disseminating more than the prescribed number of copies of Konrad's study of alienation in an urbanized society. Szelenyi and Szentjoby had to leave the country.[63]

In China the Party waged repeated campaigns to turn back tendencies to challenge the Party leadership. In 1980-1981, the CCP launched an attack on "bourgeois liberalization" in literary works. According to Hu Qiaomu, who was then in charge of Party propaganda work, this trend included the refusal to conform to socialist principles, the assertion of absolute freedom to voice "wrong" ideas, lack of interest in studying Mao Zedong Thought, and exaggeration of the Party's past mistakes. All these propensities, Hu pointed out, had been reflected in recent literary works and should be criticized.[64]

In the fall of 1983, in what was known as the campaign against "spiritual pollution," the Party tried to regain its ideological grip over a society that appeared to be slipping out of its control. The major targets of the campaign included obscene publications, pornographic videotapes, and vulgar music; literature and art that exaggerated the negative side of socialist society; and theoretical writings that spread bourgeois ideas, such as individualism and liberalism. Those who had expounded theories of alienation and humanism were forced to renounce their beliefs.[65] The practice of different forms of artistic and literary expression other than socialist realism was openly criticized. The introduction of Western theories and literature was denounced as too enthusiastic and uncritical. Love songs and long hair were even banned by some local authorities.[66]

There were two general interpretations of the political retrenchment that occurred during the reform process in state socialist countries. One held that the cause lay in the very nature of the Communist Party. It argued that the adherence to the Party leadership was a manifestation of the limitations inherent in the thinking of individual leaders and the inflexibility of the political system. The Party would never give up its monopoly of political power. Even the most reform-minded leaders themselves, this interpretation argued, were never prepared to countenance disorder in society, lack of discipline in the Party, or the spread of ideas that they regarded as subversive.

The other interpretation stressed the tactical aspect of political retrenchment. It argued that in order to keep the reform going, it was necessary to remove any targets of conservative attack. For example, Western reporters observed that although Kadar had repeatedly criticized the "false applauding" of the reforms as a "restoration of capitalism" or a "bourgeois liberalization," he sometimes appeared to be trying to convince his detractors on the left of his sincerity as a socialist rather than attempting to dispute "revisionism."[67] Even the most recognized conservative spokesman, Hu Qiaomu, argued that if the Party did not fight against bourgeois liberalization, the leftists would say, "See what has come of your policy!" and they would claim that only their leftist methods would work.[68] Stuart Schram similarly interpreted the argument of a high-ranking CCP reformer in this way: "It has been necessary to throw the young hot-heads of the democratic movement to the wolves in order to preserve the possibility for carrying out reforms in a systematic way from above."[69]

The unique position of reformers in state socialist countries determined the nature of political development. They had to operate within a constrained environment and adopt a centrist approach in pursuing reforms. To achieve the goal of reform, the Party had to relax ideological and political controls so that the people could participate and intellectuals innovate. However, if the society were genuinely free from ideological and political constraints, it might mount a challenge to the fundamental legitimacy of the Communist Party. Committing themselves to reform on the one hand and to the Party leadership on the other, the reformist leaders in both countries were constantly conducting a two-front struggle: They had to fight the orthodox left to encourage innovation and at the same time to contest the deviations of the right to preserve their power.

Commenting on China's case, Tang Tsou has described this two-front struggle as the middle course between two extreme positions. He has pointed out that although this middle-of-the-road tendency was too weak to be of any significance in the past, this moderate position in both the Party leadership and society had come to constitute the strongest political force in China. Yet following this middle course would mean frequent oscillations between advances and backlashes, repression of the left and the right, and the uneven development of liberalization and the differential reimposition of control and repression in various areas of social, political, and economic life: "The price of change will always be high and the psychological, political, and human burden of the reformer heavy."[70]

Despite the constant repression of the challenge to the Party leadership, the primary emphasis of this two-front struggle was that the major threat came from dogmatism or the leftists. Reform therefore followed a pattern of two steps forward and one step backward, with the long-term trend toward greater liberalization.

This growing liberalization is the result of two factors. One is the market-oriented economic reform, which has decentralized political and economic power. When there are alternative paths to wealth and status, not all elites stick to political power, as the totalitarian model would imply. Therefore, it is not entirely unacceptable for the Party to loosen its monopoly of political power. The second factor is the political learning of the elites. The Party leadership had been gradually adjusting to some of the irreversible changes brought by economic reform and political liberalization, redefining the meaning and forms of its leadership, and developing new institutions to accommodate changes. The centrist position that the reformist leadership adopted had taken a more liberal direction over the decades of economic and political reform. That the reformist leaders had the ability to launch far-reaching economic and political reforms testified to their flexibility. The extent of this flexibility would largely determine the outcome of political and economic reform in both countries.

Comparison

Both the Hungarian and Chinese cases demonstrate that ideological and political liberalization preceded or ran parallel with economic reform. They pointed to a common proposition: A market-oriented economic reform is ideologically incompatible with orthodox Marxism and operationally incompatible with a tightly controlled system. Therefore, the implementation of a far-reaching economic reform program requires preliminary political reform to loosen ideological controls over the formation of economic policy and relax political controls over society. These processes of ideological and political liberalization took place in the early 1960s in Hungary and the late 1970s in China. The ideological liberalization removed the constraints of dogma and involved a more pragmatic approach to Marxism. It also reduced the role of ideology altogether and promoted wider access to alternative sources of information, increased scholarly exchange with the West, and created a more open intellectual atmosphere. The preliminary political liberalization deemphasized the notion of class struggle and granted greater individual freedom to generate social support for reform programs.

Within the context of state socialism, however, preliminary political reform faces serious restrictions. Hungary had its four untouchables and China has its four cardinal principles. These shared certain sacred elements: the Party leadership, the socialist system, and Marxist ideology. The only difference was that the CCP insisted on the dictatorship of the proletariat, while the HSWP defended the principle of friendship with the Soviet Union. This difference can be explained in that the HSWP came to power with the help of the Soviet Union, whereas the CCP had experienced a long, bitter, and successful class struggle. The fourth principle—either the friendship of the Soviet Union or class struggle—thus represented the basis of power for the leadership in the given country.

In the first phase of transition from traditional state socialism, the two countries also diverged widely. Since the degree of ideological indoctrination had been greater in China than in Hungary, the process of ideological liberalization in China was more destructive to the stability of society. Breaking the stronger hold of a more dogmatic ideology in China required harsher measures. The reformist leadership launched a nationwide campaign to "emancipate the mind" in 1978. All the propaganda machines were mobilized to advocate "practice" instead of "Marxist ideology" as the criterion for testing truth. The more closed the mind, the greater the shock it would experience. The sudden exposure to alternative value systems and the striking contrast with the materialistic West amplified society's disillusionment with the status quo.

Hungary, for its part, did not experience as intensive an ideological opening. Hungary had not emphasized ideology as much as had China. Because the HSWP was not as successful as the CCP in indoctrinating the population, Marxism had never become an indigenous ideological doctrine in Hungarian society. And the role of this somewhat foreign ideology had been reduced for quite a long time in Hungary, especially following the 1956 Twentieth Party Congress of the CPSU, in which Stalinism was denounced. At the same time, religion provided an alternative belief system in Hungary. Moreover, since Hungary had never lost contact with the rest of the world, it did not experience the same shock of opening as did China.

The timing of preliminary political reform was different as well. It took twelve years for the Hungarians to prepare for economic reform after the events of 1956. Therefore, the liberating impulse of political reform was absorbed gradually. Moreover, because ideological opening preceded economic reform, the shock of ideological liberalization and economic reform did not occur simultaneously and thus did not exacerbate each other. In China, because of the urgency of reform, economic reform and ideological liberalization were introduced together only two years after the end of the traumatic Cultural Revolution. As the downgrading and redefinition of dogma was carried out in a short period of time, the dissolution of the previous ideological system was unsettling to society. Threatened by the more dynamic liberal tendencies, the authorities tended to tighten their control more often. As a result, the zigzag pattern of political development was more obvious in China.

The preliminary political reform we have discussed so far did not represent a substantial move toward political democracy in these two societies, for it still involved serious restrictions on political freedom. Yet it generated significant problems for the leadership nonetheless. One was to find a compelling ideological justification for the restructuring of the country's economic and political systems. The Party acknowledged that Marxist doctrine was not a closed system but had to evolve to meet changing circumstances and could periodically incorporate new conceptual breakthroughs. The aim was to provide a persuasive theoretical explanation of the reform program. However, discrediting the old framework of ideology did not necessarily guarantee the creation of a new ideological basis of legitimacy. Instead, it tended to produce a vacuum in the belief system, which had two consequences: a crisis of faith and a decline in public morality.

The other problem was that political liberalization was more successful in releasing political energy than in creating the means to regulate those newly released forces. Without further political reform to rebuild the basis of Party authority and to make the institutional arrangements that could channel increased participation, the liberating impulse would be destructive to Party legitimacy and lead to political instability.

NOTES

1. William F. Robinson, *The Pattern of Reform in Hungary: A Political, Economic and Cultural Analysis* (New York: Praeger, 1973), p. 51.

2. L. Szamuely, "The Second Wave of the Economic Mechanism Debate and the 1968 Reform in Hungary," *Acta Oeconomica* 33, no. 1-2 (1984): 44-48.

3. Ibid.

4. Ibid.

5. Ibid.

6. Robinson, *The Pattern of Reform in Hungary*, p. 57.

7. Ibid., p. 58.

8. Lajos Maroti, "The Building of Socialism on a Higher Level," *New Hungarian Quarterly* 12, no. 44 (Winter 1971): 4-5.

9. "Political Report of the Eleventh Party Congress," *Hongqi*, no. 8 (1977): 9-10.

10. Deng Xiaoping, "The 'Two Whatevers' Do Not Accord with Marxism," in *Selected Works of Deng Xiaoping* (Beijing: Foreign Language Press, 1984), p. 51.

11. Immanuel C.Y. Hsu, *China Without Mao: The Search for a New Order* (Oxford: Oxford University Press, 1982), pp. 44-52.

12. Helmut Martin, *Cult and Canon: The Origins and Development of State Maoism* (New York: M. E. Sharpe, 1982), pp. 81-82.

13. Ibid., p. 125.

14. Editorial commentator, "Renzhen buhao zhenli biaozhun taolun zheyike" [Sincerely making up the lesson on the discussion of truth], *Hongqi*, no. 9 (1979): 2-4.

15. Office of theoretical education, "sanzhong quanhui yilai zhongyao wenxian xuexi tiyao" [Guideline for studying the important documents since the third plenum], *Hongqi*, no. 3 (1983): 42; for more detailed discussions about the ideological development in this period, see Stuart R. Schram, "Economics in Command? Ideology and Policy Since the Third Plenum, 1978-84," *China Quarterly*, no. 99 (September 1984): 417-61; and Martin, *Cult and Canon*, chapters 7-8.

16. "Communiqué of the Third Plenum of the 11th Central Committee," *Hongqi*, no. 1 (1979).

17. Ibid., p. 17.

18. The documents of this conference were never published. Still, many of the formal speeches were subsequently published in revised versions that did not acknowledge their origin. My information comes from personal interviews with several participants of the conference, Beijing, August 1986. (Interviewees requested anonimity.)

19. *Renmin Ribao*, 7-8 December 1984, p. 1.

20. *Zhengming*, August 1986, p. 34. The interviewee who appeared in the report went by the name of Shao Ding, apparently a pen name. He was reportedly a visiting scholar at Princeton University and the representative of the Institute of Economic Reform to the United States.

21. Orville Schell, *Discos and Democracy: China in the Throes of Reform* (New York: Pantheon Books, 1988), pp. 94-97.

22. Ling Zhijun, "Qiantan bashiniandai de zhongguo baoye" [On the Chinese newspapers in the 1980s], *Renmin Ribao* (overseas edition), 21 June 1986, p. 2.

23. Robinson, *The Pattern of Reform in Hungary*, p. 95.

24. For example, W. Fellner, "Schools of Thought in the Mainstream of American Economics," *Acta Oeconomica* 18, no.3-4 (1977): 247-61; and M. Dobb, "Modern Western Theories of Economic Growth," *Acta Oeconomica* 1 (1966): 379-84.

25. Robinson, *The Pattern of Reform in Hungary*, pp. 228-29.

26. Stanley Rosen, "Prosperity, Privatization, and China's Youth," *Problems of Communism* 34 (March-April 1985): 27.

27. Alvin Toffler, *The Third Wave* (New York: Morrow, 1980).

28. Personal conversation with a graduate student from Beijing University, January 1984.

29. In 1980, two young Chinese authors, Jin Guantao and Liu Qingfeng, published an article entitled "Contemplation of History" in *Qingnian Luntan* [Youth forum]. Although the journal was banned after the first two issues, the article was copied and widely distributed among young intellectuals. Against the traditional method of class analysis, the authors tried to use the theory of cybernetics to explain the evolution of Chinese history and the reasons why it had been stagnant for so long. Their fresh, bold arguments made college students thirsty for new ideas. Although the guardians of orthodox Marxist historiography criticized the piece, the authors did not get into political trouble. They later edited a series of books entitled *Zou Xiang Weilai* [Go to the future], which introduced a wide range of Western schools of thought in the social sciences and humanities. The series was the top best seller in China for several years.

30. Rudolf Andorka, "Institutional Changes and Intellectual Trends in Some Hungarian Social Sciences," *East European Politics and Societies* 7, no. 1 (Winter 1993): 83-87.

31. Personal conversation with a member of the Institute of Development, Beijing, April 1981.

32. Janos Kornai, *Economics of Shortage* (New York: North-Holland, 1980).

33. Sandor Szorcsik, "Social Sciences, Political Science and Societal Practice," in *Politics and Political Science in Hungary*, ed. G.Y. Szoboszlai (Budapest: HSWP Institute for Social Sciences, 1982), pp. 247-63.

34. *Renmin Ribao*, 28 November 1978, p. 3.

35. For example, an "urban economic reform investigation" was conducted in conjunction with nineteen institutes and universities and attitudinal surveys with the sociology department of Beijing University. The Institute of Reform organized a series of urban economic reform surveys, examining urban enterprise behavior, fixed capital investment, consumption funds, and employment and wage systems. It also coordinated projects on the activities of enterprise directors, social reaction to price reform, the social security system, and attitudes of youth toward employment and socioeconomic life. The data base included thousands of survey samples.

36. Samuel P. Huntington, "One Soul at a Time: Political Science and Political Reform," *American Political Science Review* 82, no. 1 (March 1988): 6 and 8.

37. Leo A. Orleans, *Chinese Students in America: Policies, Issues, and Numbers* (Washington, D.C.: National Academy Press, 1988).

38. Gyorgy Aczel, "Hungarian Cultural Policy and the Hegemony of Marxism," *New Hungarian Quarterly* 12, no. 42 (Summer 1971): 3-22.

39. Robinson, *The Pattern of Reform in Hungary*, p. 226.

40. Bennett Kovrig, *Communism in Hungary: From Kun to Kadar* (Stanford, Calif.: Hoover Institute Press, 1979), pp. 402-403. Andorka, "Institutional Changes and Intellectual Trends," p. 80.

41. Kovrig, *Communism in Hungary*, p. 403.

42. Perry Link, "Intellectuals and Cultural Policy After Mao," in *Modernizing China: Post-Mao Reform and Development,* eds. A. Doak Barnett and Ralph N. Clough (Boulder, Colo.: Westview Press, 1986), pp. 81-102.

43. From 1977 to 1979, short stories with titles such as "The Class Master," "Love Should not Be Forgotten," "The Wounded," and "The Sacred Task," exposed the tragedies of the Cultural Revolution and touched the previously forbidden zones of humanism, provoking heated public controversy. The sensation came about in part because these short stories were allowed to be published.

44. Peter A. Toma and Ivan Vogyes, *Politics in Hungary* (San Francisco: W. H. Freeman, 1977), p. 15.

45. Gyorgy Aczel, "A New System of Values," *New Hungarian Quarterly* 21, no. 77 (Spring 1980): 10 (emphasis in the original).

46. Laszlo Boka, "In an Atmosphere of Humanity," *New Hungarian Quarterly* 4, no. 9 (January-March 1963): 8-9.

47. Ibid., p. 12.

48. Aczel, "A New System of Values," p. 4.

49. Robinson, *The Pattern of Reform in Hungary*, p. 79.

50. Bennett Kovrig, *The Hungarian People's Republic* (Baltimore: The Johns Hopkins University Press, 1970), p. 141.

51. Paul Lendvai, *Hungary: The Art of Survival*, trans. by Noel Clark with the author, (London: I. B. Tauris, 1988), pp. 56-57.

52. See Hu Qiaomu, "About Some Concepts of Class Struggle in the Socialist Period," in *Selected Documents Since the Third Plenum, Part I* (Beijing: People's Press, 1982), pp. 157-60.

53. The phrase "intellectuals are a part of the working class" was put into Deng Xiaoping's speech on the National Conference of Science in March 1978 by a group of theorists after quite a fight with dogmatists within the Party. Personal interview with one of the theorists, Beijing, July 1986.

54. See the "Communiqué of the Third Plenum of the 11th Central Committee," *Hongqi*, no. 1 (1979): 19. The communiqué says that the "people" are equal before the law, which leaves room for definition of "people."

55. *Beijing Review*, 21 June 1980, p. 10.

56. Office of theoretical education, "Guideline for studying important documents," p. 42.

57. *Renmin Ribao*, 12 October 1984, pp. 1, 2.

58. *Renmin Ribao* (overseas edition), 29 January 1989, p. 1.

59. Judy Batt, *Economic Reform and Political Change in Eastern Europe: A Comparison of the Czechoslovak and Hungarian Experiences* (New York: Macmillan, 1988), pp. 157-58.

60. Deng Xiaoping, "Uphold the Four Cardinal Principles," *Selected Works of Deng Xiaoping*, 1984), pp. 180-81.

61. William Robinson, "Hegedus, His Views and His Critics," *Studies in Comparative Communism* 2, no. 2 (Autumn 1969): 122-24.

62. Kovrig, *Communism in Hungary*, pp. 405-406.

63. Ibid.

64. Hu Qiaomu, "Dangqian sixiang zhanxian de ruogan wenti" (Some questions on the present ideological front), *Hongqi*, no. 23 (1981): 10-13.

65. For example, Zhou Yang made a self-criticism in *Renmin Ribao*, November 6, 1983, p. 1.

66. For some critical articles, see *Beijing Review*, 7 November 1983, p. 13; 14 November 1983, p. 4; and *Guangming Ribao*, 8 October 1983.

67. Robinson, *The Pattern of Reform in Hungary*, p. 84.

68. Hu Qiaomu, "Dangqian sixiang zhanxian de ruogan wenti," p. 3.

69. Schram, "Economics in Command?" p. 241.

70. Tang Tsou, *The Cultural Revolution and Post-Mao Reforms: A Historical Perspective* (Chicago: University of Chicago Press, 1986), pp. 251-56.

CHAPTER 4

THE POLITICAL CONSEQUENCES OF ECONOMIC REFORM

Preliminary political reform prepared the stage for economic reform. Economic reform, with its emphasis on marketization and the modification of public ownership, in turn had a substantial impact on politics, especially by creating pressure for political change in both Hungary and China. This chapter discusses three of these consequences. One was the reinforcement of ideological liberalization. By departing from traditional conceptions of economic structure, economic reform continuously challenged the previous notion of socialism and demanded its further redefinition. The effort to redefine socialism in turn reinforced the process of ideological liberalization. A second result of economic reform was the further erosion of political control. The increasing economic freedom and expansion of the market relaxed the rigid socioeconomic binding of individual citizens to the official structure and hence strengthened the society's autonomy. This growing independence smoothed the way for the forthcoming societal challenge to the Party leadership. Finally, a third effect of economic reform was the development of inflation, inequality, and corruption, which produced socioeconomic grievances. These grievances were potentially destabilizing and placed increasing political pressure on policymakers to slow down the pace of reform for the sake of stability.

Redefining Socialism

From the vast Marxist literature scholars of Marxism have synthesized the following elements of Marx's vision of the future economic system: (1)

socialization of the means of production and exchange, (2) economic planning in place of the alleged anarchy of the market, (3) valuation of goods according to their labor content, (4) abolition of money, (5) obligation of all to labor, and (6) distribution according to contribution in socialism and then according to need in communism.[1] In practice, these elements were transformed into three major principles that shaped the traditional understanding of socialism: centralized economic planning, public ownership of the means of production with state ownership as its highest level, and distribution of income according to work, which largely evolved into an egalitarian principle. Economic reform contradicted this traditional understanding of socialism in some fundamental ways. Because the regime did not want to renounce socialism as an ideology, it had to redefine socialism to make it more compatible with the economic reform program. The redefinition of these principles of socialism accompanied the process of ideological liberalization and was propelled by the ongoing economic reform. In this section, I discuss the redefinition of socialism along these three major lines: plan and market, state and nonstate ownership, and egalitarianism and incentives.

Plan and Market

Economic planning was long regarded the centerpiece of the socialist economy. Embodied in the Soviet economic model that was accepted as the orthodox road to socialism, it was intended to avoid the anarchy of overproduction and the cyclical crises characteristic of capitalist society. The rediscovery of the role of the market in a socialist economy occurred in Hungary well before the reforms of 1968. Throughout the early and mid-1960s, there were fairly free debates among East European economists about the defects of a planned economy. Although the Hungarians were the first to introduce the market mechanism into the socialist economy in practice, they were not alone in considering it.[2]

The discussion of economic reform in Hungary from the 1950s to the 1960s evolved through several stages: from blaming the economic problems on the hostile outside world and criminal sabotage, to blaming them on poor organization and lack of discipline, to citing faults in the incentive system, and finally to the realization that "the entire system of planning, decision-making, stimulation, price, credit, wages, investment, supply distribution, foreign and domestic trade must be revised, the economic mechanism itself must be changed."[3] In his article "Critique and Conception," published in 1963, Tibor Liska boldly suggested that production relations were of a market character in socialist society, that the socialist economy should be developed under the guidance of the world market, and that reform should produce a market economy. He also rejected any possibility of rational price-setting by a central authority and advocated that prices be determined purely on the basis of supply and demand.[4]

Subsequent discussions of reform in Hungary, however, did not completely follow Liska's bold argument. Full marketization was not an option at the time because of ideological limits. Instead, the debate focused on two broad alternatives: whether the Hungarian economy should retain the directive form of the planned economy or whether it should introduce market mechanisms as an indispensable part of the overall economic system.[5] As a result of empirical analyses of the failures of the centralized planning system, by the mid-1960s Hungarian economists had carried out a fundamental reappraisal of the role of the market in the socialist economy.[6] "Marxist social and economic science is making progress all the time," wrote Rezso Nyers, the Party secretary in charge of economic affairs. "In the course of this development it was gradually realized that commodity and monetary relationships have not only to be tolerated but have to be assured a decisive role in a socialist economy."[7] Bela Csikos-Nagy, director of the National Materials and Price Office, argued that Marxist economists always held the view that living and developing socialism could not be permanently encased in an unchangeable theoretical system. As he put it, "Economic reform is built up on the dual hypothesis that (1) no purposeful economic development is conceivable without central planning, and (2) no rational distribution is possible without a market."[8]

The view had become predominant in Hungary that commodity relations and the law of value must continue to operate—even prevail—in a socialist economy and must be utilized to the best advantage as levers of development. Commodity relations and the economic categories related to them, such as the market, prices, production costs, profit, and credit, should play an active part in a socialist economy, a much greater part than it had before. "The organic linking of socialist planning with the active role played by commodity and money relations," declared Nyers in 1966, "is historically unavoidable."[9]

The 1966 Party resolution on economic reform highlighted three features of the reform: (1) Day-to-day coordination of the economy would be left mainly to the market mechanism and the relationships among supply, demand, and prices; (2) central economic management would have mainly macroeconomic tasks: fixing the main macroeconomic proportions, working out development goals, and seeing to their fulfillment; and (3) firms, as buyers and sellers, would be active in the marketplace and substantially independent of the state.[10] Thus, the critical role of market in a socialist economy was theoretically established and accepted in Hungary by the end of 1966.

Although the intellectual atmosphere became much freer in the early post-Mao era in China, it was limited by the as-yet partial character of ideological liberalization. Accordingly, the Chinese did not embrace the idea of a market-oriented economy at the beginning of their economic reform. After the Third Plenum of the Eleventh Central Committee in 1978, in an effort to stimulate enterprise performance, both practice and theoretical discussions of economic reform focused on how to delegate decision-making power to local authorities and production units and how to allow local authorities, enterprises, and workers to retain profits. The reform policies after 1979 were based on the approach of "delegating powers and conceding interests to lower levels."[11] However, because the enterprises were not constrained in a competitive market context, their more autonomous operation did not necessarily conform to the good of the national economy. There appeared to be an unreasonably high number of requests from the enterprises to develop high-technology industry and strong pressure for increasing investment that ultimately led to excessive demand. Economists had to seek answers to the new problems that arose from the principle of delegating powers and conceding interests, such as the relationship between central and local authorities, the relationship between enterprise and the government, and the relationship among enterprises, as well as the actual rights and responsibilities of each side.

With the general relaxation in the intellectual atmosphere after 1978, the previously sensitive topic of marketization gradually became the center of discussion in the first few years of economic reform.[12] For example, as early as 1979, an article in *Jingji Yanjiu* (Economic studies) pointed out that the market and planning were the two mechanisms that human society had developed to regulate the economy. The article argued that the market was the result of a commodity economy, not of capitalism. The market as a regulating mechanism might provide links among production, supply, and distribution; correct imbalances; and promote competition in socialist as well as capitalist systems. The article proposed the integration of the market and planning by introducing a system of noncompulsory guidance planning, creating a flexible price system, opening markets for the means of production, allowing more job mobility, and having the enterprise assume sole responsibility for its profits and losses.[13]

Liu Guoguang, a leading economist, foresaw the need not only for a market but specifically for a buyer's market. A tight seller's market, he argued, would create too much tension for reform of a decentralized nature.[14] Another political economist, Lin Zili, elaborated along this line, saying that state planning should be implemented not by administrative methods but by a variety of economic levers, such as prices, tax rates, and interest rates, to attract and encourage enterprises to follow voluntarily the intentions of the state plan.[15] Still others called for the establishment of an economic information center, development of economic legislation and an economic judiciary system, and the free flow of labor.[16]

In these discussions the function of the state institutions in the economic system was also called into question. In 1984 an article in *Shijie Jingji Daobao* (The world economic herald) argued that the core of economic reform was to change the fundamental economic function of the state. The function of the state, according to the author, should be transformed from microlevel to macrolevel control, from administrative management to economic management, from the control of material to the control of value, and from command to coordination.[17] This argument was very similar to that stated in the HSWP's "Resolution on Economic Reform" in 1966, which advocated the reduction of the state's constant interference in microeconomic affairs.

These academic discussions soon led to the official redefinition of socialism. The "Resolution on Economic Reform," adopted by the Third Plenum of the Twelfth Central Committee in October 1984, was a milestone in China's economic reform. The socialist economy was redefined as "a planned commodity economy based on public ownership, in which the law of value must be consciously followed and applied."[18] In the mid-1970s, the market was considered to be the embodiment of capitalism and the antithesis of socialism, and minor rural market activities and peasant sideline production for local markets were criticized as the "tails of capitalism."[19] The acceptance of the market mechanism in the socialist economic system thus represented a major change in the official Marxist economic theory in China.[20] Chinese economists considered the adoption of the concept of "commodity economy" as an ideological breakthrough, for it meant the Party acknowledged that the market mechanism should play an important role in a socialist economy.

The political report of the Thirteenth Party Congress held in 1987 went a step further, presenting a new formula: The state regulates the market, and the market guides the enterprise. According to this formula, the state would regulate the relationship between supply and demand through economic, legal, and (if necessary) administrative means and create a favorable economic and social environment to which enterprises would respond and make correct managerial decisions accordingly. The report held that the socialist market system should include not only markets for consumer and capital goods but also markets for other essential factors of production, such as capital, labor, technology, information, and real estate.[21] The following paragraph from the report clearly represented the Party's ideological stand on this issue: "Some of the things we have introduced in the process of reform, such as expanded markets for means of production, funds, technology and labor service and the issuance of stocks and bonds, are phenomena which are not peculiar to capitalism but are bound to appear in the wake of large-scale, socialized production and the development of a commodity economy."[22]

Thus "commodity economy" entered into the official vocabulary of both Hungary and China.[23] But no matter how widely the market was accepted as an integral part of a socialist economy, that did not mean that full-fledged marketization of the economy was underway. In fact, both the theory and the practice of central planning were far from disappearing. Thoroughgoing marketization was still beyond the limits of ideological acceptance. Moreover, the introduction of markets into a centrally planned economy created confusion and malfunctions in the system. The leadership and most economists considered a mixture of plan and market as the most desirable solution.

State and Nonstate Ownership

Public ownership of the means of production was another characteristic of orthodox state socialism. After the revolution, all state socialist regimes, without exception, confiscated the major means of production that had previously been owned privately and developed their own structure of ownership. The predominant part of this new structure was the state ownership of major industrial and commercial enterprises (and some agricultural farms); the second level consisted of collective ownership of agriculture and some small industrial and commercial enterprises; at the bottom of this structure was some residual private ownership in the retail and service sectors.

For years, state ownership was considered the highest level of public ownership and the best exemplification of socialism in both concept and practice. The state enterprise occupied a privileged position in the planning system. Not only did it have priority in obtaining investment, raw materials, and labor supply from the state, but its employees also enjoyed better welfare programs, such as better medical care, job security, and retirement subsidies, and therefore higher social status.[24] Economic reformers, in seeking a more effective incentive system to promote more efficient production and a livelier economy, experimented with various reforms of ownership and management. Because such experiments needed either theoretical guidance beforehand or ideological justification afterward, the redefinition of state ownership became necessary.

In 1967, prior to the introduction of basic and far-reaching economic reform in Hungary, there was an ideological debate on the nature of the cooperative in a socialist society. The "dogmatic" beliefs that only what was owned by the state could be considered "consistently" (i.e., completely) socialist property and that cooperative property represented a lower grade of ownership were labeled "obsolete" and "erroneous."[25] Both the state enterprise and the agricultural cooperative were declared to be equally full-fledged socialist organizations. Participants formulated the thesis that both state and cooperative property should be regarded as consistently socialist.

On the surface, such arguments may seem trivial. However, the ideological "upgrading" of the cooperatives touched the core principle of socialism, that is, the appropriate forms of social ownership. During the economic reform, as collective ownership assumed equal importance with state ownership, the private sector also gained greater recognition. "Besides the socialist sector having decisive superiority," Nyers stated, "the private sector will have to be maintained even in the future in its present supplementary role."[26]

During the first wave of Hungarian economic reform (1968-1972), however, the ideological stand on the issue of diversified ownership was not as forceful as that on the question of marketization. The resolutions of 1966-1968 hardly touched upon the necessity for competition among state, cooperative, and private enterprises in the economy. Questions related to the transformation of the ownership system and to property rights escaped attention—in part because the problem had not been acknowledged, and in part for tactical reasons. At the time, reform in these areas was still considered incompatible with the prevailing image of socialism.

In the 1970s the term "second economy" emerged in Hungarian economic literature. The "first economy" referred to the governmental agencies, officially registered nonprofit institutions, state-owned firms, and cooperatives. The "second economy" referred to the formal and informal private sector.[27] According to Istvan Gabor, the second economy was independent from the dominant form of ownership (i.e., state ownership) and was also separate from the dominant form of management (i.e., large enterprises). Instead, it was centered in small-scale cooperative enterprises (five to ten members) and involved mainly family enterprises. Gabor regarded the second economy as an important but not a dominant activity within the national economy, as having a complementary and auxiliary character. It was an "invisible" or less visible economy that produced incomes that could not be or were only partially registered by the tax office.[28] While the second economy could be discussed as an economic issue, there was no attempt to find a theoretical justification for its existence. Although the Hungarian government had officially endorsed the important role of the second economy in building socialism in Hungary in a HSWP Politburo resolution in 1980, it deliberately left the ideological

assessment of the second economy ambiguous, as recognition of privatization remained politically unacceptable.[29]

It was only in the 1980s that an interest in property relations began to
emerge in theoretical discussions. There were two groups of proposals
relating to these issues. One recommended an administrative system in
which state property rights would be exercised by a property-supervising
ministry. The other group advocated the establishment of more firms
operating on the basis of direct interest in preserving and increasing
property (general partnerships, limited liability companies, and joint-stock
companies) and economic competition among the various forms of
enterprise.[30]

A proponent of the second school of thought, economist Marton Tardos
argued that market efficiency could be secured only if the government
rallied individuals and social groups behind their interest in increasing the
value of their property. The reform of property rights, according to Tardos,
should include the transformation of collective enterprise, which in many
places bore the same traits as the state enterprises, and the promotion of
private enterprises, which were "the only sphere of the economy which has
performed dynamically." Citizens must increasingly save, he pointed out,
and invest their savings.[31] This would be inconceivable without a policy that
encouraged the activity of private capital and the recognition of the profits
from private capital. It was important to ensure that the citizens had trust in
a legal order that protected private property. Tardos was convinced that the
"development of the new forms of enterprise and of cooperatives, the
appearance of diverse groups of shareholders, and the growing security and
weight of private property in the economy, may bring about substantial
changes in the development of the country and the socialist economy."

Similar to the Hungarian case, at the very beginning of reform in China
collective ownership (especially in agriculture) was said to be a legitimate
form at that stage of development. There was thus no need to transform it
into a higher level of ownership, as in the past practice of upgrading the
level of ownership from village to brigade and commune.[32] During the
ensuing rural reform, the system of collective ownership was downgraded
even further by contracting collective property to individual households.

China's rural reform did not begin with a clearly designed formula but
developed spontaneously in some villages, was later endorsed by the central
leadership, and then finally was put into theoretical perspective.[33] After 1979
the Chinese implemented a contracting system to replace the previous
collective ownership in the countryside. The key concept was that individual
households contracted with either the brigade or the production team to
work specific areas of the collective fields (or forests, fish ponds, or
orchards), promising to deliver to the collective a specified quota of grain

(or other produce or even money). Anything above the contracted quota could be sold independently by the household. Although this effort might not be called full privatization, it was without doubt the decollectivization of agriculture.

It was only after the attempt to implement market mechanisms that people fully realized that ownership reform was indispensable to successful market operations. Dong Furen, then the director of the Institute of Economics of the Chinese Academy of Social Sciences, argued that the normal functioning of the market required that each participating unit have independent economic interests so that it could be self-motivated and that each unit possess independent decision-making power so that it could respond to market signals. All these requirements raised the very basic question of ownership.[34] Li Yining, an economics professor at Beijing University, made the most influential argument on this topic. He insisted that "economic reform could fail because of the failure of price reform, but it would succeed only due to the reform of ownership, not to the success of the price reform."[35] Other scholars also held that if the enterprise were only given power and a share of profits but lacked clearly defined property rights, and if the enterprise were responsible only for its profits but not for its losses, it would not behave as expected in a market system.[36]

The 1984 resolution on economic reform clearly called for the separation of ownership from the power of operation. "One of the main reasons why the state exercised excessive and rigid control over enterprises in the past," the resolution explained, "was to equate the concept of their ownership by the whole people with the concept of their direct operation by the state institutions." The resolution recommended the "establishment of various forms of the economic responsibility system with contracted jobs as the main content" in urban enterprises.[37] The separation of ownership and management was a formula to devolve operational autonomy and responsibility to the enterprise without a change of ownership. Considering the strong ideological resistance to large-scale privatization, the separation of ownership and management marked significant progress.

A share-holding system (or "stockification"), which was first introduced in China in 1985 as a means of raising funds, was later considered by some to be a solution to the problem of ownership. The advocates of stockification argued that a share-holding system would clearly define the property relations of the enterprise; establish a checking mechanism among producers, owners, and managers; and hence rationalize enterprise behavior. Moreover, if the enterprise workers bought the shares, they would care about the management and production of the enterprise.[38] Some also pointed out that it might justify the existence of large-scale private enterprise, from an ideological point of view, if the public held the shares.[39] The redefinition

of the property rights of large enterprises remained the most difficult part
of the discussion of ownership reform, as it related to the question of how
to evaluate the property in monetary terms.

An official position on the question of ownership was finally presented
in the political report of the Thirteenth Party Congress in 1987. China was
said to be in the primary stage of socialism, during which it was particularly
important to develop diverse sectors of the economy, provided that public
ownership remained dominant. It emphasized again the separation of
ownership from managerial authority for state enterprises. Cooperative,
individual, and private sectors of the economy were all encouraged to
expand. Since the private sector of the economy promoted production,
stimulated the market, provided employment, and helped in many ways to
meet people's needs, the report claimed, it was a necessary and useful
supplement to the public sector.[40]

Despite occasional bold arguments for large-scale privatization that
appeared in academic publications and symposiums,[41] the main thrust of the
discussion of property rights was to criticize the defects in the traditional
understanding of public ownership and to create an ideological space for the
existence of other forms of ownership. The official view was that public
ownership should be the predominant part of the national economy and that
other forms of ownership, no matter how indispensable, could only be
supplementary. The official view further recognized that the operation of
state enterprise should be reformed in some feasible ways yet to be
developed.

Egalitarianism and Incentives

The orthodox socialist principle of income distribution was "to each
according to his work" instead of "to each according to his work and
capital." Yet it had evolved in practice into a principle of egalitarianism
—equal pay regardless of work accomplished—which became a firmly held
socialist ethic. The reformers believed that the lack of material incentives
was one cause of economic inefficiency and therefore sought to reform the
egalitarian practice in income distribution. The attack on egalitarianism was,
therefore, to many theorists, a return to genuine Marxism, whose principle
of "to each according to his work" seemed to justify material incentives and
income differentials.

In theory this principle had two meanings. First, in a socialist community, the only source of personal income was labor, and the incomes arising
from the private ownership of the means of production ceased to exist. A
much larger number of theoretical questions arose in connection with the
second and more classical interpretation of distribution according to work.

This interpretation implied that income should be distributed according to the amount of work accomplished. That was, more work should be paid more and less work should be paid less. The rediscovery of the original principle of socialist distribution usually went back to this latter interpretation, which justified income differentiation.

In Hungary the ideological foundation of income differentiation was reconsidered early in the reform process. According to a study group commissioned by the Hungarian National Technical Development Committee, rising wage levels would effectively stimulate an increase in performance and productivity only if they occurred in a "selective" manner. In other words, the desire of the individual to strive for higher qualifications and to work more efficiently and skillfully depended to a large extent on wage differentials.[42] In order to prepare for such reform, the principle of equality was redefined: "Socialism is a society of equality and not of egalitarianism. Socialist equality does not mean the equal distribution of goods, but rather that the elimination of class disparities must guarantee everyone an equal opportunity to succeed."[43] Reformers established the principle that within certain limits, average wages should be more differentiated among enterprises; personal incomes, where necessary, should be differentiated according to skill and responsibility; and the financial rewards of higher qualifications, knowledge, and responsibility should increase.[44]

The Chinese made the same conceptual change with regard to egalitarianism and material incentives. Realizing that egalitarianism only destroyed the incentive to work hard, the media persistently attacked "eating from the same big pot" and stressed the values of "competition" and "equality of opportunity." Theorists found that Marx had never denounced material interest and that the Party should work for the material benefits of the people.[45] "To each according to his work" was again emphasized with "more pay for more work and less pay for less work."[46] This indicated the toleration of large differences in income distribution. The policy of encouraging some people to improve their income sooner than others was stressed as the only road to prosperity for the whole society. Common prosperity was the ultimate goal of socialism, the resolution on economic reform of 1984 reiterated, but it could not and would never mean absolute egalitarianism or that all members of society would become better off simultaneously.[47]

Once economic reform permitted private ownership, share-holding, and private employment, it became impossible not to allow people to earn income on the basis of their capital holdings. Therefore, the political report of the Thirteenth Party Congress stated clearly that it was important to have diverse forms of distribution, provided that distribution according to work and earnings from individual labor remained the principal form. In addition to this main form of distribution, the report claimed, there could be other legitimate forms. For example, when enterprises issued bonds to raise funds, buyers received interest; when shares were issued, share-holders received income in the form of dividends; enterprise managers received additional income as compensation for risk-taking; and owners of private enterprises employing a certain number of workers received some unearned income.[48] With the objective of common prosperity, the report encouraged some people to prosper earlier than others through honest work and lawful business operations.

Although they welcomed the adoption of material incentives as part of the reform policy, Hungarian intellectuals acknowledged the contradiction between efficiency (the basic rationale of economic reform) and equality (a long-accepted socialist principle) in income distribution. Janos Kornai noted that this dilemma would be exacerbated by economic reform but could offer no effective solution.[49] The apparent conflict between socialist ethics and a policy that fostered or tolerated large income differentials also caught the attention of Chinese scholars. Debates over "social justice" (*shehui gong-ping*), a term that first appeared in 1986, became more frequent.[50]

Resistance to the policy that encouraged income differentials also came from below. Having become accustomed to the practice of egalitarianism, people had difficulty accepting large income gaps. The traditional concept that more income should be earned by more and better work and not by speculation and no work contributed to the popular resistance to income differentiation. For the leaders, the promotion of income differentials was a delicate issue because it threatened to arouse socioeconomic grievances. As we will see later in this chapter, such grievances over inequality were potential causes of social instability.

In summary, the redefinition of socialism in Hungary and China followed a largely similar trajectory. In both countries the discussions about the role of the market progressed from seeing the market as a supplement to planning, to viewing it as equally important, and finally to giving the market a predominant role in the economy. The Hungarians arrived at this conclusion prior to the implementation of reform, whereas the Chinese took nearly ten years to do so. The debates about ownership were much less straightforward in both countries. The issue was absent from the first wave of reform discussions in Hungary in the 1960s and 1970s, and although the Chinese had practiced ownership reform as a major component of their reform program, they did not spent much time discussing it. The theoretical discussions of ownership reform in both countries remained ambiguous most of the time and were very much a matter of ex post facto rationalization in China and Hungary alike. It seemed that the notion of public ownership had a stronger ideological hold than the concept of central planning. Or it may well have been that giving up state ownership presented more practical difficulties or a more serious threat to political power. The discussions on the distribution system moved from disclaiming egalitarianism and returning to the original Marxist principle of "to each according to his work," to the acceptance of income from sources other than one's work. This did not create many ideological difficulties but caused practical problems later.

Despite all the theoretical and practical restrictions, the controversies outlined here reveal that the essential definition of socialism was modified in Hungary and China; both moved away from the Stalinist notion of socialism to a significant extent. The continuous effort to redefine socialism was a part of the ideological liberalization that was propelled by the ongoing economic reform. It grew out of the ideological necessity to legitimize the fundamental changes that had occurred or were expected to occur in the economic system. Socialism was not challengeable, but what constituted socialism was subject to discussion.

The relatively free debate among intellectuals about the definition of socialism reinforced ideological liberalization. The difficulties and uncertainties involved in economic reform demanded more creative thinking from intellectuals and an environment that would induce frank discussion of policy alternatives. As a result, the Party had to enlarge the range of ideological tolerance in the realm of economics. Although the freer intellectual atmosphere in the economic sphere did not automatically spread to other fields, it did inhibit retrogression in other areas. It was unlikely that the Party could maintain orthodox Marxism in the political sphere while it was continuously revising it in the economic sphere. Since the political and economic components of Marxism were inextricably linked, the redefinition of socialism not only enlarged the space for further innovations in the economic system, but also created the possibility of redefining the Party leadership in the political system. (The changing definition of the political system and the content of Party leadership are discussed in chapter 6.)

Economic Pluralization

The rigid central planning economic system organized society and the economy according to a single administrative hierarchy. With no right to private productive property, little freedom to choose jobs, and no alternative sources of goods and services, members of society were economically dependent on the state and the state's representatives, that is, the leaders of each work unit. Before the reform, factories provided their employees not only with work but also with housing, medical treatment, child care, transportation, recreation, and consumer goods that were not readily available through other channels.[51] In similar fashion rural leaders exercised broad control over the economic fortunes of peasants, such as their work assignments, their access to loans, their opportunities for outside employment, and often the size and location of their private plots.[52] The economic dependence of people on their work units in turn created political dependence, for deviant political behavior could be punished economically. Officials of a work unit had ample opportunity to distribute more goods and services to workers and peasants in their favor while giving less to those who were less compliant. This patron-client relationship was of course highly asymmetrical, the unit leaders enjoying considerable arbitrary power over their subordinates.

In order to increase the flexibility of the economy, reformers introduced new forms of ownership, increased labor mobility, and created alternative sources of goods and services. By marketizing the economic structure, these efforts altered the social relations that had been associated with the centralized planning and distribution system, raising the possibility of a more flexible social order. The decentralization and pluralization of economic power weakened the effectiveness of political control and strengthened the autonomy of the society vis-à-vis the state.

Changes in Ownership

Corresponding to the theoretical discussion of the property rights reform, economic reform involved a diversification of kinds of ownership. This aspect of reform should not be characterized simply as privatization. Generally, ownership reform had four aspects: first, decollectivization of agriculture, which was especially dramatic in China; second, privatization of the retail and service sectors; third, destatization of some small or mid-sized enterprises and separation of ownership and management in large enterprises; and fourth, encouragement of foreign sole ventures or joint ventures.

As noted above, in the first reform wave, from 1968 to 1972, ownership reform received a very modest place on the Hungarian agenda. It was during the second wave of reform, starting in the late 1970s, that reformers paid more attention to the issue. During the reform, agriculture remained socialized. State and collective farms cultivated some 85 percent of the land and contributed about 66 percent of the agricultural output; individual households held 15 percent of the land and yielded 33 percent of the output. But as Jan Prybyla argued, the state and collective sector was "significantly privatized in terms of de facto property rights."[53] Within the state and large cooperative farms, various forms of subcontracting or the outright sale of land and specialized tasks to small cooperatives were developed. "De facto privatization of state and collective farms and small cooperatives was combined with the de jure privatization of plots and small farms."[54] According to Kornai, a remarkable division of labor between cooperatives and private household farms evolved in which the cooperatives concentrated more on grain and fodder, which could be produced most efficiently by large-scale operations, while private household farms focused on labor-intensive products where small-scale operations succeeded better.[55]

Private household farming was once regarded in Hungary as a bourgeois remnant that should be replaced by collective forms of production. Now private household farming, which produced a large portion of meat, dairy and other animal products, and fruits and vegetables, was declared a permanent component of agriculture under socialism. With few exceptions, there was no legal restriction on selling output, and prices were determined by supply and demand on the free market for foodstuffs.

In contrast to the Hungarian case, the change in the forms of ownership in rural China was quite dramatic and massive. The household responsibility system, in which land was contracted to individual households, covered 99.96 percent of the 5.69 million production teams of the entire country in 1987. Although the responsibility system was not implemented under the banner of ownership reform, the contracting of collective property by individual households was its key attribute since the very beginning. A large portion of rural property was either contracted to or owned by individual households. The total value of rural property was estimated at 3 trillion yuan as of 1986, of which 2 trillion was land collectively owned and contracted out to peasant households. For the rest, peasant households owned 55 percent of the productive fixed assets, 90.6 percent of the housing, and more than 60 percent of the cash and savings in kind.[56]

The massive change in the form of ownership in the Chinese countryside after the late 1970s to a large extent released the peasants, who comprise a majority of the population in China, from strict administrative control. It therefore provided a favorable background for a relaxed social environment. One critical result was that it released surplus labor from agricultural production. As long as peasant families fulfilled their quota, it did not matter how much labor or how many working hours they put in. This gave the peasants enormous flexibility to engage in nonagricultural activities.

In the cities, economic reform encouraged private ownership in the retail and service sectors in both Hungary and China. In 1986 the maximum number of employees for each private enterprise in Hungary, apart from family members, was raised from seven to fifteen or in some cases to twenty. This was a small number for those accustomed to private market economies but large in comparison with other state socialist countries. It meant the legalization of "small capitalism." There were in fact private firms with more than a hundred or even 1,000 employees in the country.[57]

A new form of enterprise appeared in Hungary in the 1980s: the business work partnership (BWP). Small-scale co-ops owned by the participants, the BWPs provided badly needed services such as plumbing and auto repairs.[58] They represented a deliberate effort to legalize formerly illegal economic activities or to be tolerant of ambiguous cases that were regarded as socially useful or at least not harmful. In 1983 a large portion of residential construction and services were provided by the private sector, and about 33 percent of active working time was spent in the private sector in 1984.[59] It was also believed that altogether 1.2 million man-years were spent in the legal private economy by an economically active population of 5.2 million people. Many more million years were spent in semipublic, semiprivate or extralegal private activities.[60] According to Prybyla, the Hungarian Party and state came to terms with the informal private sector to a greater extent than did their Chinese counterparts: "The Hungarians were really the first to quietly practice Deng Xiaoping's dictum that it doesn't matter whether a cat is black or white so long as it catches mice."[61]

The number of individual laborers in China grew from 0.15 million in 1978 to 6.59 million in 1988. Their proportion in the total work force rose from 0.2 to 4.6 percent during the same period. Although they were outnumbered by the labor force in state and collective enterprises, their impact on the society was much larger than their numbers. In 1988 they contributed 17.8 percent of total retail sales and owned the majority of enterprises engaged in retail sales, catering, and services. Since these sectors were closely related to daily life, they not only made life easier, but also created a more relaxed and pluralized environment. With the opening of the private sector in the cities, people were able to resign from state enterprises and open their own businesses. It was true that it took courage to risk a secure job and benefits, but the private sector nevertheless provided an alternative for people when they had trouble with their unit or leaders.

The rapidly increasing number of individual households and private enterprises, which are outside of central planning, enlarged the marginal autonomy of the society vis-à-vis state control. Unlike enterprise managers in the state sector, small entrepreneurs could not be dismissed by Party secretaries and were not likely to be Party members. For example, as of 1988, of the 140,000 self-employed individuals in Beijing, only 640 (0.45 percent) belonged to the Party.[62]

The third aspect of ownership reform was the destatization of some small- and medium-size enterprises and the separation of ownership and management in large ones. In the early 1980s, the Hungarian government adopted a comprehensive program to develop "new forms of business."

Within a few years, more than 10,000 new small enterprises emerged (in forms like "petty cooperatives" and "independent contract work associations") in a country where the number of state and cooperative enterprises had been counted in hundreds rather than in thousands for decades.[63] A characteristic feature of the Hungarian reform was experimentation with different mixed forms, combining state ownership with private activity or private ownership. One such form was leasing, which was widely applied in trade and in the restaurant sector. Fixed capital remained state owned, but the business was run by a private individual selected by auction, who paid a rent fixed by a contract as well as taxes. The individual would keep the profit or cover the deficit at his or her own risk. In 1984 about 11 percent of the shops and 37 percent of the restaurants were leased in this way.

Another popular form was the enterprise business work partnership (EBWP). Under the EBWP, people employed by a state-owned firm did some extra work under special contract for extra payment but in some sense within the framework of the employer state-owned firm. In many instances the members were allowed to use the equipment of the firm.[64] The purpose of creating this new form was clear: It gave a legal framework for certain kinds of activities that were formerly illegal. This was also a way for managers to increase wages when the wage fund was fixed and thus to retain skilled workers. The number of such units increased rapidly from 2,775 in 1982 to 17,337 by the end of 1984.[65]

In China, from 1985 to 1987, all firms with fixed assets of less than 1.5 million yuan and annual profits of under 200,000 yuan were contracted out or leased to individuals or cooperatives for periods of up to five years.[66] They were granted relatively broad rights of business decision-making, including decisions about the distribution of their profits. Various efforts to reform the ownership and management of large industrial enterprises, such as share-holding and contracting, were also experimented with in China.

Because of the complexity and scale of industrial production, however, the reform of large state enterprises in both China and Hungary did not produce visible success. The size of the assets, the soft budget constraints, and the huge financial burdens to keep up welfare for employees and retirees all hindered efforts to increase efficiency of large state enterprises.

The last category in the pluralization of ownership was the authorization and encouragement of sole and joint foreign ventures. More than seventy firms were owned jointly by the Hungarian state and foreign private business in 1987.[67] At first, cautious Chinese leaders intended to limit the scope of foreign investment in their country to particular organizational forms and particular geographic regions. Yet over time, virtually every part of China became eligible for foreign investment. About 16,000 joint venture enterprises were approved by 1988, and the number of sole foreign venture enterprises reached 1,230.[68]

One distinctive feature of the ownership reform in China was the decentralization of decision-making and profit-retaining power to local governments. While the ownership of most enterprises remained in the hands of government, the decentralization nonetheless gave local governments incentitives to be more competitive in their economic activities.[69] The rapid expansion of the township and village enterprises is a fascinating example of local governments' economic vigor.[70] Although local governments and entrepreneur cadres did gain more arbitrary power because they controlled more resources, individual employees, too, had greater autonomy. In the changing macroenvironment, in which labor mobility had increased greatly and the sources of supply had multiplied, individual workers obtained much more bargaining power and opportunities than they had had before the reform.

Labor Mobility

Increased job mobility and consequently enhanced population mobility represented another change brought about by economic reform. These were even more important for the growing autonomy of the society than the change in the forms of ownership, because freer labor mobility reduced the degree of personal attachment of the employees to the unit and to individual leaders.

At the peak of bureaucratic centralization in Hungary, labor was closely tied to the workplace. Kornai pointed out that there were various restrictions: administrative prohibitions on changing jobs, prohibitions against taking employment in cities without a special permit, and distribution through employers of many goods and services such as housing, child care, recreation, food rations or food, and other consumer goods.[71] The same was true in China. Under the previous system, jobs were assigned for a lifetime.[72]

The reformers soon realized that without a freer labor flow, it was impossible to talk about self-management of the enterprise and therefore impossible to contemplate the desired functioning of the market. The uninhibited flow of the factors of production was a necessary condition for a market system to be efficient and to maintain an equilibrium. Labor was one of these production factors. In the course of reform in Hungary, the restrictions on individuals choosing and changing jobs were abolished. Remnants of the restrictions on the distribution of goods and services still existed in housing, health care, and child care. These were, however, less binding than before.

The freer labor policy resulted in high resignation rates, which reached 15.7 percent in Hungary in 1982, as compared, for example, to 7 percent in Czechoslovakia in the same year.[73] Income and opportunities offered by the formal and informal private sector attracted labor away from state-owned firms. Those who were willing to work harder for the sake of higher consumption could enter the second economy. People held two or three jobs. There was a popular saying in Hungary describing such a situation: "On the first shift—that is to say, doing your main job—you save energy so as to be able to earn enough money on your second shift—working on the side, that is—to be able to build a house on your third shift."[74]

Since China had a huge labor reserve, individual workers never had as much bargaining power vis-à-vis enterprises as did their Hungarian counterparts. With a heavy population pressure, China had stricter controls on population movement. Not only was the work assignment for a lifetime, but it was also very difficult to change the household registration upward (e.g., from rural to urban or from small city to large city). Economic reform loosened such restrictions.

In rural China economic reform authorized the creation of the fast-growing township and village enterprises, which provided job opportunities for peasants. In 1988 about 49 million peasants, or 8 percent of the agricultural labor force, worked in the township and village enterprises.[75] Economic reform also permitted the peasants to resettle and assume employment in the cities. Between 1979 and 1985, a total of 45.8 million members of the rural work force switched to nonagricultural activities. During the same period, the urban population showed a net increase of 127 million, in addition to which there was a floating population of between several hundred thousand and one million who stayed in the cities year-round looking for jobs. The annual figure of those who left the rural areas for temporary employment in cities amounted to six million. Of the jobs newly created in the cities and towns each year, approximately one million were filled by peasants. About one-fifth of the rural labor force changed their employment, place of residence, or even social status under the economic reform.[76]

After several years of experimentation, the minister of labor and personnel announced that, effective October 1986, new workers would be hired only on a contractual basis in China's state enterprises.[77] The prevailing practice, which provided permanent employment despite workers' job preferences and performance, would thus be phased out in favor of a new category of state employee less dependent on the work unit for basic necessities. The number of contractual workers in state enterprises rose from 3.5 million in 1986 to 9.9 million in 1989, accounting for 10 percent of the work force of state enterprises in the latter year.[78]

Although the reform of the labor system was intended primarily to revitalize the enterprise, it enhanced the freedom of choice among individual workers. For the first time, as one reporter put it, not only could the employers fire the employees, but the employees could also "fire" the employers, that is, they could quit. The new life opportunities also awakened individual consciousness. With reform offering people the chance to choose their jobs, people started to reevaluate their abilities, real and potential, making them less satisfied with their situations. A catchword of the time was "to realize self-worth." According to a news report, almost everyone surveyed felt mistreated relative to their talents at their jobs.[79] One survey showed that more than 60 percent of the people wanted to change their occupations.[80] According to the Ministry of Labor, the number of successful job transfers in forty-four labor markets was 1.07 million between 1986 and 1988.[81]

The freedom to choose a job was a crucial condition for individual autonomy. Without such a basic individual right, there could be little freedom of thought or freedom of speech, for what one said and did would affect one's career, salary, and social welfare. The growing possibility of labor mobility also expanded people's awareness of their individual worth and rights. It heightened their capacity to identify with others and to imagine themselves improving their social status and mastering their environments.

Alternative Sources of Supply

A third basic change introduced by economic reform was the pluralization of the sources of goods and services. This was closely related to the greater labor mobility. In state socialist societies, the basic wage was low, and a large portion of income was realized in the form of state subsidies and social welfare that were distributed largely through the workplace. Increasing labor mobility would be impossible without changing the system of supply. Once people were no longer wholly dependent on only one source of supply, they could begin to have freedom of choice.

The encouragement of private ownership in the retail and service sectors helped create alternative sources of goods and services. In 1983, 87 percent of repair and maintenance services in Hungary were performed by the second economy. In China a similar pattern emerged. The number of free markets in China increased from 33,302 in 1978 to 71,359 in 1988, with urban free markets rising from zero in 1978 to 12,181 in 1988.[82] The rapid expansion of free markets undermined the rigid food rationing system that had restricted population mobility. In 1978 the proportions of state, collective, and other (private, joint venture, etc.) in the total value of retail sales were 55 percent, 43 percent, and 2 percent, respectively; by 1988 the mix was 39 percent, 34 percent, and 27 percent.[83] This implied that the sources of goods and services for daily life had multiplied tremendously.

Kornai observed that "the great achievement of the Hungarian reform is the significant extension of choices." Consumers had far more choice as the domain of bureaucratically rationed goods and services became narrower (although it was not eliminated entirely). Within the nonstate sector, prices conveyed the consumers' signals to the producers, who responded with changes in supply.[84]

Housing was a serious problem in almost all socialist societies.[85] The trend in the prereform system was toward public housing. All apartment houses were nationalized; tenancy was rationed by the bureaucracy. The average living space per capita in China in 1978 was 4.2 square meters, barely enough room for a bed. As a result of government efforts to meet the popular housing demand, by 1988 it had increased to 8.8 square meters, which was scarcely more adequate. The shortage of housing bound people to their units and their leaders, the only source of housing, and restricted the mobility of the society.

Under economic reform, housing was to be gradually commercialized and privatized in both countries. Individuals could invest in their own private housing instead of waiting for a bureaucratic allotment. In Hungary 71.4 percent of the total housing stock was in private ownership by 1980. In 1984, 85.7 percent of the new dwellings built were private.[86] In China the commercialization of housing was also underway. With heavy population pressure, however, the realization of such plans may take much longer. Low incomes and limited bank savings in China also restricted the development of private housing.

The commercialization of the supply of goods and services also commercialized social relations. Those who had money could almost get anything they wanted, a privilege previously reserved for those with access to political power. This was the first step away from the political monopoly on social life and in turn produced two side effects. One was the erosion of public morality. Money talked everywhere, and "gratitude money" became the way to acquire anything in shortage, as reflected in the facetious remark that in Hungary "everyone is building his own socialism."[87] The other was the income gap between the private sector and the state sector. Both corruption and inequality produced socioeconomic grievances (discussed in the following section).

As Milton Friedman has pointed out, the development of the market greatly reduces the range of issues that must be decided through political means that tend to require substantial conformity.[88] The introduction of market relations into ownership, labor mobility, and the supply of goods and services reduced the dependence of individual citizens on the official structure, enhanced the scope of individual choices, stimulated individual consciousness, and ultimately prepared for the birth of a civil society.

Economic marketization broke the monopoly of Party secretaries and organizational cadres over assignments and promotions and eroded their powers of patronage. The changes in the managerial orientation to profit-making as a result of reform lessened the political dependence of the employees. Reform also provided opportunities to accumulate wealth for certain sectors of the society and eventually a growing middle class. At the very least, it provided an ultimate escape for those who really had trouble with the leaders of their work units. The regime was confronted by a growing population of individuals who were outside the Party-controlled distribution of rewards and promotions in state-owned units.

However, private ownership may not be the engine for democracy that some would like to believe. One must bear in mind that in a society that had been accustomed to secure jobs and social benefits, not many cared to risk their medical care, sick leave, low but secure wages, and so forth to go into private business, especially when the fate of private enterprises remained unclear. The size of the private sector has thus remained so disproportionately small compared to the state sector that it has hardly become a force for democracy. A wealthy and politically significant middle class, if it emerges, may come from a hybrid form of ownership; thus, its political orientation may be different from that of the West.

Although increasing economic freedom and pluralization in the society do not necessarily stimulate active demands for democracy, they nevertheless created a more autonomous society that the Party was less able to manage by traditional means. They undermined the administrative/economic control that the Party had so effectively imposed on the society. With more freedom to grow their own grain, to buy things on an open market, or to quit and move to another workplace, people felt a greater sense of liberty than before to hold their own political views and refuse to conform to the Party's line. The Party needed new means of control compatible with a more autonomous civil society, for without such control, the social unrest that had grown out of economic grievances was likely to develop into a crisis.

Socioeconomic Grievances

Besides increasing ideological flexibility and societal autonomy, economic reform produced uncertainties, disorientation, and instability. Among the major consequences of economic reform were inflation, inequality, and corruption, all of which were evident in both China and Hungary to various degrees.

Inflation

The relaxation of price controls was an indispensable part of a market-oriented economic reform. However, soaring retail prices became a common phenomenon of daily life in China in the late 1980s. From 1984 to 1987, China's retail price index rose by an average of 7.4 percent annually, but in 1988 prices officially jumped 21 percent compared with a year earlier. Unofficially, but more realistically, the inflation rate was close to 40 percent in 1988 and early 1989. As inflationary pressure in China intensified, the prices of vegetables and meats, in particular, climbed to previously unknown heights. For example, vegetable prices in large cities in the first half of 1988 rose by about 50 percent. In September 1988, the prices of meat, poultry, and eggs were 46 percent higher than in August 1987. Such price hikes affected the daily lives of China's wage earners. A survey of households conducted by the State Statistical Bureau discovered that the share of urban and rural residents whose real incomes had been eroded by inflation doubled from 1986 to 1987, rising from 20 percent to 40 percent.[89]

There were different explanations for the primary causes of inflation in China. One argued that inflation was caused by price reform and changes in the structure of the economy associated with reform. In 1979 the Chinese government started to adjust the artificially low prices of agricultural goods. The state purchase prices of farm products were increased by 20.1 percent in 1979 and again by 8.1 percent in 1980. The general level of purchase prices of farm products increased by 77 percent between 1978 and 1986.[90] The decontrol of food prices that the regime introduced in 1985 permitted peasants to sell certain foodstuffs in cities at whatever price the market would bear, pushing up urban food prices. The prices of energy, raw materials, and other primary products were also raised, which led to a chain reaction, contributing to inflation.

Another explanation attributed the cause of inflation to excess demand brought on by overextended investment by state enterprises. As the reform transferred more and more income power to the provinces and enterprises, the center had less and less command over financial resources. Excessive investment, a rapidly expanding wage and bonus bill, and huge government subsidies were then translated directly into the state's budget deficits. This led to the overissue of currency to cover the deficits, which in turn caused inflation.[91]

On this matter, reform in Hungary proceeded much more smoothly than in China. From the very beginning, the Hungarian reformers were aware of the destabilizing effects of inflation in the wake of the liberalization of the price system. A comprehensive reform of consumer prices was delayed, and a policy of "permanent but gradual" price modifications was adopted. While the proportion of production materials with fixed prices fell from 70 to 35 percent in the first five years of reform, the ratio of consumer goods with fixed prices declined only from 53 percent to 50 percent.[92] This strong state control of consumer prices was to prevent inflation. Reformers also put into the reform package tight wage controls according to which managerial incomes would be reduced if there was an increase in average wage.[93] These wage controls served the dual purpose of checking both cost and demand inflation. With labor costs under tight control, enterprises were not forced to raise product prices. The limits on wage increases also stabilized the level of consumption and brought about a manageable aggregate demand. As a result of these measures, price increases were kept at 1.6 percent from 1968 to 1973 and 7.5 percent from 1978 to 1984.[94] Controlled market prices helped to avoid certain sociopolitical grievances but at the same time limited the effects of the reform. In 1985 Hungary experienced a sharp consumer price increase, with dairy products up by 28-29 percent, meat and vegetables by 9-18 percent, urban transportation fares by 55-60 percent, and postal service by 85 percent.[95] Yet by then the population's financial and psychological tolerance of inflation had risen. The Hungarians seemed to have greater tolerance of inflation than did the Chinese, as discussed later in this chapter.

Inequality

One basic principle of the reform was to link increases in wages and salaries directly to increases in productivity in each enterprise. The purpose was to encourage inequality as a means to achieve efficiency. This policy led to greater wage differentials, and the income inequality was further exacerbated by inflation. Those on fixed incomes, such as pensioners, of course suffered the most from inflation.

The designers of the Hungarian reform attempted quite consciously to reallocate rewards among different social groups (e.g., managerial strata and manual workers, skilled and unskilled workers). For the majority of the personnel of an enterprise, year-end bonus could not exceed 15 percent of annual wages, while the top management could get as much as 85 percent.[96] The sharp increase in bonuses paid to management at the expense of workers caused complaints. As Robinson has observed:

> When those in top posts became the recipients of profit shares ten to fifteen times greater than those of the workers and lower level employees, the dissatisfaction and discontent of the latter reached great dimensions. Their anger, however, was directed not only at the gross disproportions, in monetary rewards, but also at the system of categorization per se. It was, they felt, a deliberate

affront and an attempt to create a new class system, with the workers henceforth to be labelled as third-class citizens.[97]

Because of such strong resentment, this system was abandoned one year after being put into practice. The reformers then designed a less transparent bonus scheme, and through 1972 managerial incomes continued to rise compared to those of workers.

Another income gap in Hungary was that between the state sector and the private sector. The position of urban blue-collar workers in the state sector steadily deteriorated relative to almost all other major social groups. Meanwhile, peasants, artisans, and the self-employed took advantage of reform policies to make dramatic improvements in their standing.[98] Wage differences between the state and cooperative sectors were considerable. In the construction branch, for example, the average wage in state enterprises went up by 19.6 percent from 1967 to 1971, compared with 35.1 percent in cooperative enterprises.[99] Some research results revealed that there were those whose income was ten to twelve times the average.[100] At one end, there were private entrepreneurs with attractive private houses in elegant neighborhoods and vacation villas with swimming pools and late-model BMWs parked in front. On the other were people who slept three or four to a room with the toilet at the end of the hall.[101]

It had become clear by the beginning of the 1970s that there existed serious sociopolitical constraints on further increasing income inequalities in Hungary. In autumn 1970 the government launched a campaign against various "abuses" of the freedoms allowed by the new system. In 1973 an 8-percent increase in the wages of manual workers was introduced.[102] By 1975-1976, the central authorities tightened control over both the average level of money wages and income differentials within the state sector, using a set of guidelines that established a minimum increase for the lowest wage categories and a maximum increase for other wage categories, beyond which a steeply progressive tax would be levied. Between 1970 and 1975 income differentials narrowed because of these measures. The ratios among top managers, middle-level managers, and workers were 270:164:94 in 1970 and 234:128:94 in 1975.[103] After 1972 the emergence of greater job mobility and the growing ability for state employees to hold second jobs in the private sector reduced grievances over income disparities.

In contrast to Hungary, in China egalitarianism expanded within the state sector. According to a survey conducted by the State Bureau, the ratio of salaries between junior and senior fellows in research institutes in forty-eight cities changed from 1:3 to 1:2 from 1985 to 1988; between junior and senior doctors in hospitals from 1:3 to 1:2.2; between assistant professors and professors from 1:4.1 to 1:2.1; and between staff members and bureau-

level officials from 1:3.1 to 1:1.6.[104] Bonuses became the universal
compensation for everyone and an important source of additional income;
the proportion of bonuses in total income increased from 9.8 percent in 1978
to 34.1 percent in 1987.[105] This trend toward narrowing the gap between
workers and managers may be due in part to a more cohesive work unit
culture in China, within which the work unit leaders were not as insulated
from pressure for more or less equal incomes.

Instead, inequality in China was most obvious between the state sector
and the emerging private sector. The gap was widest between the workers
in state enterprises that were the mainstay of the planning system and those
in private enterprises or acting as individual laborers, a group that was
created or enlarged by the reforms. In 1988 about 10 percent of the nation's
12 million self-employed industrial and commercial workers earned over
10,000 yuan a year (an average worker earned 1,200 yuan a year), and 1
percent of these earned far more—hundreds of thousands of yuan. On the
average, self-employed workers earned more than twice as much as those
employed in the state sector.[106]

Not only did the people in the private sector have more opportunities to
make money, but they were also less hurt by inflation than those in the state
sector. According to economic theory, inflation redistributes income.
Inflation was tantamount to taxation for those who lived on fixed salaries.
In China this group included large numbers of intellectuals, teachers, and
doctors. High-income recipients, on the contrary, were mainly the self-
employed, owners of private enterprises, and staff members of Chinese-
foreign joint ventures.

One group that appeared to be particularly underprivileged in terms of
monetary income and opportunity to appropriate state assets for personal
purposes in China consisted of rank-and-file academics. They were the
principal beneficiaries of the relaxation of the intellectual climate after Mao,
but their status, as measured by both social prestige and the ability to
purchase goods, remained low. The popular saying in China was "the
experts who make missiles earn less than the peddlers who sell eggs; the
barbers who wield razors earn more than the surgeons who use scalpels."
Those who worked in productive enterprises obtained bonuses under various
names in addition to their wages, but those who worked in academic or
government institutions received only a basic salary. In 1978 state workers
in occupations that required specialized knowledge earned on the average 2
percent more than manual workers; by 1986 manual workers earned on the
average 10 percent more than intellectual workers, and the disparity
continued to grow.[107] An increasing number of intellectuals sought second
or third jobs to supplement their formal income, and many resented these
economic trends.

Corruption

One product of the process of introducing market relations into a destitute bureaucratic system was corruption. Corruption, according to Huntington, is behavior of public officials that deviates from accepted norms in order to serve their private ends. In China and Hungary, corruption took two forms: popular and official. Popular corruption involved almost everyone, from police officers to doctors and even garbage collectors, who to some extent held certain power and exercised it to gain illegal economic benefits. Popular corruption reflected the general decline of public morality, the topic of the next chapter. Official corruption involved officials at every level of government who used their influence and positions for the economic betterment of themselves and their families. Official corruption, especially at high levels, was a cause of much dissatisfaction among ordinary people.

The introduction of market mechanisms in the course of economic reform generated new sources of wealth and an easier flow of money and consumer goods, but it was unable to create new rules of the game or, even when the rules were in place, to persuade people to observe them at the same pace. Although corruption, bribery, theft, influence peddling, extortion, and petty favoritism had existed under state socialism, they reached a stunning scale as the binding norms weakened and as the blending of plan and market greatly expanded opportunities for profiteering and speculation.

The bureaucratic monopoly of inside information and access to scarce or allocated goods allowed the official corruption in China to develop to an unprecedented extent. As enterprises obtained freedom to expand new profit-making activities, all levels of bureaucracy rushed to establish their own corporations. Some 250,000 of 360,000 new companies organized under the reforms by mid-1987 were involved in the sale and resale of scarce commodities and production materials, profiting from the disparities between state and market prices.[108]

Official documents acknowledged that corruption was a serious problem at all levels and repeatedly called for a clean government. The Supreme Court of China established a minimum criterion of corruption of 10,000 yuan for the prosecution of a corruption case. From 1982 to 1988, 190,000 such cases were prosecuted.[109] According to another report, more than 65,000 government officials were prosecuted for corruption from 1983 through 1992.[110]

One form of activity reported was local officials' regular extortion of "contributions" from private enterprises, foreign concerns, or state-owned enterprises. Leading officials took advantage of their posts and pocketed the legal sales commissions under various pretexts instead of delivering them to the state. Foreign investors, particularly Hong Kong businesspeople, spoke of routine demands for kickbacks, bribes, or other "fees" to complete a deal. Foreign executives frequently felt compelled to give gifts of cameras, televisions, and other high-tech equipment to their Chinese partners or hosts.[111] Some officials reportedly wanted cash delivered in person or deposited in their Hong Kong bank accounts.[112] Children of top leaders figured prominently in this trend. Sons and sons-in-law of Deng Xiaoping and Zhao Ziyang and other high-ranking officials were involved in corporations that engaged in profiteering and reportedly made huge amounts of money. Rumors concerning secret Swiss bank accounts of various leaders circulated widely.

Corruption, according to Huntington, may not necessarily be a negative factor in the process of modernization in a given country. For example, it may provide immediate, specific, and concrete benefits to groups that might otherwise be thoroughly alienated from the society.[113] In China's case the group was the cadres whose previous political privileges diminished during economic reform. Corruption thus might have been conducive to the maintenance of a stable political environment and one way of surmounting bureaucratic regulations that hampered economic expansion. But because it violated their sense of fairness and resulted in gross inequality, corruption was the most deeply hated consequence of reform among the Chinese population. According to a 1988 survey of twenty-eight provinces and cities, 78.1 percent of the people said that they most resented government corruption and were most concerned about the punishment of corrupt officials.[114]

Even though one would suspect the same corrupt behavior existed among officials in Hungary as well, few accounts are available in English. There have, though, been a large number of reports on corruption among ordinary citizens of society, which I take up in the next chapter.

Tolerance, Perception, and Expectations

High inflation rates and huge income differentials exist in countries other than state socialist ones, and official corruption is rampant in many Third World countries. But people in some countries appear less accepting of inflation, inequality, and official corruption than people in others. Chinese citizens' tolerance for inflation, for example, was very low. This was true for several reasons. First, per capita income for ordinary Chinese was about 900 yuan ($290) in 1988, of which 80 percent went for daily consumption (food 60 percent, clothing 13 percent, and rent and utilities 8 percent).[115] If inflation soars, the impact on basic living conditions is disastrous. In addition, although the freedom to change jobs in China started to expand, the majority of the population had only a limited ability to adapt to rising inflation by finding more profitable work. Third, few assets were available to the Chinese people to allow them to preserve the real value of their monetary wealth, and it was therefore difficult for consumers to avoid losses in the value of their savings produced by inflation.

These same factors explain why Hungarians had greater tolerance for inflation. First, at $2,100 (in 1988), their per capita income was much higher than that of the Chinese, and the effect of the inflation of consumer prices was far less because daily consumption constituted a smaller portion (food 25 percent, clothing 9 percent, and rent and utilites 10 percent) of Hungarians' income.[116] Second, their job mobility was greater, and many people were engaged in the second economy, making Hungarians better able to adjust to inflation. Third, with the privatization of housing, more and more people put their savings into real estate and were able to preserve the real value of their wealth, which lessened the impact of inflation.

The low tolerance of economic difficulties was not so much a problem of real poverty as the perception of it. Martin King Whyte has argued that "what matters most is not equality per se, but equity—that is, whether people are perceived as getting what is due them, and whether existing inequalities are seen as just and fair."[117] As Ted Gurr has pointed out, the fundamental cause of frustration is an imbalance between what one gets and what one considers one's due. The greater the scope of relative deprivation, the more likely is violent behavior. According to a public opinion survey conducted in 1982, 95 percent of the respondents believed that there were rich and poor people in Hungary.[118] In a survey of thirty-three cities in China in 1987, 88.7 percent of the respondents believed the income gap had widened, 67.6 percent believed their own income had dropped, and 71.6 percent of workers believed their social status had fallen.[119]

The visible hand of government in creating economic hardship was another cause for social resentment. In principle, as some scholars have pointed out, the reward system was much more pronounced under socialism, since it was much easier than under capitalism for the people to see a direct link between their rewards on the one hand and political decisions and power on the other. Presumably, inequalities arising from the operation of the market were less transparent, since the market appeared to be a highly impersonal distribution mechanism, governed by principles that had nothing to do with the will of the Party.[120] However, during the process of economic transition, the role of the government remained strong, since it was the government that introduced all these reform measures. The government was blamed for inflation and inequality, as these phenomena were seen to have arisen from political decisions.

Whatever the academic controversies over its positive and negative functions during economic development, corruption was intolerable to the masses, who perceived it as illegitimate. The Confucian tradition of virtuous officials has had a particularly lasting impact on Chinese society, which has high expectations for clean government. Official corruption also fostered the widespread perception that reforms had merely provided cadres with new opportunities but excluded ordinary people from enjoying the benefits.

Economic grievances were also a product of unfulfilled expectations. High expectations from reform were generated primarily by two causes. The first was the leadership's promise of rising living standards so as to build societal support for the reform program. It was politically convenient deliberately to inspire, or at least not to discourage, high expectations for economic reform. Second, the early successes of economic reform, such as the rural reform in China, also tended to generate optimistic expectations. Social surveys in 1987 showed that nine years after the inauguration of economic reform in China, people's expectations had increased. Social expectations concerning the reform no longer focused solely on higher income; people expected to participate in social life, to raise their social status or realize their self-worth, to gain more freedom in choosing jobs, and to acquire benefits through fair competition.[121] A survey conducted by the Reform Institute in 1988 found "the masses' expectations of the benefits from the reform kept rising in a straight line, while the level of the masses' subjective appraisal of the improvement of their living standard kept decreasing." The institute warned that the gap between people's expectations and the ability of the government to fulfill them was potentially destabilizing.[122]

One paradox here was that people had more and higher expectations regarding the new system but were not prepared to give up all the benefits that had come along with the old one. For example, people expected a rapid rise in wages under the reform, while at the same time they expected virtually complete price stability as had existed under the old system. This paradox highlighted the continuation of the social contract that had developed under state socialism, under which people took the state welfare system for granted. Society's continued insistence on this kind of social contract posed tremendous obstacles to successful market reform.

These economic grievances had several political implications. First, as Kornai had warned, inflation and other economic misconduct were good excuses for a conservative retreat, providing conservative leaders with the pretext to suppress market forces and revive tight administrative control.[123] For example, the political pressure from trade unions against inequality brought about by the New Economic Mechanism was a major reason reform in Hungary drew to a halt in 1972. The decision represented the clear priority of a politically acceptable income distribution and a minimum rate of increase of living standards for all major groups in the population, with special concern for manual workers.[124] There were similar cases of retreat, though smaller, in China.

Second, economic grievances destroyed the people's confidence in the leadership. The legitimacy of the Party was further undermined as the Party failed to live up to the expectations of the masses. A study of changes in social contentment in Hungary indicated that 92 percent of the people interviewed in 1976 expected their living standards to improve; but in 1979, after prices increased, this proportion plummeted to only 14 percent; in 1981 to 9 percent; and at the beginning of 1984 to a mere 4 percent.[125] The unprecedented extent of inflation and corruption in post-Mao China reminded people of the inflation and corruption in the late 1940s when the Kuomintang government finally lost its control over China. The analogy was quite widespread among the population in 1988 and 1989.

As James Davies has pointed out, the actual state of socioeconomic development is generally less significant than the expectation that past progress, now blocked, can and must continue in the future. Political stability and instability are ultimately dependent on a state of mind, a mood, in a society. It is the dissatisfied state of mind rather than the tangible provision of "adequate" or "inadequate" supplies of food, equality, or liberty, he argued, that produces the demands for further political change and even revolution.[126]

Dissatisfaction brought about the third political implication of socioeconomic grievances, that is, it generated instability. Judy Batt has commented that the whole area of prices and incomes became a political minefield for reforming state socialism.[127] Inflation eroded the standard of living of politically important urban residents, contributed to bureaucratic corruption, weakened support for the political leadership, and brought sporadic violence. For example, the gap in income between state employees and private employees in China began to stir up protests and complaints, as reflected in the strikes by Beijing bus drivers over the higher salaries received by the employees of collectively owned taxi companies. Some 200 strikes, each involving more than 1,000 workers, are believed to have occurred in the first half of 1988 alone.[128] Opposition to government corruption was a major motivation behind the 1989 student demonstration in China and the most powerful slogan that mobilized millions of citizens in Beijing to take to the streets to express their resentment. Since the social tolerance of inflation, inequality, and corruption was relatively higher in Hungary, unrest caused by social grievances was not as widespread as in China.

Comparison

This chapter has discussed three political consequences of the economic reform: the redefinition of socialism that reinforced ideological liberalization; economic pluralization that further relaxed political control; and the emergence of socioeconomic grievances that imposed heavy pressures on the political leadership.

With the introduction of the market mechanism and the change in the ownership structure, economic reform not only required a preliminary ideological liberalization, but also propelled the redefinition of socialism to legitimize the fundamental changes that occurred or were expected to occur in the economic system. The image of socialism, therefore, was liberalized. Because of the uncertainties involved in economic reform, the Party showed greater ideological tolerance in the realm of economics, which in turn sustained a general momentum toward a freer intellectual atmosphere.

Economic marketization—the diversification of the structure of ownership, the expansion of labor mobility, and the proliferation of the sources of supply of goods and services—reduced the monopoly of Party secretaries and organizational cadres over assignments and promotions and eroded their powers of patronage. As a result, it relaxed the rigid binding of individual citizens to official structure, enhanced the range of individual choices, stimulated individual consciousness, and ultimately prepared for the birth of a civil society.

Economic reform also created new problems. Price reform brought about overt inflation in China and a constant threat that shadowed the reforms in Hungary. The encouragement of the private sector in the economy produced income inequality and facilitated corruption. It created a fast-growing sector whose employees earned much more than workers in the traditional state sector. The coexistence of multiple sectors in the economy, a dual-track price system, and multiple channels for distribution seemed to invite corruption. The lack of proper rules in economic operation also allowed some people to use illegal means to obtain economic benefits.

Inflation, inequality, and widespread corruption exemplified a dilemma of the economic reform. Economic reform was implemented to raise the living standard of the population. However, at least in the short run, it turned out that reform measures lowered the living standard of many families who found that their real income declined relative to rising prices. Economic hardship was exacerbated by people's low tolerance for such phenomena and their high expectation for an ever-rising living standard. The low tolerance was caused by the inertia of the long-practiced socialist egalitarianism; the high expectation was generated by the real or promised growth of income to be brought about by the reform. These expectations turned out to be dangerous when economic reform failed to bring about the much-anticipated betterment.

Economic and political reform had different impacts upon different social sectors. Despite the perceived relative decline of income by certain social groups, economic reform raised the absolute living standard for the general population. People enjoyed greater freedom in the more relaxed political environment. Yet some groups benefited more than others. Peasants were the beneficiaries of rural reform, even though they started to run into increasing difficulties in selling grains and obtaining loans and paying taxes levied by local authorities. Individual households and private entrepreneurs engaged in commerce and industry were the major beneficiaries of economic reform in that they accumulated wealth at an astonishing rate. Government officials in general were losing the arbitrary powers they had before the reform, yet overall they were not necessarily the losers, as they could use their positions to obtain personal gain in the economic transition.

Conversely, urban population, especially those who worked in the state sector, felt the negative consequences of reform. They had enjoyed job security and all kinds of welfare benefits under traditional state socialism but were in a disadvantageous position in the economic reform, especially when marketization provided opportunities to prosper to those who were outside the state planning system, not those who were within. Intellectuals more than any other group welcomed ideological liberalization, but they became victims of economic reform in that their salaries stagnated. The gains and losses of different social groups during the reform would affect their willingness to challenge the regime, as discussed in chapter 5.

There were also differences between the reform experiences in Hungary and China. The astronomical rate of inflation in China in part reflected the rapid price reform, lack of wage controls, and a lax monetary policy. The relatively controlled inflation rate in Hungary indicated that a carefully designed reform scheme and proper policy could make a difference. The tight wage controls in the Hungarian reform package reduced enterprises' motivation to raise product prices to make up labor costs and stabilized the level of consumption, which brought about a manageable aggregate demand.

Official corruption was more evident in China than in Hungary. It was a target of public resentment, and the government repeatedly vowed to eliminate it. The dual-track price system fostered widespread corruption, since the same products or materials had both a planned price and a market price, which created opportunities for speculation. The collapse of moral self-constraint as a result of the crisis of faith and the much lower living standard of government officials in China also served as likely causes for rapacity. It appeared that official corruption in Hungary was less serious, as there were fewer vocal complaints about it.

Although inflation and corruption in Hungary were not as serious as in China, inequality was a far larger problem in Hungary. The social resentment toward the income gap between industrial workers and managers was one major cause of the suspension of economic reform in the early 1970s. When the economic reform later resumed, income inequality remained visible, especially between workers in the private sector and those in the state sector. By the 1980s, however, resentment over inequality had weakened, as the booming second economy started to provide more opportunities for accumulating wealth. In Hungary, with its tight labor supply, many state employees held a second or even a third job in the second economy. Thus, their energies were largely channeled into efforts for their own betterment. This was less possible in labor-abundant China.

Compared to Hungary, China had less tolerance for either inflation, inequality, or corruption. In economic terms, low personal incomes in China meant less capacity to absorb price hikes, and more restricted job mobility made it more difficult to adjust to price increases. In cultural terms, this intolerance was not only fostered by the protracted propagation of equality as a socialist ethic, but was also deeply rooted in the Chinese tradition of worrying not about scarcity but inequality. Consequently, social discontent assumed a more explosive nature in China than in Hungary.

On the road of transition, state socialist systems were hindered by ideological, political, social, economic, and even psychological obstacles that occasioned zigzag patterns in almost every sphere of reform. The process of reform entailed many paradoxes: The state tried to extricate itself from its past paternalistic function, but the society continued to hold it responsible for many things for which it had been responsible in the past. Private ownership was permitted, but not everybody was able or willing to partake of it. Choices of jobs were greater, but not many people would accept the risk in labor mobility. In short, the implicit social contract of state socialism became one of the most serious obstacles in the economic transition. The psychological and institutional adjustments to the transition took much longer than people had imagined at the beginning.

NOTES

1. Morris Bornstein, "Ideology and the Soviet Economy," in *Comparative Economic Systems*, ed. Jan S. Prybyla (New York: Meredith, 1969), pp. 81-82.

2. For example, during the same period, there was a similar discussion in Czechoslovakia that became the prelude to what was known as the Prague Spring in 1968. Among the active Czechoslovak economists were Ota Sik, Evzen Lobl, and Radoslav Selucky. See the discussion by Judy Batt, *Economic Reform and Political*

Change in Eastern Europe: A Comparison of the Czechoslovak and Hungarian Experiences (New York: Macmillan, 1988).

3. Ibid., pp. 136-148.

4. L. Szamuely, "The Second Wave of the Economic Mechanism Debate and the 1968 Reform in Hungary," *Acta Oeconomica* 33, no. 1-2 (1984): 47.

5. Ibid., p. 54.

6. Batt, *Economic Reform and Political Change in Eastern Europe*, p. 147.

7. Rezso Nyers, "Social and Political Effects of the New Economic Mechanism," *New Hungarian Quarterly* 10, no. 34 (Summer 1969): 4-5.

8. Bela Csikos-Nagy, "Socialist Economic Theory and the New Mechanism," *New Hungarian Quarterly* 8, no. 28 (Winter 1967): 40.

9. Rezso Nyers, "The Comprehensive Reform of Managing the National Economy in Hungary," *Acta Oeconomica* 1, no. 1 (1966): 21.

10. Gabor Revesz, *Perestroika in Eastern Europe: Hungary's Economic Transformation, 1945-1988* (Boulder, Colo.: Westview Press, 1990), p. 61.

11. Wu Jinglian, "Choice of Strategy in China's Economic Reform," paper presented at the annual meeting of the American Economics Association, Chicago, December 1987.

12. See, for example, articles by Liu Guoguang and Lin Zili in *Jingji Yanjiu*, nos. 10 and 11 (1980); article by Yang Jianbai in *Jingji Yanjiu*, no. 1 (1981); and a series of articles in *Jingji Yanjiu*, nos. 6, 7, and 8 (1982).

13. Liu Chengrui, Hu Naiwu, and Yu Guanghua, "Jijua he shichang xiangjiehe shi woguo jingji guanli gaige the jiben tujing" [The integration of planning and market is the basic path for our reform of economic management], *Jingji Yanjiu*, no. 7 (1979): 37-46.

14. Liu Guoguang, "Luelun jihua tiaojie yu shichang tiaojie de jige wenti" [On some questions of plan coordination and market coordination], *Jingji Yanjiu*, no. 10 (1980): 3-11.

15. Lin Zili, "Shehuizhuyi jingji tiaojie lilun tantao" [An exploration of the theory of socialist economic coordination], *Jingji Yanjiu*, no. 11 (1980): 19-32.

16. *Renmin Ribao*, 31 October 1980.

17. *Shijie Jingji Daobao*, 23 April 1984.

18. *Beijing Review*, 29 October 1984, p. VII.

19. The term "tails of capitalism" (*zibenzhuyi weiba*) was coined during the Cultural Revolution. It implied that nonplanned individual economic activities, such as rural market exchange and sideline production, were remnants of capitalism.

20. For some detailed discussion on the debate over the concept of market in post-Mao China, see Robert C. Hsu, "Conceptions of the Market in Post-Mao China," *Modern China* 11, no. 4 (October 1985): 436-60.

21. *Beijing Review*, 9-16 November 1987, pp. 33-35.

22. Ibid., p. 33.

23. The choice of this term rather than straightforward "market" reflected the ideological consideration. To redefine socialist economy as a full-scale market economy was ideologically unacceptable at the time.

24. The higher social status of state ownership before the reform in China was reflected in views regarding marriage: It was considered an inappropriate match for someone employed in state-owned enterprise to marry a worker from a "collectively owned" factory.

25. William F. Robinson, *The Pattern of Reform in Hungary: A Political, Economic and Cultural Analysis* (New York: Praeger, 1973), pp. 60-62.

26. Nyers, "The Comprehensive Reform of Managing the National Economy in Hungary," p. 35.

27. "Informal private sector" refers to private enterprises that were not registered.

28. Istvan Gabor, "The Second (Secondary) Economy," *Acta Oeconomica* 22, no. 3-4 (1979): 291-311.

29. Akos Rona-Tas, "The Second Economy as a Subversive Force: The Erosion of Party Power in Hungary," in *The Waning of the Communist State: Economic Origins of Political Decline in China and Hungary*, ed. Andrew Walder (Berkeley: University of California Press, 1995), pp. 61-86.

30. Marton Tardos, "Economic Organizations and Ownership," *Acta Oeconomica* 40, no. 1-2 (1989): 17-37.

31. Ibid.

32. See the communiqué of the Third Plenum of the Eleventh Central Committee of the CCP.

33. Fixing quotas for each household—the rudiments of a responsibility system—was first practiced by peasants of Guzheng County, Anhui Province, in 1978. It was written up into a report "Dawn in the Countryside: China's Hope" by a group of young people and passed along to the central leadership. In 1980 Premier Zhao Ziyang read their report and called it "an extremely clear account of the problems in the countryside." The responsibility system was introduced nationwide since 1981.

34. Dong Furen, "Suoyouzhi gaige yu jingji yunxing jizhi gaige" [Ownership reform and economic operation mechanism reform], *Xinhua Wenzhai*, no. 4 (1986): 58-65.

35. *Beijing Ribao*, 19 May 1986.

36. Liu Guoguang, "Guanyu suojouzhi guanxi gaige de ruogan wenti" [Several questions on ownership reform], *Xinhua Wenzhai*, no. 3 (1986): 66-69.

37. *Beijing Review*, 29 October 1984, pp. III-XVI.

38. Tong Dalin, "Gufenhua shi shehuizhuyi qiye de yige xinjidian" [Stockification is a new supporting point for socialist enterprises], *Xinhua Wenzhai*, no. 10 (1986): 63-64.

39. Chen Weishu, "Shehuizhuyi gongyouzhi jiegou de liangzhong xuanzhe" [Two choices for the structure of socialist public ownership], *Xinhua Wenzhai*, no. 10 (1986): 65-69.

40. *Beijing Review*, 9-15 November 1987, pp. 25, 36.

41. The demand for privatization was so popular that on the eve of the Seventh National People's Congress in 1988, the Party had privately persuaded the deputies not to raise the matter in the congress. (Conversation with Wan Rennan, former president of China's Sitong Company, 28 October 1989, Washington, D.C.)

42. Robinson, *The Pattern of Reform in Hungary*, p. 367.

43. Ibid., p. 314.

44. K. Falus-Szikra, "Wage Differentials in Hungary," *Acta Oeconomica* 25, no. 1-2 (1980): 172.

45. *Renmin Ribao*, Special Commentator, "How Marxists Look at Material Interests," *Peking Review*, 13 October 1978, pp. 5-10.

46. *Renmin Ribao*, Special Commentator, "Implementing the Socialist Principle 'To Each According to His Work'," *Peking Review*, 4 August 1978, pp. 6-15.

47. *Beijing Review*, 29 October 1984, p. XII.

48. Ibid., 9-15 November 1987, pp. 27, 36.

49. Janos Kornai, "The Dilemmas of a Socialist Economy: The Hungarian Experience," *Cambridge Journal of Economics* 4, no. 2 (1980): 147-57.

50. For example, see Zhou Weimin and Lu Zhongyuan, "Xiaolu youxian, jiangu gongping" [Efficiency first, and take justice into consideration at the same time], *Jingji Yanjiu*, no. 2 (1986): 30-37; and Jin Pei, "Yi gongping cujin xiaolu, yi xiaolu shixian gongping" [Use justice to promote efficiency, use efficiency to realize justice], *Jingji Yanjiu*, no. 7 (1986): 78-82.

51. Andrew Walder, *Communist Neo-Traditionalism: Work and Authority in Chinese Industry* (Berkeley: University of California Press, 1986).

52. Jean Oi, "Communism and Clientalism: Rural Politics in China," *World Politics* 37, no. 2 (1985): 238-66.

53. Jan S. Prybyla, "To Market, To Market . . ." *Issues and Studies* 23, no. 1 (January 1987): 73.

54. Ibid.

55. Janos Kornai, "The Hungarian Reform Process: Visions, Hopes, and Reality," *Journal of Economic Literature* 24, no. 3-4 (December 1986): 1702.

56. Economic Research Report by the Comprehensive Problems Group of the Institute of Development, "Nongmin, shichang, he zhidu chuangxin: baochandaohu banian hou nongcun fazhan mianlin de shenceng gaige" [Peasants, the market, and innovation in the institution: On the deep structural reform in rural areas after eight years of fixing output for each household], *Jingji Yanjiu*, no. 1 (1987).

57. Ivan Volgyes, "Hungary: A Malaise Thinly Disguised," *Current History* 84 (November 1985): 365.

58. Prybyla, "To Market, To Market . . ." p. 76.

59. In addition to the category indicating how many people were in the private sector, Hungarian statistics show how much time was spent in the private sector or how much work was accomplished by the private sector. This suggests that with a tight labor

supply, people usually work for both the state and private sectors. State and private sectors shared active labor time instead of the number of laborers. This is less the case in labor-abundant China.

60. Prybyla, "To Market, To Market . . ." p. 77.

61. Ibid., p. 79.

62. Connie Squires Meaney, "Market Reform in a Leninist System: Some Trends in the Distribution of Power, Status, and Money in Urban China," *Studies in Comparative Communism* 22, no. 2/3 (Summer/Autumn 1989): 216.

63. Tamas Bauer, "Economic Reform Within vs. Beyond the State Sector," manuscript, 1987.

64. David Stark, "The Micropolitics of the Firm and the Macropolitics of Reform: New Forms of Workplace Bargaining in Hungarian Enterprises," in *State Versus Markets in the World-System*, vol. 8 of *Political Economy of the World-System Annuals*, eds. Peter Evans, Dietrich Rueschemeyer, and Evelyne Huber Stephens (Beverly Hills: Sage, 1985), pp. 247-73.

65. Kornai, "The Hungarian Reform Process," p. 1709.

66. Prybyla, "To Market, To Market. . ." p. 74.

67. *Radio Free Europe Research* (*RFER*) 12, no. 4, 30 January 1987, p. 11.

68. Liu Jiazhen, "Woguo liyong waizi de huigu yu zhanwang" [Retrospect and prospect of the utilization of foreign investment in our country], *Renmin Ribao* (overseas edition), 28 February 1990, p. 2.

69. Shaoguang Wang, "The Rise of the Regions: Fiscal Reform and the Decline of Central State Capacity in China," in *The Waning of the Communist State: Economic Origins of Political Decline in China and Hungary*, ed. Andrew Walder (Berkeley: University of California Press, 1995), pp. 87-113; and Susan Shirk, *The Political Logic of Economic Reform in China* (Berkeley: University of California Press, 1993).

70. Andrew G. Walder, "China's Transitional Economy: Interpreting Its Significance," *China Quarterly*, no. 144 (December 1995): 963-79; and Jean Oi, "The Role of the Local State in China's Transitional Economy," *China Quarterly*, no. 144 (December 1995): 1132-49.

71. Kornai, "The Hungarian Reform Process," p. 1713.

72. This physical attachment to the working unit could be portrayed by an account in which the author pointed out that "in our organizations, quite a number of professional people do not like their jobs. But the leader is resolved not to let them go." The author relates, "A friend of mine who has been applying for a job transfer unsuccessfully for over ten years was once told by his boss: 'there is no point arranging it for you since you are here on orders from above. Why should we go out of our way to find another person when we have you here? You are ours, and you stay where you are'"; Chen Wenxi, "Freedom of Job Choice Essential," *China Daily*, 6 November 1986. There is yet another account in which a young worker who wanted to transfer to another workplace he thought was more suitable for him was asked by his unit to bail himself out for 1,000 yuan. *Renmin Ribao* (overseas edition), 12 July 1987, p. 1.

73. Kornai, "The Hungarian Reform Process," p. 1714.

74. Paul Lendvai, *Hungary: The Art of Survival* (London: I. B. Tauris, 1988), p. 76.

75. State Statistical Bureau of China, *A Statistical Survey of China 1989* (Beijing: China Statistics Press, 1989), p. 35.

76. Economic Research Report by the Comprehensive Problems Group of the Institute of Development, "Nongmin, shichang, he zhidu chuangxin."

77. *Renmin Ribao* (overseas edition), 3 September 1986, p. 1.

78. Ibid., 4 March 1989, p. 1.

79. Wang An, "Zhongguo, yige shiyi zhi zhong de gongchang" [China, a working place with a billion people], *Renmin Ribao* (overseas edition), 7 January 1988, p. 3.

80. *Renmin Ribao* (overseas edition), 3 January 1987.

81. Ibid., July 1988, p. 4.

82. In China "free market" refers to the markets (most of them daily) in which local residents sell their own products, such as meat, vegetables, and handicrafts. "Free" means outside the state planning system.

83. State Statistical Bureau of China, *A Statistical Survey of China 1989*, p. 76.

84. Kornai, "The Hungarian Reform Process," p. 1714.

85. See Ivan Szelenyi, *Urban Inequalities Under State Socialism* (New York: Oxford University Press, 1983).

86. Kornai, "The Hungarian Reform Process," p. 1708.

87. Peter Toma, *Socialist Authority: The Hungarian Experience* (New York: Praeger, 1988), p. 135.

88. Milton Friedman, *Capitalism and Freedom* (Chicago: University of Chicago Press, 1962), p. 15.

89. Jan Prybyla, "China's Economic Experiment: Back from the Market?" *Problems of Communism* 38 (January-February 1989): 4.

90. Li Yunqi, "China's Inflation," *Asian Survey* 29, no. 7 (July 1989): 655-68.

91. For a good discussion of inflation in China, see Barry Naughton, *Growing Out of the Plan: Chinese Economic Reform, 1978-1993* (New York: Cambridge University Press, 1995), pp. 247-52.

92. Ivan Berend and Gyorgy Ranki, *The Hungarian Economy in the Twentieth Century* (London: Croom Helm, 1985), p. 242.

93. Richard Portes, "Economic Reforms in Hungary," *American Economic Review: Papers and Proceedings* 60 (1970): 307-313.

94. Kornai, "The Hungarian Reform Process," p. 1720.

95. "The Price Increase That Came in from the Cold," *RFER* 10, no. 7, 15 February 1985, pp. 3-4.

96. David Granick, *Enterprise Guidance in Eastern Europe: A Comparison of Four Socialist Economies* (Princeton, N. J.: Princeton University Press, 1975), pp. 266-67.

97. Robinson, *The Pattern of Reform in Hungary*, pp. 148-49.

98. Henryk Flakierski, "Economic Reform and Income Distribution in Hungary," *Cambridge Journal of Economics* 3, no. 1 (1979): 24, and table 3.

99. Richard Portes, "Hungary: Economic Performance, Policy and Prospects," Joint Economic Committee, 95th Cong., 1st sess., *East European Economics Post Helsinki* (Washington, D.C.: U.S. Government Printing Office, 1977), p. 786.

100. Toma, *Socialist Authority*, p. 116.

101. Revesz, *Perestroika in Eastern Europe*, pp. 18-19.

102. Flakierski, "Economic Reform and Income Distribution," p. 26.

103. Laura D'Andrea Tyson, "Aggregate Economic Difficulties and Workers' Welfare," in *Blue-Collar Workers in Eastern Europe*, eds. Jan Triska and Charles Gati (London: George Allen & Unwin, 1981), p. 115.

104. Jiang Zemin, "Renzhen xiaochu shehui fenpei bugong xianxiang" [Seriously fight against the phenomenon of unfairness of social distribution], *Xinhua Wenzhai*, no. 7-8 (1989): 55-58.

105. State Statistical Bureau of China, "Changes in the Life-Style of Urban Residents," *Beijing Review*, 14-21 November 1988, p. 30.

106. Dai Yannian, "Dealing with Unfair Income Gaps," *Beijing Review*, 15-21 August 1988, pp. 7-8.

107. Prybyla, "China's Economic Experiment," p. 6.

108. Connie Squires Meaney, "Market Reform and Disintegrative Corruption in Urban China," in *Reform and Reaction in Post-Mao China: The Road to Tiananmen*, ed. Richard Baum (New York: Routledge, 1991), pp. 124-42.

109. Qi Dajun, "Bingrugaohuang de fuhua" (Incurable corruption), *Zhongguo Zhi Chun*, no. 81 (February 1990): 37-39.

110. *Yearbook on Chinese Communism 1993* (Taipei: Institute for the Study of Chinese Communist Problems, 1994), P8—2.

111. Ibid.

112. Meaney, "Market Reform and Disintegrative Corruption," pp. 130-31.

113. Samuel Huntington, *Political Order in Changing Societies* (New Haven: Yale University Press, 1968), pp. 68-71.

114. Qi, "Bingrugaohuang de fuhua," p. 38.

115. World Bank, *World Development Report 1990* (Oxford: Oxford University Press, 1991), p. 196.

116. Ibid., p. 197.

117. Martin King Whyte, "Social Trends in China: The Triumph of Inequality?" in *Modernizing China: Post-Mao Reform and Development*, eds. A. Doak Barnett and Ralph N. Clough (Boulder, Colo.: Westview Press, 1986), pp. 103-123.

118. Toma, *Socialist Authority*, p. 115.

119. John P. Burns, "China's Governance: Political Reform in a Turbulent Environment," *China Quarterly*, no. 119 (1989): 498.

120. Frank Parkin, *Class Inequality and Political Order* (London: Paladin, 1975); and Flakierski, "Economic Reform and Income Distribution," p. 17.

121. Wei Qun, and Duan Yue, "Yinmi wangguo zhong de jige wenti: zoufang zhongguo shehui diaocha xitong" [Several questions in the hidden kingdom: a visit to China's social survey system], *Zhongguo Qingnian*, November 1987, p. 13.

122. Burns, "China's Governance," p. 491.

123. Kornai, "The Hungarian Reform Process," p. 1724.

124. Portes, "Hungary," pp. 787-89.

125. Toma, *Socialist Authority*, p. 146.

126. James C. Davies, "Toward A Theory of Revolution," *American Sociological Review* 27, no. 1 (February 1962): 5-19.

127. Batt, *Economic Reform and Political Change in Eastern Europe*, p. 258.

128. Prybyla, "China's Economic Experiment," p. 4.

CHAPTER 5

SOCIETAL CHALLENGES TO THE POLITICAL ESTABLISHMENT

Previous chapters have discussed how ideological and political liberalization set the stage for economic reform and how economic reform reinforced ideological liberalization, created a more autonomous society, and generated socioeconomic grievances. This chapter examines the ways in which these five factors—ideological liberalization, political liberalization, economic reform, a more autonomous society, and socioeconomic grievances—produced societal challenges to the existing political establishment in the two countries.

The societal challenge is defined here as demands raised by various sectors of society that cannot be met by the existing political system and therefore create pressures for systemic reform. The societal challenge took several forms in Hungary and China. One was a passive challenge, manifested in an increasingly alienated society that withdrew its moral support for the regime. This mass alienation was characterized by a crisis of faith, a decline of public morality, and occasionally mass protests. The passive challenge was usually fluid, volatile, and without clear objectives.

The second form of societal challenge was indirect, promoted by the emergence of a more autonomous society. Unlike the passive challenge, which merely involved withdrawal from the existing system, the emerging autonomous society in reforming state socialist countries demanded space for its very existence in ways that did not fit with the previous ideological or political frameworks. It demanded the recognition of group and individual interests as legitimate and the imposition of certain limits on the arbitrary power of the Party and the state.

The third form was an active challenge, that is, the articulated political demands to the government raised either by outspoken intellectuals or by an organized protest movement. It was made possible by political liberalization, which involved greater official tolerance of diverse political opinions and loosened control over individual and group activities. Because of its concrete and confrontational character, the active challenge produced the most visible clash with the political establishment. Whether such conflict produced greater liberty and democracy depended to a large extent on the strength and strategies of the protest movement and on the flexibility of the political establishment.

The Passive Challenge: Mass Alienation

The notion of mass alienation refers to the citizenry's disassociation from and rejection of the meanings, norms, and values that define the system in which they live. In Hungary and China, mass alienation was characterized by a crisis of faith in communism and the Communist Party and by a strong sense of normlessness: the perception that norms have lost their regulative force and that socially unapproved means are necessary to achieve one's goals. This sense of normlessness led to the decline of public morality and to widespread popular corruption.

Communist regimes used two basic justifications to persuade their populations to accept and identify with their system. One was the ideological claim that socialism and communism were the inevitable results of the scientific laws of historical evolution. The other justification was socioeconomic performance, reflected in the system's ability to provide economic prosperity and social justice for its citizens. Although the improvement of the living standard was not at all impressive, state socialism did provide its population a cradle-to-grave welfare system featuring full employment, health care, free education, and retirement plans. (Because of the huge population, only urban state employees enjoyed such benefits in China.)

Over the years, both the ideological and socioeconomic justifications were seriously eroded. According to Marxist ideology, the socialist system was supposed to provide a more genuine political democracy and a higher level of economic development than capitalism. However, the state socialism that was practiced in China and Hungary failed to provide satisfactory political and economic services to its people. There were no effective checks on the abuse of political power, and the planned economy consistently generated a shortage of consumer goods. The gap between theory and reality became a major source of mass alienation, which led people to question the values and norms that the regimes sought to promote. As a result, there developed a pronounced feeling of "us" versus "them" in the people's attitude toward the regime.[1] Ordinary people increasingly expressed indifference to officially propagated values, retreated into private life, concentrated on material and personal interests, ignored social norms, and occasionally held open protests.

In Hungary increasing mass alienation was deepened by a severe national crisis in which the Communist Party exhausted most of its political credibility and the people became disillusioned: The brutal Soviet suppression of the 1956 Hungarian uprising shattered the population's faith in the Party, a faith that was relatively weak in the first place. When universities were reopened in Hungary in the spring of 1957 after the shock of 1956, Laszlo Boka observed that the young people that lined the benches in the lecture halls and seminar rooms were "grim, apathetic and inaccessible."[2] He also had some experience with a friend's two sons. The twenty-four-year-old son argued with his father (who was a Party member) all the time, holding him responsible for what happened during the Rakosi era. But his younger brother simply did not see the point of arguing. He said, "My brother is an idiot, we don't speak the same language [as our father]."[3]

In 1963 a young Hungarian poet, Ferenc Baranyi, published "The Ballad of the Pampered Youth." In the poem he expressed resentment toward the older generation, who were always telling him that the old days were much worse than the youth of today could ever imagine. The young people did not want to compare their lives with those of thirty years before but with advanced countries or the promise of tomorrow. A well-known Hungarian writer, Peter Veres, commented that "our youth are weary of the constant preaching about the coming of a socialist utopia."[4]

As William Robinson observed in the early 1970s, Hungarian youth were, as a group, politically apathetic, indifferent to ideology, and mainly interested in studying subjects that would advance them professionally and financially. Material comforts attracted them, but the construction of socialism left them uninspired.[5] The Party frankly admitted that communist ideology was not taken seriously by young people. Young Hungarians had what was termed a "secondary ideology" or an "everyday ideology," which was characterized by individualism and abstention from politics.[6] Young people followed Western fads, wearing blue jeans and listening to rock music. They pursued material rewards offered by the system, but their pursuit lacked ideological content or appreciation for the regime.

Radio Free Europe conducted a series of surveys among Hungarian travelers in the West in the 1970s. Surveys indicated that 50 percent thought that socialism worked badly in Hungary (38 percent thought it worked well), and 59 percent believed that democracy in the West worked well (13 percent thought it worked badly). In hypothetical free elections, only 5-10 percent preferred the Communist Party, whereas 42 percent would have voted for a democratic socialist party, 27 percent for a Christian democratic party, 17 percent for a peasant party, and 6 percent for a conservative party.[7]

The loss of faith in the Communist Party was also reflected in the increasing resurgence of religion, which spread to all social strata and age groups. According to a survey conducted by Miklos Tomka of the Mass Communications Institute of Hungarian Radio in 1984, even though as many as 80 percent of all believers had long ago stopped actively practicing their religion, their faith remained unshaken and in many cases had perhaps strengthened. The chairman of the State Office for Church Affairs, Imre Miklos, admitted that the Communist Party was to blame for this situation because atheistic Marxist-Leninist ideology had been unable to provide a compelling alternative to religion. In its efforts to change the attitude of the young Hungarians who had become disenchanted and cynical because of the difficult situation in their country, the state authorities had reluctantly reached the conclusion that they needed the support of the churches not only for maintaining national unity but also to carry out much-needed social and charity services.[8]

Although the people of China had been more thoroughly indoctrinated, they, too, became greatly disillusioned after ten years of the Cultural Revolution. In May 1980 *Zhongguo Qingnian* (Chinese youth), an official monthly of the Central Committee of the Communist Youth League, published a letter entitled "Why Is Life's Road Getting Narrower and Narrower?"[9] The writer, a young worker, openly confessed her loss of faith in the Communist ideals she had cherished in her youth. She saw that there was no longer genuine trust between people and argued that human nature was selfish, that people performed seemingly selfless actions for selfish reasons. Over the next few months, some 60,000 young people from all over China responded to the letter, echoing the author's despair. The letter illustrated the so-called crises of faith, trust, and confidence among the young generation, which was thereafter often referred to as the "lost generation." The letter's central themes—the arbitrariness of China's political system, the destructive effects of politics on human relationships, the desire for recognition of the individual's worth in a collective society—recurred again and again in the literature of the reform period.

The crisis of faith was reinforced by ideological liberalization in the initial stage of reform, during which Marxism and communist ideals further lost their cohesiveness and effectiveness, and alternative value systems were presented. The crisis of faith was most serious among young people. It expressed itself in terms of opposition to all the values that had been promulgated in the past: political apathy as against political commitment, individualism as a negation of the long-taught value of collectivism, and materialism and consumerism as opposed to idealism and asceticism.

In China the loss of confidence in the Communist Party accompanied the rapid relaxation of ideological control that followed the extreme indoctrination during the Cultural Revolution. It proved very difficult to discredit past practices without discrediting the Communist Party itself. It was equally difficult to show the need for economic reform and Western technology, on the one hand, without nullifying the myth of the superiority of socialism, on the other. For example, before the reform, the official word preached that two-thirds of the world's population were living in misery and that the Chinese were the happiest people in the world, thanks to the leadership of the Communist Party. This was the ideological basis for the Party's right to rule. Later, when people were astonished by the much higher living standard of the Western and newly industrialized countries, they tended to attribute China's backwardness to socialism and the Party as well.[10] The unfavorable comparison with the economic performance of the industrialized and newly industrialized countries undermined the credibility of socialism and the Communist Party and fostered young people's expectations for a utopian capitalism. Opinion surveys showed mixed ratings for the Party. In one such survey of university students in Guangdong in 1988, only one-third of them agreed that becoming a Party member was "life's ideal," another third were "indifferent," and 24 percent thought that it was better to be a "nonparty personage." Although 71.8 percent agreed that Marxism-Leninism was scientific "but needed to be continuously developed," 14 percent thought it was obsolete.[11]

Individualism was in vogue among Chinese youth from the inauguration of reform, with Jean-Paul Sartre the most popular philosopher on university campuses. Self-realization was the catchword among youth throughout the decade of reform. A bold declaration of individualism appeared in a speech given by a young poet at a university: "The secret of my success is being faithful to my own feelings. I am what I am. I don't let myself be pushed around. I want to be myself in my poetry."[12] Deng Xiaoping later commented that one such speech had destroyed all the ideological and political work the Party had done among the students.[13] An indicator of growing individualism was that the most popular song among the younger generation in prereform China, "We Are the Successors of Communism," was replaced ten years after the implementation of reform by a song entitled "I Am a Lonely Wolf from the North." According to Wuer Kaixi, a student leader in the 1989 student movement in China, the students found meaning in the image of the lonely wanderer trapped in a bitter, empty landscape. Wuer remarked that "in recent years Chinese college students have been rebellious against all sorts of authority. The favorite word among the youth in China is 'No.'" Wuer believed that young people were "lost and disoriented."[14]

A further indicator of mass alienation in both Hungary and China was the decline of public morality and the rising enthusiasm for material wealth aroused by economic reform. To be sure, popular corruption had previously existed under state socialism. As the formal system could not provide adequate goods and services, people became adept at using connections and back doors. In addition to vertical patron-client links, there were horizontal relationships that involved circles of friends and friends of friends. Together they comprised a web of supply and demand relations outside both the market and planning system. During the economic reform, popular corruption developed on a much larger scale.

In Hungary popular corruption became a way of life. People generally knew what the going rate was for various goods and services. A bed in hospital called for a 1,000-forint bribe, surgery required a bribe of between 2,000 and 10,000 forints, whereas for some small favors a pack of cigarettes or a bottle of wine might suffice. Almost 80 percent of the estimated 100,000 million forints of so-called invisible income in Hungary was connected to some form of corruption.[15] In the spring of 1983 the Hungarian Television Science Club organized a debate about Hungarian society in the 1980s. The reaction of the viewers was that "money reigns in Hungary."[16] In the past a tip was the reward for extra service, nowadays, if you were lucky your tip would secure you no more than the prescribed quality or the minimum service. Elemer Hankiss, a well-known sociologist and a member of the Hungarian Academy of Sciences, listed a catalogue of the items that could be obtained only through bribery: material goods, services, licenses and concessions, job positions, and even the "conditions of autonomous human existence" (absence of fear, feeling of security, and opportunities).[17] Hankiss concluded that everyone was corrupting everyone else throughout Hungarian society.[18] People developed various schemes to beat the system, from obtaining foreign currency accounts to traveling abroad.[19]

There were numerous similar examples of popular corruption in China, from bribing a police officer to cancel an arbitrarily issued ticket to bribing a garbage collector to remove the trash promptly. Bribes began to be routinely required in big cities to install phones, start electric service, get mail delivered, or receive medical attention. Corrupt public behavior went together with the worship of money. The Party slogan "Look to the future" was popularly transformed to "Look for money," which had the same Chinese pronunciation (*xiang qian kan*). Money was no longer seen as the symbol of evil and the bourgeoisie but a guarantee of happiness.[20] A sociology student at Beijing University even found a Marxist justification for it: He argued that according to Marxist theory money was the concentration of average social labor and thus to worship money was to worship social labor, so there was nothing wrong with it.[21] Sometimes the greed for money exceeded basic moral considerations. There was one report of bystanders bidding for a price to rescue someone who had fallen into the water.[22]

The sense of normlessness was further reinforced by the fusion of public and private spheres of life developed in state socialist systems. There was considerable confusion about the difference between entrepreneurship and crime. On the one hand, many people detested entrepreneurs because they thought that private enterprise involved illegitimate economic activities and criminal conduct. On the other, many believed that the new authorization for entrepreneurship and private enterprise could legitimize any economic crime. In many cases people interpreted the lifting of the restrictions that sustained the totalitarian regime as an invitation to violate some of the basic principles necessary for the survival of any society, regardless of its ideological foundations. Entrepreneurs obtained profits by cheating their customers. There were numerous instances of the sale of fake medications, fake wine, and fake cigarettes. Although swindled customers would never come back, there were plenty of new customers to cheat.

People developed a negligent attitude toward work in the public sector and a lack of responsibility toward public property and public affairs. There was a strange phenomenon in China: State enterprises kept losing money, but their workers continued to receive more bonuses. Managers wanted to appear to lose money so that they would not have to deliver their profits to the state but distributed them as bonuses to their workers instead.[23] Pilfering became widespread. Workers in the state enterprises often sold factory property to the half dozen so-called recycling stations that were usually established outside the factory gate.[24] Social resentment also led to slow-downs in the workplace, resulting in decreased productivity. It was reported that the productivity rate in China reached its lowest point in early 1989 just before the student movement.[25]

Together, the crisis of faith, the decline of public morality, and social grievances formed a passive challenge to the party leadership. They reflected a society that was more and more difficult to control, and they challenged the capacity of the existing political institutions to respond effectively to the discontent. The passive challenge did not pose an acute threat to the regime but rather a chronic one. Without major disruptions, the regime could possibly have lasted without instituting political reforms.

A more serious consequence of mass alienation lay not in the erosion of the Party's legitimacy, for a regime could survive without legitimacy for a long while, but in the potential for the alienation to inflame popular upheaval. Although mass alienation was basically a withdrawal from the existing system, it could explode into massive protest in a crisis situation. In a critique of "aggregate-psychological" theories of revolution, Theda Skocpol argued that "no matter how discontented an aggregate of people may become, they cannot engage in political action unless they are part of at least minimally organized groups with access to some resources."[26] The passive challenge to the political establishment discussed here was thus not sufficient for a revolution and posed no immediate physical threat to the regime. But it exerted a constant pressure for the regime to prevent any minimally organized groups from emerging and any crisis from developing.

Another consequence of mass alienation was its long-lasting effect on the building of a normal market and a credible political system. Once it became a pattern of thinking and behavior, it would persist for a long time. It was a psychological and behavioral pattern that, although created by one institutional environment, could affect the formation and functioning of new institutions. The disrespect for rules and the tendency to cheat the system would produce a corrupt market system—an anomic framework in which market transactions are undertaken through irregular or unsanctioned means, such as the abuse of official positions, the manipulation of personal connections, bribery, or the use of violence by criminal organizations. Mass alienation would also eventually impede the construction of stable democratic institutions.

As the old basis of legitimacy eroded, the Party needed to establish a new basis of legitimacy. One possible solution was to fill in the spiritual void left by the fast-declining communist idealism. But within the frameworks of state socialism, even a reforming one, the Party was crippled in finding an alternative. It had to insist on the validity of communist ideals, regardless of how few people believed in them, while at the same time looking for something supplementary. Because religion was excluded on an ideological basis, the Party tried to invoke patriotic feelings in the population. In China the love of the homeland was written into the "Resolution on Spiritual Civilization" of 1986 as one component of "socialist spiritual civilization." The Party hoped that if people loved their country, they would love the Party as well. It was true that nationalist sentiment was stronger than the communist ideal among the population, as expressed in the protest against Japanese imports in 1985, the dispute between Chinese and African students over black students' dating Chinese in 1987, and occasional riots at sports events involving foreign teams. However, few equated the country with the Party. Stanley Rosen found that "unquestioning loyalty toward the Communist Party . . . declined at the expense of independence of thought and judgement, respect for talent, and a patriotism separated from Party leadership."[27]

The Hungarian government had to walk a more delicate line in encouraging nationalism as an alternative to communism. Allowing for a degree of patriotic pride and self-respect bolstered the legitimacy of the regime. It would have been politically suicidal, however, for the government to incite anti-Soviet or anti-Romanian sentiment. Several hundred thousand Hungarian minorities lived in neighboring countries, especially in Romania; any strong nationalist appeal would seriously endanger Hungarian relations with these socialist allies.

The promotion of nationalism was largely unsuccessful. Even if it had been effective, nationalism was far from adequate as an alternative for Marxism. It might hold the nation together for a period of time but would be unable to create the norms necessary for the regular functioning of society and the market.

Political reform might serve better to shore up the legitimacy of socialism and defuse a possible social explosion. Stephen White suggested that with poor economic performance, the economic bases of legitimacy decline in importance. It may prove possible to shift some of the burden of legitimation from purely economic performance to other political or procedural bases, such as the enlargement of political participation by electoral reform, encouragement of corporatist structures of interest articulation, or increased dialogue and consultation between the leadership and the society.[28] These political reform measures may alleviate the degree of mass alienation, rebuild legitimacy, and prevent a crisis situation from developing into massive upheaval. The pressures created by mass alienation made political reform desirable. Whether the leaderships in Hungary and China would or would not respond to these pressures depended on their flexibility as well as their limits.

The Indirect Challenge: The Emergence of Civil Society

Political liberalization and economic reform produced another challenge to the existing political establishment by promoting the emergence of a civil society. The concept of civil society, with its origins in G.W.F. Hegel, Karl Marx, Antonio Gramsci, Jürgen Habermas, and many others, has been variously defined as including nongovernmental autonomous economic organizations; public and voluntary religious, cultural, and political organizations; independent news media; and occupational and professional societies.[29] The common denominator is the autonomy of individuals and groups vis-à-vis the state. Closely related to the concept of civil society is that of a public sphere, conceived as the forum in which private individuals come together as a public, debating matters of general interest.[30] The public sphere can be viewed as an arena existing between the civil society and the state, in which the two interact.

Although both a civil society and a public sphere may exist independently, neither can function effectively without the other. Without a public sphere to debate various societal interests and to interact with the state and hold it accountable, civil society will have no institutionalized political voice and will remain impotent. Without a coherent civil society, a public sphere will be dominated by a disorganized mass society, in which individuals are not directly related to one another through societal groups but are readily available for mobilization by political elites or counter-elites.[31] The public sphere will function more effectively if private individuals come together in an organized fashion through a civil society.

In order to adequately reflect the complexity of the relationships between state and society during the reform period, we can further distinguish among various types of civil society and public spheres. The existence of autonomous social, economic, and cultural organizations may imply the existence of a civil society. But it does not necessarily involve the existence of a specifically political society, which exists only if there emerge voluntary associations and social movements that intend to influence state decisions or to obtain a share of state power.[32] Along the same lines, a managerial public sphere, in which private citizens and associations discuss and autonomously regulate the distribution of collective goods and services, should be distinguished from a political public sphere, in which public discussions concern the activities of the state.[33]

One implication of this analysis is that different types of civil society and public spheres pose different degrees of challenge to state power. A civil society and a managerial public sphere may not pose a direct threat to an established regime. Indeed, in some cases an enlightened party-state may allow or even encourage their existence so as to relieve the overburdened government of some of its functions. In contrast, the formation of a specifically political society and a political public sphere does pose a challenge to the state's monopoly of political power. They constitute a political realm that is essential to the achievement of democratization but that most authoritarian regimes are extremely reluctant to permit. In the following analysis, I will use the term "noncritical realm" to refer to the existence of a civil society and a managerial public sphere and the term "critical realm" to refer to the combination of a political society and a political public sphere.

Improving Economic and Political Conditions

Certain preconditions must be met if formal autonomous organizations are to develop. Political conditions are the most important. In societies without the right of association, the emergence of groups would be suppressed, limited, or deterred. Economic conditions are also crucial to these types of organizations; since formal organizations require facilities and equipment, financial resources are essential to their successful operation.

Lacking favorable political and economic conditions, prereform state socialist societies had very few autonomous social organizations. The absence of a supportive political condition was served by an ideological justification for a monistic social structure. Orthodox Marxism recognized only the Communist Party as the representative of the interests of the whole human society. Moreover, the one-party system, performing both administrative and economic functions and taking charge of the political, economic, cultural, and social life of the country, was believed to preclude the need for other autonomous organizations. The constitution of each communist country guaranteed freedom of association, but the political opposition was deprived of constitutional rights. If other organizations existed, they only helped the Party manage its work and were hierarchically organized under the monistic leadership of the Party.

Economic conditions were restricted by the state socialist economic structure. The Communist Party had successfully nationalized and collectivized all the principal means of production in industry and agriculture. The allocation and distribution of materials, products, and services were controlled by a bureaucratic hierarchy that merged with the Party organizations. The monopoly of economic resources in the hands of the state administrative hierarchy and the work unit largely eliminated the financial possibility for the existence of social organizations not subject to Party supervision.

Facing the emergence of diverse interests during the process of economic reform, the official attitude toward organized social activities gradually relaxed. Reformers in both the Hungarian and Chinese leaderships gradually embraced the notion of pluralism (the details of which are discussed in the next chapter). Although the Party was still ambivalent about the legitimate existence of organized interest groups, restrictions on the right of association came under growing criticism in Hungary after 1987, and some parts of the media acted as a prime vehicle for such criticism. The Committee on Constitutional Law of the People's Patriotic Front became a forum in which some of the country's prominent legal experts pressed the case for effective legal guarantees of the right of association. They argued that legal registration should be the only prerequisite for the establishment of an association, meaning that no political conditions should be attached to their existence.[34]

The necessity for legislation concerning social organizations had not yet caught the attention of lawmakers in China. As a country that had just begun to establish its legal system and that to a large extent was still accustomed to unlawful and arbitrary decisions by individual leaders, China still had a long way to go toward establishing and effectively enforcing such legislation. However, the ambiguity in ideological assessment and legislation of autonomous social organizations left some space for the development of social organizations.

It is self-evident that if an organization is financially sponsored by the government, it would be hard for the organization to secure its autonomy from the government. One promising implication of economic reform for the formation of a civil society was the pluralization of available financial resources. The emergence of a managerial public sphere was promoted not just by the relaxation of governmental controls over society but also by the creation of greater private wealth that could be used for public purposes. Some people in the private sector who obtained a great amount of wealth under the economic reforms donated part of their fortune to public projects, such as education, entertainment, and transportation facilities. This opened the possibility for them to sponsor other artistic, social, or even political activities.

In 1982 a case that the Western press described as "unprecedented for a communist country" was reported in Hungary. A seventy-eight-year-old man whose wealth was estimated to be 10 million forints offered his millions to have a public swimming pool built in Obuda, a suburb of Budapest. In an interview with Radio Budapest, the millionaire, who remained unnamed, said that he had acquired his wealth by honest means, for the most part through smart investments and by "saving every penny." He claimed that he wished to "leave something for posterity" and explained that he did not want to give his wealth to his relatives because he believed in "self-acquired gain."[35]

A decree issued on 1 September 1987, made it possible for individuals to establish private foundations in Hungary. Donors would have the right to appoint a board of trustees to administer the endowment or even to establish an institution to do so. Foundations were required to place their assets into an account at the national savings bank, where they would earn the highest interest rate of 10.5 percent.[36] As of 1987, more than 120 foundations had been registered with the Hungarian Ministry of Culture, their total assets amounting to almost 50 million forints. Fifty foundations registered at the Ministry of Health, their assets reaching nearly 100 million forints.[37]

International foundations as well were active in Hungary. One of the most powerful, the Soros Foundation, was established by a Hungarian-American with a declared goal of promoting "the development of Hungarian society . . . by expanding opportunities for cultural creativity, public education, and new initiatives." The foundation granted scholarships to Hungarian scholars and students to study in the West, sponsored Hungarian participation at conferences in the West, and helped provide Hungarian institutions with instruments, spare parts, and materials for scientific research. In 1987 the foundation's largest award ($400,000) went to Hungary's National Institute for Management Training. Other gifts included $200,000 to the management school of the Skala Department Store and $40,000 to the Hungarian Chamber of Commerce. The Soros Foundation also financed the publication of Hungarian works on the social sciences, donating $8,000 for the translation into English of the works of Oszkar Jaszi and Istvan Bibo. It also gave financial support to members of the so-called democratic opposition. Between 1986 and 1987, the Soros Foundation funded a total of 801 individual and institutional projects (out of 2,350 applications received).[38]

In China there was no sign of the development of private foundations. Only a few foreign foundations (from Hong Kong, Europe, and the United States, including the Soros Foundation) operated in China, mainly for educational purposes. But the pressure on private entrepreneurs to donate money to public projects was heavy: The traditional values of community, the trend toward egalitarianism, the fear of an ensuing political movement that might change the current policy and denounce individual wealth all pushed those who became rich to give part of their wealth to the public. Some bold entrepreneurs even began to set foot in the political sphere, though in an unsophisticated manner. For example, when Liu Binyan was expelled from the Party, a hotel owner, in defiance of the official line, invited Liu and his family to take a vacation at one of his establishments.[39]

In February 1989 the *New York Times* reported that "the calls for a more democratic system are coming not just from students and intellectuals but from a new social class of wealthy entrepreneurs" who "are helping to finance the incipient democratic movement and provide logistical support. Just in the last month, owners of private businesses have twice underwritten gatherings of intellectuals to discuss democracy." According to this report, a businessman offered the equivalent of thousands of dollars to bolster democratic activities.[40]

The prospect of new financial resources for independent groups depended largely on the development of a multisectoral economy, that is, on the development of economic pluralism, and on the extent to which the entrepreneurs (private or collective or even state) had the power to appropriate their money. It was also related to the political situation, for people could form associations only when they were sure that doing so would not cause them political trouble.

The Development of a Noncritical Realm

After 1949 most of the numerous associations that existed in Hungary before the communist takeover were dissolved by the communists as incompatible with the new social order; others were forced to merge with regime-sponsored organizations. However, local and nonpolitical associations began to stage a steady comeback when the political climate eased during the 1960s and 1970s. In the early 1980s, a group of Hungarian political dissidents founded a private philanthropic charitable organization known as the Foundation to Assist the Poor (SZETA). SZETA collected money, food, and clothing and organized fund-raising campaigns, charity concerts, and exhibitions. It not only distributed donations to the poor but also began to act as a pressure group in defense of the less fortunate, offering legal advice and lobbying the government for more extensive welfare programs. The government attempted to co-opt SZETA into the existing bureaucratic framework but failed.[41] The organization finally lost steam when it was unable to secure continuous contributions from private sources.

In step with the general trend in Europe, two other societal initiatives gained momentum in Hungary in the 1980s: the peace movement and the environmental movement. The independent Peace Group for Dialogue was established in 1982, recruiting primarily among university students and carrying on an antinuclear campaign through private meetings, distributions of leaflets, and an attempt to organize a peace march. The Peace Group for Dialogue defined itself as nongovernmental and nonoppositional, but a Politburo resolution in March 1983 stipulated that the independent peace movement be merged into the official National Peace Council.

Public outcry over a Hungarian-Czechoslovakian-Austrian Danube project developed into another movement in the 1980s. Protesting the serious ecological implications for the surrounding land of a 30-kilometer-long diversion of the river, an environmental group called the Danube Circle formed. In 1986, the circle claimed that it had collected some 10,000 signatures on petitions opposing the project. A group of intellectuals signed an open letter to the Austrian public concerning the environmental cost of the project.[42]

The protests surrounding these three issues—domestic poverty, world peace, and the environment—were not directly confrontational, but they did express an independent public opinion and therefore ran into conflict with the government. Although the Hungarian government stifled two of the movements and the other died when its funds were exhausted, their failure did not spell the bankruptcy of a middle-of-the-road strategy, as some scholars have suggested.[43] The emergence of an independent public opinion and autonomous social organizations, if only temporarily, provided experience for society and provided the precedent for their subsequent expansion.

In the late 1980s, with a much relaxed political atmosphere, social groups in Hungary mushroomed. By 1988 Hungary had 6,570 associations with a total membership of two million. Most of the 300 national associations (which had the largest membership) and approximately 40 percent of all associations were established by the authorities. But the rest were autonomous local associations consisting mostly of artistic, scientific, sports, hobby, and neighborhood groups.[44] For a small country with a population of about 10 million, the 4,000 nonofficial associations were a substantial number. There were self-proclaimed independent trade unions, such as the Democratic Movie Union, with 400 members, for the purpose of defending the interests of film, television, and video markets, and the Democratic Union of Scientific Workers, with 2,500 members, which claimed to uphold the interests of those who worked in science. There were also populist groups, such as the Peter Veres Society, with 1,500-2,000 members and an avowed purpose to address the problems of the Hungarian countryside.[45]

In China the loosening of both ideological and political control provided a more relaxed atmosphere for the formation of various groups, and economic pluralization made them financially viable. Cultural and social clubs, societies, and associations proliferated. For example, from 1981 to 1984 in Shanghai, the number of officially registered social groups grew from 628 to 2,627, an increase of more than 300 percent.[46]

The case of consumer associations in China provides an example of the development of a noncritical realm under state socialism. Economic reform increased the role of the market, and industry and commerce saw unprecedented activity. But along with greater economic dynamism came shoddy workmanship, the use of inferior materials, the substitution of poor-quality goods for high-quality ones, forgery, underweight goods, shortchanging, arbitrary prices, and forced combinations of goods.[47] To protect their interests, consumers began to organize their own associations. In 1988 there were 1,088 such consumer associations in China, which received 200,000 complaints and helped consumers receive compensation worth 47 million yuan.[48] In one sense, the consumer associations were the product of the societal demand to protect private consumer interests; in another, they relieved the Party and government of some of the burden of consumer protection.

The state structure remained the determining framework for these consumer associations. All the consumer associations were affiliated with various levels of government, had semiofficial status, and were funded by the government commerce departments. The associations were responsible for managing extragovernmental affairs, and yet their authority came largely from their official affiliations. Personal intervention by the Party leaders, rather than any institutionalized legal recourse, was the most effective way to battle with irresponsible enterprises, as most enterprises were susceptible to Party and government orders. At the same time, however, consumer associations also increasingly pursued their interests outside official channels. They resorted to the mass media to create pressure from public opinion, which most of the enterprises dared not ignore.[49] Media reports of bad quality could force a private enterprise to close down as consumers stayed away from its products.[50]

The dual status of the consumer associations and their dual strategies for protecting consumer interests reflected a period of transition and confusion in China. Social groups lacked organizational resources, which had previously been systematically monopolized by the state socialist system. They needed legal status, organizational expertise, technical facilities, communication networks, financial resources, and a sense of belonging and mutual trust among their members. To acquire such resources, the newly emerging social groups had to rely either on the state or on traditional organizations. Most of them affiliated with parts of the official establishment, such as government agencies or formal business corporations, that could provide them with a legitimate title and share their financial expenses. Therefore, most social organizations, too, had a dual status and dual financial sources.[51] Other grass-roots organizations, which lacked personal or institutional connections with the state, affiliated with family, clan, or religious organizations.[52] These traditional organizations, usually based on blood or spiritual bonds, provided a sense of belonging and mutual trust and sometimes offered local political standing and connections as well.

Another interesting phenomenon in China was the emergence of unofficial research institutes sponsored by big business, which was possible only after the political liberalization and economic reform. Two such research institutes later played a role in organizing democratic activities. One was the Sitong Institute of Social Development, sponsored by the Sitong Group (a computer company). The institute worked intensively on proposals for socialist parliamentary democracy, revision of the constitution, and the reform of public ownership and related legislation. Cao Siyuan, the director of the institute, was the first to call for an enterprise bankruptcy law for China and participated in drafting the law. After the bankruptcy law aroused heated discussion in the National People's Congress (NPC) Standing Committee, Cao Siyuan sent every committee member a book he had written explaining bankruptcy and made a call on each of them to lobby for the bill.[53] This represented a new form of intellectuals' participation in politics, in contrast to holding high government positions or taking to the streets.

The other group was the Beijing Institute of Economics, which was established in 1987 with the financial support of the Beifang Group, a printing and distribution company. Most members of the institute were participants of the Democracy Wall Movement of 1978-1979, which had been officially suppressed. The institute published a series of theoretical works on urban economic reform. Together with *Jingji Ribao* (Economic daily) and the Research Center on China's Public Opinion, it conducted many large-scale social surveys, such as the "Survey of Political Psychology of Chinese Citizens" and the "Survey of Political Perception and Attitude of the Deputies of the National Peoples' Congress." It bought out *Jingjixue Zhoubao* (Economic weekly) and turned it into a mouthpiece for its ideas. It also opened a correspondence school of administration that registered students by the thousands.[54] Both the Sitong Institute of Social Development and the Beijing Institute of Economics exerted their influence as independent groups and functioned quite well, but they became involved in the turbulent student movement in 1989 and were shut down during the subsequent repression.

In sum, economic reform and political liberalization created greater room for the development of civil society in both China and Hungary. Although societal autonomy grew, however, the state remained the determining framework in at least three ways. First, the state's acceptance of the necessity for and legitimacy of social groups was a fundamental precondition for their emergence. The emergence of more autonomous social groups was not achieved without the authorization, encouragement, and sponsorship of the reformist political elite. Second, most social organizations, the building blocks of civil society, still relied heavily on the state for organizational resources, such as legal status, staff members, and financial support. And third, administrative intervention continued to be one of the major means of resolving conflicts of interest among social and economic organizations. The duality of these social organizations has made many observers question their autonomy. It is true that they did not obtain the kind of independence that groups in the West have. Yet if we use as reference point the old state, in which these organizations performed only official functions or did not exist at all, we see an obvious trend toward autonomy for the society.

While the similarities between the experiences of China and Hungary are striking, there are also differences. For example, many more private foundations were created in Hungary than in China. The emergence of organized sources of private funding made a much greater contribution to the development of a civil society than did the individual actions of generous rich people. Moreover, many grass-roots organizations in rural China, and even among urban intellectual circles, were based primarily on family ties and personal connections rather than on open membership and formal constitutions. The lack of a corporate sense in such organizations may undermine their effectiveness. Conversely, the existence of numerous cultural and sport clubs and associations in Hungary indicates a higher degree of self-organization.

The emergence of a civil society is not equivalent to the development of, nor do they necessarily lead to the creation of, political oppositions. Some scholars see a positive relationship between the two, arguing that in permitting the emergence of a civil society, reforming state socialist regimes have begun a gradual process of embourgeoisement, in which former proletarians are transformed first into members of the bourgeoisie and then into citizens.[55] In contrast, other scholars assert a more negative relationship, believing that by signing "an implicit nonaggression pact" with society, the state has allowed citizens the limited pursuit of private and egoistic ends in exchange for their abstention from political activities.[56]

In fact, both views may be partially correct. For most people, the provision of greater economic benefits does outweigh the continued restraints on political participation. For the majority, managing their own social and economic affairs without engaging in politics may be completely acceptable. However, politics has always been the preoccupation of a minority. In the end, it is this minority that shapes the political evolution of state socialist societies. The enlarged societal and economic autonomy provides this minority with the basis to strive for the creation of a political space, even in defiance of the state's preferences. Destatization of the economy also offers this minority the ability to live without state support and the material resources to form autonomous political organizations. On balance, therefore, the emergence of a more autonomous civil society plays a positive role in the promotion of political reform.

The Active Challenge: Articulated and Organized Protest

Political Opposition in Hungary

In well-functioning democracies, political opposition works within the system. Yet the conventional definition of political opposition in Eastern European countries tended to assume the existence of independent groups of individuals, acting in a more or less organized fashion outside the system and posing direct or indirect challenges to their governments from without.[57] Political opposition under state socialism first of all opposed the rules of the political game and therefore were not tolerated and themselves refused to work within the system.

However, as George Schopflin has argued, comparatively little of this conventional definition applied to Hungary. In Hungary, according to

Schopflin, after the initiation of political liberalization in the early 1960s, and especially after the implementation of economic reform in the late 1960s, the political limits on intellectual activity, on the expression of criticism, and thus the ability to exert pressure on the government from within appeared to be sufficiently loose to permit the existence and functioning of what Schopflin termed a "paraopposition." By this he meant an opposition that did not overtly question the ideological bases of the system but played a semiautonomous political role permitted by that system.[58]

The Hungarian leadership upheld a thin and changeable dividing line between permissible criticism and proscribed dissent, as Janusz Bugajski and Maxine Pollack have observed. This demarcation shifted according to current political requirements and was frequently tested by the opposition in its attempts to extend the reformist debate. Hence, Hungary's dissenting intelligentsia was often referred to as a "semilegal" opposition.[59] The more flexibility the current system had (or was believed to have), the more intellectuals tended to work within the existing framework. Because of early programs of political liberalization and economic reform, Hungary had created an environment far more tolerant of semilegal opposition.

In the 1960s a so-called Budapest School composed of New Left Marxist sociologists and philosophers sought to develop the intellectual legacy of Gyorgy Lukacs and to apply their ideas to the practice of Hungarian society. In the early 1970s, when economic reform was halted, there was a reversal of the recent cultural liberalism, and the group's criticisms were declared to be ideologically unacceptable. In May 1973 several leading members of the Budapest School of Marxist philosophers—including Andras Hegedus, Angnes Heller, Mihaly Vajda, Gyorgy Markus, Gyorgy Bence, Janos Kis, and Maria Markus—were dismissed from their academic posts, and Hegedus, Vajda, and Kis were expelled from the Party.

Alongside the reintroduction of economic reform in the late 1970s, the regime's attitude toward dissident intellectuals also appeared to be entering a new stage of tolerance. Although the majority of dissidents were blacklisted from professional employment and their writings banned from authorized publications, the regime at first did little to obstruct their efforts to establish a "second sphere" of public opinion through the creation of "free university" lecture courses, samizdat publications and journals, an alternative bookshop (or "samizdat boutique," as it was called), and the independent voluntary organization SZETA. By 1982 the "democratic opposition," as Hungary's dissidents were calling themselves, were publishing their own quarterly magazine, *Beszelo* (News from inside), duplicated in over a thousand copies and with a circulation probably ten times that number. They even launched an independent publishing house, the AB Independent Publishers, to make available to the Hungarian public the works of Hungarian and foreign authors banned by the official censors.

Despite their divisions and disagreement, the opposition groups in Hungary shared two general strategies. The first was the emphasis on the creation of the institutions of civil society and a sphere of open debate and opinion. They began with an interest in the questions that were not directly political, such as helping the poor and Hungarian nationalities in Romania. The goal of the opposition was the extension of the public sphere and using economic reform to carve out a greater free space for society.[60]

The second strategy was to cooperate with reformists within the Party leadership. The opposition realized that Hungary could increase its external independence and internal pluralism only if economic reforms were not delayed. In other words, market-oriented economic reform not only was one of the objectives of the opposition but also created a relaxed environment for the existence of the opposition. The stance of the "democratic opposition" toward the regime was therefore far from totally hostile. It recognized that the only safeguard for their new-found freedoms in the medium term was the continuing advance of reform. It even offered advice to the regime on how to develop and pursue its own program. In an influential article written in the spring of 1982, one of the leading theorists of the opposition, Janos Kis, argued that the Hungarian leadership was in fact better prepared and qualified to promote changes than the leading circles of other East European states and that the population itself was not as alienated from the regime as in most other socialist countries. Consequently, he optimistically suggested, "There might be far better chances in Hungary for reaching a compromise settlement between the Government and the people than there were in Poland in 1980-81."[61]

After Mikhail Gorbachev came to power and initiated *glasnost* in the Soviet Union, political reform became an increasingly popular topic in all circles of Hungarian life. In June 1985 forty-five intellectuals, including writers, actors, sociologists, historians, and economists representing a wide range of oppositional political thought, gathered in secret at a campsite near the village of Monor, some fifty kilometers southeast of Budapest, to discuss the nation's future. It was the first time that proponents of such diverse political views and priorities had come together not only to voice their criticism of the present communist system but also to identify current problems, to examine their causes, and offer carefully considered, specific solutions.[62] Although it produced no dramatic breakthroughs, the meeting in Monor was an event of major significance. It showed that despite sometimes wide differences of opinion on particular issues, sufficient common ground to plan and coordinate strategy existed among the various opposition groups in Hungary. It was also a powerful reminder that the political opposition in Hungary had become an increasingly well-organized and dedicated force with which the regime had to contend.

The opposition staged political demonstrations, either on important national anniversaries or in support of dissident calls for democracy and free speech. They sent protest letters or statements of support to the government, other communist regimes, opposition groups in neighboring states, Western governments and organizations, and international forums. Dissidents arranged several large meetings to discuss reform and expand the reach of the opposition.

Starting in the mid-1980s, several dissident journals began to campaign for political pluralism in Hungary. In 1986 the outspoken publication *Demodrata* (Democrat) issued a draft program calling for major political reform and institutionalized pluralism. In June 1987 after prolonged consultation with different strands in the "democratic opposition," the leading unofficial journal *Beszelo* published a very sophisticated proposal for political reform. The basic premise of the sixty-page document, entitled "Social Contract," was simple: For economic reform to be successful in Hungary, political reform was essential; and in order for political reform to succeed, the Party must give up its monopoly on power and make society an equal partner in political life. The document's authors acknowledged that the one-party system would remain in Hungary for the immediate future. At the same time, they said, a degree of pluralism would be possible if the Party were made accountable to the people through a series of controls and legal guarantees.[63]

Shortly after the publication of this program, around 150 Hungarian populist writers and reformist economists gathered on 27 September 1987, in Lakitelek in southeastern Hungary. Imre Pozsgay, president of the PPF, was the main speaker at the meeting. He said that Prime Minister Karoly Grosz was willing to enter into a constructive dialogue with the participants in the spirit of the government's new program for economic reform. Pozsgay called on them to formulate their own alternative program for radical reform, saying that the government was ready and willing to consider it. Mihaly Bihari, a political scientist, described the present "socialist" system as a self-complacent dictatorship that pretended to be a democracy. In the end, the meeting at Lakitelek passed a resolution to form the Hungarian Democratic Forum.[64]

The Hungarian Democratic Forum held its first meeting on 30 January 1988, in Budapest's Jurta Theater, attended by some 500 people from a wide range of backgrounds and representing differing ideological views. At the end of the meeting, the Democratic Forum adopted a statement on political reform, asking for an end to the "unchecked monopoly of power" and measures to prevent any organization or individual from rising above the constitution and the law. It issued specific proposals to reform the country's political system, including the drafting of a new electoral law, a listing of citizens' rights and a guarantee that they would be honored, the creation of a constitutional court, and the reform of the National Assembly to become an openly functioning, democratically elected parliament responsible only to the electorate. The statement was sent to Hungary's official media for publication but never appeared there.[65]

As the political situation became further relaxed in the late 1980s, there appeared to be a more pronounced focus on political and organizational work among Hungary's dissidents. In its 12 November 1988 issue, *Heti Vilaggazdasag* (World economy weekly), the popular weekly of the Hungarian Chamber of Commerce, listed the new political organizations that had been established during the 1980s. The list included the Society of Followers of Bajcsy Zsilinszky with 500 members and a goal of creating a coalition between the reform wing of the HSWP and the alternative organizations; the League of Young Democrats, with 1,600 members, whose objective was to create "a social alliance, grouping together politically active, radically reform-minded youth groups and individuals;" the Network of Free Initiatives, with 1,500 members, calling for the self-organization of civil society, independent of the state; the Leftwing Alternative Association, with 300 members, claiming to reject both the Stalinist and the bourgeois course and seeking to establish a self-governing society; and the New March Front, with no "members" but only "participants," aiming to reform the political institutional system, increase the role of popular associations, and reassess the history of the recent past.[66]

This political opposition did not exist free of political harassment and repression, even in the late 1980s. Dissidents periodically received stiff warnings from the authorities, and the police often confiscated their publications. However, the political opposition in Hungary had much more breathing room than did dissidents in China. The semilegitimate status of Hungarian opposition groups was the result of their less confrontational approach and greater tolerance on the part of the Hungarian Party leadership. The interactions of the two sides later produced an outcome very different from that in China.

The Protest Movement in China

The articulated political demands of intellectuals are an important part of the active challenge to the political establishment in state socialist societies. In China intellectual dissent has largely been influenced by its precedents in Chinese tradition.[67] One characteristic of traditional intellectual dissent was the belief that it was the responsibility of intellectuals to assume the role of critics vis-à-vis the government: Intellectuals were obligated to speak out when the government deviated from Confucian ideals. As Merle Goldman has argued, however, Confucianism justified critics of government on moral grounds but did not legally guarantee an opposition.[68] Thus, another characteristic of this tradition was the lack of institutional standing for intellectual dissent. The formation of a group to fight for views was regarded as disruptive. Lacking a corporate entity or autonomous organization with sufficient power to exert influence, intellectual dissent took the forms of either total withdrawal or individual criticism.[69]

Intellectuals in China were also heirs to the May Fourth Movement, which sought to create a Westernized culture as a solution to China's social, political, and economic problems in the early decades of the twentieth century. For the first time, during the 1910s and 1920s, educated Chinese who believed in freedom of expression and individual rights formed their own intellectual and cultural communities.[70] This was what Goldman and Timothy Cheek called "the model of the May Fourth intellectual": politically committed but intellectually autonomous.[71]

In short, Chinese intellectuals inherited a dual tradition. During the long premodern history, intellectuals considered themselves closely related to, if not part of, the ruling elite. In late imperial and early republican periods, a civil society emerged, along with a public sphere of debate and opinion in which intellectuals could participate.[72] The intellectual dissent in post-Mao China followed this dual tradition. On one side, encouraged by the ideological liberalization, many intellectuals joined the reformist leadership to promote economic and political liberalizations, in a fashion strikingly similar to their counterparts in Hungary. There was a proliferation of think-tanks, such as the Institute of Economic Reform, Rural Policy Research Office (later changed to Rural Development Center of the State Council), and the Institute of Economics of Chinese Academy of Social Sciences. These think-tanks absorbed many talented and ambitious young and middle-aged intellectuals, and they became part of the reform elite in China.

At the same time, some intellectuals began to break from the traditional pattern of loyal dissent and to assume a more independent role in the society, following the May Fourth spirit. They started to organize collective activities and groups to voice their political demands. The Democracy Wall Movement in 1978-1979, the student demonstrations in 1986-1987, the petition for general political amnesty in 1989, and the student movement in 1989 all directly raised political demands to the regime outside official channels.

In late 1978, while the official line was cautiously demystifying Marxism-Leninism-Mao Zedong Thought from above, a more radical protest movement arose from below. The movement was encouraged in part by the new ideological openness; however, it did not confine itself to the officially set boundaries. It was the first to challenge the Cultural Revolution, Chairman Mao, and the Communist Party. As Xidan Democracy Wall in Beijing served as the backdrop for posters expressing sharply dissenting views, the movement was referred to as the Democracy Wall Movement. The arguments and political stands presented in the posters varied from moderate to radical. The moderate ones did not go beyond the official limits at that time, calling for wide-ranging political reforms and the elimination of feudal remnants, as well as the specific reversal of verdicts of the Cultural Revolution. But the radical ones were highly critical of Marxist ideology and the Chinese government. The centerpiece of the Democracy Wall Movement was the call for more freedom and human rights, mainly civil liberties.[73]

In addition to putting up posters, participants in the Democracy Wall Movement distributed leaflets, published periodicals, made public speeches, and contacted the foreign press. As many as 180 unofficial political groups and periodicals mushroomed throughout the country from November 1978 to March 1979.[74] Among the most popular periodicals that emerged from the movement were *Tansuo* (Explorations), *Qimeng* (Enlightenment), *Siwu luntan* (April fifth forum), and *Beijing Zhi Chun* (Beijing spring). The Democracy Wall Movement also encouraged (if not directly organized) a series of demonstrations, sit-downs, and hunger strikes seeking to redress grievances that originated in the Cultural Revolution.

The most radical and eloquent advocate of democracy during those hectic months was the editor of *Tansuo*, Wei Jingsheng. His now-famous wall poster, "Democracy: The Fifth Modernization," was later published in *Tansuo*. "If the Chinese people wish to modernize, they must first establish democracy and they must first modernize China's social system," Wei argued; "Democracy is not a mere consequence, a certain stage in the development of society. It is the condition on which the survival of productive forces depends."[75]

Regarding it as a show of popular support for its reform program and against the orthodox opposition, the reformist leadership tolerated and even endorsed the Democracy Wall Movement. However, when the movement questioned not only the evils of the Cultural Revolution but also the authority of the Communist Party, it went beyond the limits of official toleration. In early 1979 the Party leadership imposed restrictions on political and ideological liberalization, with Deng Xiaoping proclaiming the

Four Cardinal Principles (adherence to Marxism-Leninism-Mao Zedong Thought, socialism, the people's democratic dictatorship, and the Party leadership) in March. Thereafter, the movement was officially prohibited, and several of its leading members were arrested. Wei Jingsheng was sentenced to fifteen years in prison, accused of selling military information to foreigners during the Sino-Vietnamese War.[76]

In his analysis of the Democracy Wall period of 1978-1979, Andrew Nathan concluded that virtually none of the protesters was demanding Western-style democracy but seemed to envision a more responsive yet still essentially authoritarian political system.[77] By 1986, however, increasing numbers of Chinese intellectuals began to regard multiple political parties, competitive elections, checks and balances on the state power and the Party's power, and independent interest groups as necessary features of democracy. Although Wei Jingsheng remained in prison, the views he expressed in 1978-1979 had become widespread by 1986. The sphere of permitted public discourse had been expanded to include the ideas of the rule of law, separation of powers, and even pluralism. Carefully worded suggestions that China might have something to learn from Western models in this regard were also tolerated. The freer discussion of political reform inspired student demonstrations for more democracy at the end of the year.

In December 1986, students from the University of Science and Technology in Hefei, Anhui Province, became sharply disillusioned when they found that the local Party cadres had arbitrarily controlled the election of deputies to the provincial People's Congress. Frustrated by the undemocratic practice in those local elections, the students launched a protest on 5 December. While some students in these demonstrations simply complained about poor school conditions, most expressed their concerns about politics. They hung posters with such slogans as "No democratization, no modernization!" and "Give me liberty or give me death!" Within four weeks, student demonstrations broke out in at least eleven other cities across China, including Shanghai and Beijing. The demonstrations persisted for several weeks from early December 1986 to early January 1987.

After a short period of hesitation, as the ranks of the demonstrators swelled, the authorities launched a campaign against "bourgeois liberalization." Party General Secretary Hu Yaobang was dismissed, accused of being lax toward unorthodox ideological tendencies.[78] Three distinguished intellectuals (Fang Lizhi, Liu Binyan, and Wang Ruowang) who had sharply criticized the Party were subsequently expelled from it.

By forcefully demanding democracy and freedom, the student demonstrations in 1986-1987 were a direct and concerted challenge to the Party leadership. Compared to the Democracy Wall Movement in 1978, the protest movement in 1986-1987 was significantly larger, participants

numbering in the thousands. The student movement also adopted a more
open and popular form of protest by holding public demonstrations, whereas
the participants in the Democracy Wall Movement had acted more like a
conspiratorial group. The difference may well be attributed to the relaxation
in the political atmosphere between 1978 and 1986. Still, the student
demonstrations of 1986-1987 remained poorly organized and lacked clear
short-term objectives, not to mention strategies for achieving them.

In early 1989 the protest forces shifted their attention to human rights.
On 6 January 1989, Fang Lizhi petitioned Deng Xiaoping to release all
"political prisoners" to mark the upcoming fortieth anniversary of the PRC;
he sent a similar letter to the Western press.[79] At about the same time, two
young literati, Bei Dao and Chen Jun, collected the signatures of some
thirty-three noted scholars and writers on a petition demanding amnesty for
political prisoners, including Wei Jingsheng. Another "letter of opinion,"
signed by forty-four scientists and scholars (among them nuclear physicists
Wang Ganchang and Lu Liangying), who demanded the release of political
prisoners and proposed structural reform of the political system, was
submitted to the Standing Committee of the NPC. Chen Jun also planned to
use the scheduled April 1989 meeting of the NPC to submit "A Report on
Amnesty '89."[80] The shift of many of China's most prestigious intellectuals
to a pro-Wei position ten years after his arrest, Nathan commented, signaled
how far the conflict between the regime and the intellectuals had
developed.[81]

Although the petition movement did not directly challenge the political
authority of the Party, the regime was caught off-balance by the emergence
of independent political opinion of this sort. The Propaganda Department of
the Central Committee ordered news media not to cover the event. The
order itself in a way reflected the relaxed atmosphere at the time, for
without it the official press might have reported the movement. After a short
period of hesitation, the government awkwardly denied the existence of any
political prisoners and on that basis declared the demands for an amnesty
groundless. In order to deter the development of a human rights movement
in China, the regime clumsily prevented Fang Lizhi from attending a
banquet hosted by U.S. President George Bush in Beijing to which Fang had
been invited, confiscated an international petition to the NPC delivered from
Hong Kong in support of the amnesty drive, and used a weak pretext to
expel Chen Jun from the country.[82]

Despite the organized activities to promote democracy, no independent
political organizations existed in China, not because the tradition of
intellectual dissent disdained such groups, but because the Communist Party
did not allow any political organizations outside its control to survive. Any
independently organized political activities were ruthlessly suppressed, and

dissident groups had to go underground or operate overseas. The only stable political opposition group until 1989 was organized in the United States in 1983: The Chinese Alliance for Democracy (CAD) was established by a group of Chinese students who were involved in or had various connections with the Democracy Wall Movement. It was relatively well organized, with a permanent headquarters and full-time staff in the United States and a clearly stated charter to promote democracy, freedom, human rights, and pluralism. It published a monthly magazine *Zhongguo Zhi Chun* (China spring) and organized some political activities, such as testifying before congressional committees and holding demonstrations in front of the Chinese embassy and consulates. The organization and its publication were strongly rejected by the Chinese government and were banned from China. A member of CAD was arrested in Shanghai in 1986 under the accusation of distributing "counterrevolutionary propaganda materials."[83]

A collision between the increasingly vocal society and the political establishment in China occurred in the spring and summer of 1989. The development and the mechanisms that led to the bloody outcome and gravely wounded reform in China are discussed in chapter 7.

Comparison

The societal challenges discussed in this chapter occurred in three forms. The first was the passive withdrawal of the population from the official ideological framework, resulting in the crisis of faith, the decline of public morality, and social resentment over government policies. Although this passive challenge to the political establishment posed no immediate physical threat to the regime, it seriously undermined the effectiveness of the ruling regime. It created pressures for the regime to rebuild or at least repair the basis of its legitimacy through institutional reforms. Moreover, if popular discontent became widespread and if even minimally organized groups had access to some resources, then the discontented masses could present a more active challenge. The long-lasting effect of mass alienation could also impede the eventual construction of a normal market system and democratic institutions.

The second type of societal challenge was represented by the incipient civil society, which contested the Party's monopoly of power in an indirect but more active manner. Independence, or potential independence, against state power lies at the heart of the concept of civil society. Civil society does not simply exist outside state control but is also a self-regulated society organized into forms such as parties, interest groups, professional associations, or autonomous work units. It challenges the existing political establishment by developing an autonomous space, undermining the previous monistic organizational concept and structure, and demanding new concepts and institutional adaptations to incorporate emerging social pluralism.

The third form of societal challenge raised pointed political demands, placing much more pressure on the establishment for further political reform than the other two types. In both China and Hungary, part of the intellectual community tended to cooperate with the reformist leadership and tried to initiate change from within the system. This phenomenon, rarely observed in other countries, occurred because political liberalization and economic reform in these two societies had created considerably larger space for the intellectuals to act at least partially within the system.

There were also some basic dissimilarities between the societal challenges in the two countries. The most basic difference is the stronger institutional orientation that existed in the societal challenges in Hungary. Both the civil society and political opposition were more institutionalized than their Chinese counterparts, which were usually based on familial and personal connections. This difference is due in part to official tolerance. Oppositional organizations were strictly prohibited in China, while the Hungarian opposition enjoyed a semilegal status and gained a more stable institutional basis. The different attitudes of the two regimes created two quite different patterns of opposition. The more flexible attitude of the Hungarian establishment produced a "paraopposition": It worked on the fringes of the system, made moderate demands, and was willing to compromise with the government. The more rigid attitude of the Chinese establishment produced another pattern: Some intellectuals operated well inside the system, working for incremental change from within; while others worked well outside the system (not just on the fringe) but without the ability to organize.

Second, the more stable institutional basis for opposition in Hungary was also due to the strategies the opposition adopted. The political opposition in Hungary put more emphasis on nonpolitical issues, such as helping the poor and environmental protection, to enlarge its living space together with the growing civil society. Lacking an institutional standing, the Chinese protest movement seemed to have no strategies at all. Although a civil society was emerging in China, the protest movement had not yet consciously considered it part of its strategic thinking and did not actively attempt to build or enlarge it.

Third, because of the absence of an organizational basis, the Chinese dissidents resorted mainly to individual endeavors or temporary movements. This also made them more vulnerable: Individuals were easily singled out for punishment, and spurts of political activity created instability that often exceeded official tolerance and provoked repression. They also tended to sustain the momentum of their protests as long as possible in the belief that this would reduce the subsequent repression. This strategy often radicalized the movement. In contrast, Hungarians waged demonstrations on some important occasions but withdrew promptly. The 1956 incident had taught the opposition groups in Hungary to be more realistic about the Soviet presence and therefore to exercise more self-restraint.

As the previous discussion has indicated, the strengths and weaknesses of the opposition movements are a factor of their relations with the political establishment. The flexibility of the political leadership and institutions, to be discussed in the next chapter, was of great importance in determining of the strength of and the interactions with societal challenges and thus the outcome of political change.

NOTES

1. There are plenty of discussions about the categories of "us" and "them" in state socialist societies. For example, Miklos Haraszti, *A Worker in a Worker's State*, trans. Michael Wright (New York: Universe Books, 1978); Alexander Zinoviev, *The Reality of Communism* (New York: Schocken Books, 1984); and Andrew Walder, "Workers, Managers and the State: The Reform Era and the Political Crisis of 1989," *China Quarterly*, no. 127 (September 1991): 468-70.

2. Laszlo Boka, "Impatient Youth," *New Hungarian Quarterly* 5, no. 16 (Winter 1964): 3-4.

3. Ibid., p. 7.

4. Ivan and Mary Volgyes, *Czechoslovakia, Hungary, Poland: Crossroads of Changes* (New York: Thomas Nelson, 1970), pp. 83-93.

5. William F. Robinson, *The Pattern of Reform in Hungary: A Political, Economic and Cultural Analysis* (New York: Praeger, 1973), p. 272.

6. "Hungarian Youth Rejects Marxist Ideology," *Radio Free Europe Research (RFER)* 9, no. 42, 19 October 1984, pp. 2-3.

7. Bennett Kovrig, *Communism in Hungary: From Kun to Kadar* (Stanford, Calif.: Hoover Institute, 1979), p. 430.

8. Peter Toma, *Socialist Authority: The Hungarian Experience* (New York: Praeger, 1988), p. 184.

9. Pan Xiao, "Weishenmo rensheng de lu yue zou yue zhai?" [Why is life's road getting narrower and narrower?] *Zhongguo Qingnian*, May 1980.

10. After the Cultural Revolution, China sent many delegations to foreign countries. When the delegations came back with the report that in the West even a working-class family could have a house, refrigerator, TV, and automobile, people were astonished. In China only those above the rank of vice-minister could enjoy such luxuries.

11. John Burns, "China's Governance: Political Reform in a Turbulent Environment," *China Quarterly*, no. 119 (1989): 497-98.

12. Ibid., p. 25.

13. Deng Xiaoping, "Concerning Problems on the Ideological Front," *Selected Works of Deng Xiaoping* (Beijing: Foreign Languages Press, 1984), p. 367.

14. "To Be Young and in China: A Colloquy," *New York Times*, 7 October 1989, p. 11.

15. "The Causes and Extent of Corruption in Hungary," *RFER* 12, no. 34, 28 August 1987, p. 14.

16. Toma, *Socialist Authority*, p. 143.

17. Paul Lendvai, *Hungary: The Art of Survival* (London: I. B. Tauris, 1988), p. 90.

18. Ibid., p. 91.

19. Toma, *Socialist Authority*, pp. 87-114.

20. Rosen, "Prosperity, Privatization, and China's Youth," p. 12.

21. Personal interview, Beijing, 1983.

22. Lu Tao and Wang Bing, "SOS, linghun de jinji hujiao" [Emergency call from souls], *Zhongguo Qingnian*, July 1988, p. 28.

23. Yang Manke, "Sanshitian mudu dalu guai xianzhuang" [Thirty days of witnessing a strange situation on the mainland], *Zhongguo Zhi Chun*, no. 103 (December 1991): 60-62.

24. Guo Ji, "Dalu kanshanzhe shuo" [What they're talking about on the mainland], *Zhongguo Zhi Chun*, no. 103 (December 1991): 63-69.

25. *Renmin Ribao* (overseas edition), 4 January 1989, p. 1.

26. Theda Skocpol, *States and Social Revolution: A Comparative Analysis of France, Russia, and China* (New York: Cambridge University Press, 1979), p. 10.

27. Stanley Rosen, "Value Change Among Post-Mao Youth: The Evidence from Survey Data," in *Unofficial China: Popular Culture and Thought in the People's Republic*, eds. Perry Link et al. (Boulder, Colo.: Westview Press, 1989), pp. 193-216.

28. Stephen White, "Economic Performance and Communist Legitimacy," *World Politics* 38, no. 3 (April 1986): 471.

29. Mayfair Mei-hui Yang, "Between State and Society: The Construction of Corporateness in a Chinese Socialist Factory," *Australian Journal of Chinese Affairs*, no. 22 (July 1989): 35; John Keane, ed., *Civil Society and the State: New European Perspectives* (London: Verso, 1988), pp. 19-20; and David Strand, "Protest in Beijing: Civil Society and Public Sphere in China," *Problems of Communism* 39 (May-June 1990): 2.

30. Jürgen Habermas, *The Structural Transformation of the Public Sphere: An Inquiry into a Category of Bourgeois Society*, trans. Thomas Burger (Cambridge: The MIT Press, 1989), p. 27.

31. William Kornhauser, *The Politics of Mass Society* (New York: The Free Press 1959), pp. 32-33.

32. The emphasis on a distinctive political society rather than a blanket civil society is borrowed from Grzegorz Ekiert, "Democratization Processes in East Central Europe: A Theoretical Reconsideration," *British Journal of Political Science* 21, no. 3 (1991): 285-313.

33. The distinction between a managerial public sphere and a political public sphere was brought to my attention by William Rowe's article "The Public Sphere in Modern China," *Modern China* 16, no. 3 (July 1990): 309-29, and by my subsequent correspondence with him.

34. "Calls for Wider Right of Association Multiply," *RFER* 13, no. 7, 19 February 1988, pp. 7-10.

35. "Hungary's New Rich," *RFER* 9, no. 3, part 2 of 2, 20 January 1984, pp. 22-29.

36. "Private Foundations Proliferate," *RFER* 13, no. 2, 15 January 1988, pp. 35-39.

37. Ibid.

38. Ibid.

39. Liu Binyan's speech at Johns Hopkins University, 1 December 1988.

40. *New York Times*, 21 February 1989, pp. A1, A13.

41. Ivan Szelenyi and Robert Manchin, "Social Policy Under State Socialism: Market Redistribution and Social Inequalities in East European Socialist Societies," in *Stagnation and Renewal in Social Policy: The Rise and Fall of Policy Regimes*, eds. Martin Rein, Gosta Esping-Andersen, and Lee Rainwater (New York: M. E. Sharpe, 1987), pp. 133-34.

42. Tony Judt, "The Dilemmas of Dissidence: The Politics of Opposition in East-Central Europe," *Eastern European Politics and Societies* 2, no. 2 (Spring 1988): 208.

43. Vladimir Tismaneanu argued that the failure of the peace and environment movements in Hungary proved that the efforts to avoid the appearance of a political opposition, a strategy adopted by both movements, is a utopian illusion under an authoritarian regime. Vladimir Tismaneanu, "Unofficial Peace Activism in the Soviet Union and East-Center Europe," in *In Search of Civil Society: Independent Peace Movement in the Soviet Bloc*, ed. Vladimir Tismaneanu (New York: Routledge, 1991), pp. 1-53.

44. "Calls for Wider Right of Association Multiply," *RFER*, pp. 7-10.

45. Gabor Revesz, *Perestroika in Eastern Europe: Hungary's Economic Transformation, 1945-1988* (Boulder, Colo.: Westview Press, 1990), pp. 130-31.

46. Chen Jinluo and She Dehu, "Social Groups Are an Important Force for Building Socialist Democratic Politics," *Renmin Ribao* (overseas edition), 29 April 1988.

47. Forced combination of goods was a common practice in China. The shops usually required the customers to buy certain commodities that were difficult to sell as the condition for purchasing the goods that were in higher demand.

48. *Renmin Ribao* (overseas edition), 9 March 1989, p. 1.

49. Huo Da, "Wan Jia You Le" (The sadness and happiness of thousands of households), *Xinhua Wenzhai*, no. 3 (1987): 120-40.

50. Personal communication with a former reporter from *China Consumer's Daily*, Beijing, May 1992.

51. The survey sample of Xiaoshan City, Zhejiang Province, China showed that of ninety-nine social organizations, six were official, twenty-four were non-official, and sixty-nine were semiofficial. Cited from Wang Ying et. al., *Shehui Zhongjianceng: gaige yu zhongguo de shetuan zuzhi* [Middle layer of the society: reform and China's social organizations], (Beijing: China Development Press, 1993), pp. 333-42.

52. Economic Research Report by the Comprehensive Problems Group of the Institute of Development, "Nongmin, shichang, he zhidu chuangxin: baochuandaohu banian hou nongcun fazhan mianlin de shenceng gaige" [Peasants, the market, and innovation in the institution: On the deep structural reform in rural areas after eight years of fixing output for each household], *Jingji Yanjiu*, no. 1 (1987): 3.

53. Pamphlet distributed by Cao Siyuan when he was in the United States in 1989.

54. Zhao Jun, "Zhongguo Zhengtan Zhinang Xinshengdai" [New generation of think-tank in China's political arena], *Zhongguo Zhi Chun*, no. 75 (August 1989): 45-47.

55. Ivan Szelenyi, "Eastern Europe in an Epoch of Transition: Toward a Socialist Mixed Economy?" in *Remaking the Economic Institutions of Socialism: China and Eastern Europe*, eds. David Stark and Victor Nee (Stanford, Calif.: Stanford University Press, 1989), p. 222.

56. Ekiert, "Democratization Processes in East Central Europe," pp. 285-313.

57. George Schopflin, "Opposition and Para-Opposition: Critical Currents in Hungary, 1968-78," in *Opposition in Eastern Europe*, ed. Rudolf L. Tokes (Baltimore: Johns Hopkins University Press, 1979), p. 142.

58. Ibid., pp. 142-86.

59. Janusz Bugajski and Maxine Pollack, *East European Fault Lines: Dissent, Opposition, and Social Activism* (Boulder, Colo.: Westview Press, 1989), p. 128.

60. Josef Gorlice, "Introduction to the Hungarian Democratic Opposition," *Berkeley Journal of Sociology: A Critical Review* 31 (1986): 117-65.

61. Bill Lomax, "Hungary—The Quest for Legitimacy," in *Eastern Europe: Political Crisis and Legitimation*, ed. Paul G. Lewis (London: Croom Helm, 1984), pp. 68-110.

62. "Hungarian Opposition Groups Hold Meeting to Discuss Nation's Future," *RFER* 11, no. 8, February 21, 1986.

63. "Democratic Opposition Announces Program for Political Reform," *RFER* 12, no. 34, 28 August 1987.

64. "Democratic Forum Proposed by Populist Writers and Other Intellectuals," *RFER* 12, no. 48, 4 December 1987.

65. "Hungarian Media Fails to Publish Appeal For Political Reform," *RFER* 13, no. 6, 12 February 1988.

66. Revesz, *Perestroika in Eastern Europe*, pp. 130-31.

67. Frederick Wakeman, "The Price of Autonomy: Intellectuals in Ming and Ch'ing Politics," *Daedalus* 101 (Spring 1972): 35-70.

68. Merle Goldman, *China's Intellectuals: Advice and Dissent* (Cambridge: Harvard University Press, 1981), pp. 1-17.

69. Ibid.

70. Merle Goldman, "Dissident Intellectuals in the People's Republic of China," in *Citizens and Groups in Contemporary China*, ed. Victor C. Falkenheim (Ann Arbor: Center for Chinese Studies, University of Michigan, 1987), p. 162.

71. Merle Goldman and Timothy Cheek, "Introduction," in *China's Intellectuals and the State: In Search of a New Relationship*, eds. Merle Goldman, Timothy Cheek, and Carol Lee Hamrin (Cambridge: Harvard University Press, 1987), p. 3.

72. Rowe, "The Public Sphere in Modern China," pp. 318-26.

73. For details, see James D. Seymour, *The Fifth Modernization: China's Human Rights Movement, 1978-1979* (New York: Human Rights Publishing Group, 1980).

74. Cao Changqing, "Kangzheng de shengyin: minban kanwu" [Voice of protest: unofficial periodicals], *Beijing Zhi Chun*, no. 7/8 (December 1993/January 1994): 23-27.

75. Orville Schell, *Discos and Democracy: China in the Throes of Reform* (New York: Pantheon Books, 1988), pp. 206-207.

76. *Beijing Review*, 26 October 1979, pp. 6-7.

77. Andrew Nathan, *Chinese Democracy* (New York: Alfred A. Knopf, 1985).

78. *Beijing Review*, 26 January 1987, p. 5.

79. *Zheng Ming*, April 1989, pp. 6-10.

80. Su Wei, "Nage chuntian de gushi" [The story of that spring], *Zhongguo Zhi Chun*, no. 110 (July 1992): 9-12.

81. Andrew J. Nathan, "Chinese Democracy in 1989: Continuity and Change," *Problems of Communism* 38 (September-October 1989): 24.

82. Ibid.

83. For the incident, see *Zhongguo Zhi Chun*, no. 44 (February 1987); and Andrew Nathan, *China's Crisis*, (New York: Columbia University Press, 1990), pp. 88-94.

CHAPTER 6

THE ADAPTABILITY OF THE POLITICAL ESTABLISHMENT

Adaptability—the capacity to adjust to the challenges that arise in one's environment—is vital in order for a person, an organization, or a system to survive. The leaderships of Hungary and China introduced economic reform and political liberalization to adjust the functions of the Party and the state in response to the challenges raised by national political crises and deteriorating economic performance. During the course of economic and political reforms, new challenges to the legitimacy of the Party leadership and to social stability arose, which constituted new tests of the adaptability of the political establishment in both countries.

The communist parties in Hungary and China reacted by initiating further changes in two major areas. The first was ideological adaptation, which involved the redefinition of the notion of Party leadership. The second was institutional adaptation, aiming at increasing the responsiveness of the political institutions by granting more autonomy to mass organizations, opening more channels for consultation and dialogue, and vitalizing the representative system. This chapter discusses these efforts and their limitations.

Ideological Adaptation: Modifying the Notion of Party Leadership

The ideological liberalization ushered in at the beginning of economic reform in Hungary and China constituted only the first stage in the Party's ideological adaptation. As noted in chapter 3, the preliminary ideological liberalization involved a more pragmatic approach to Marxism, including widening the range of interpretation of Marxism, reducing the emphasis on class struggle, and authorizing contact with the outside world. These steps, however, did not directly challenge the notion of Party leadership that lay at the core of communist doctrine. Rather, the need to revise this concept arose later in the course of economic reform and political liberalization. The feasibility and desirability of preserving absolute Party leadership in an economically marketizing society, the relationships between the Party and government, and the connection between the state and the society all underwent reexamination and, ultimately, transformation in both countries. As part of the official redefinition of Party leadership, authorities introduced the concept of pluralism and the recognition of the need to check the power of the Party leadership.

At the beginning of the economic reform, pluralism was firmly rejected in Hungary on the grounds that it could be used as an ideological weapon by "splitters," undermining the leading role of the Party and destroying its unity with other Marxist-Leninist parties.[1] The idea of separate or conflicting interests was ridiculed on the grounds that the working class, which allegedly owned and operated the basic means of production, could hardly come into conflict with itself.

But as economic reform redistributed economic resources and social mobility reassigned social status, certain sectors developed different categories of interests. The previous assumption that there could be no differences of interest among the people began to fade, for it could not explain short-term clashes of various legitimate interests among the people. In response to these developments, the leaderships in both countries gradually embraced the notion of pluralism, acknowledging the legitimate existence of diverse interests. The two leaderships also promised to provide legal protection and institutionalized mechanisms for interest articulation. As we will see later, this ideological acceptance of the existence of a plurality of interests was accompanied by the acknowledgment that the power of the Party was limited and that the Party and government should be more representative and responsive.

In the early years of economic reform, the notion of pluralism made scattered appearances in official articles and speeches in Hungary. Although it did not readily accept the notion at first, the Hungarian Party leadership did encourage a greater role for the trade unions and other local collective interests.[2] In the 1980s, when the political climate became more relaxed, the Hungarians began to elaborate on the notion of pluralism more and more systematically, and the existence of plural interests was officially accepted. Rezso Nyers, the architect of Hungarian economic reform who was dismissed in the early 1970s and returned to influence in the early 1980s, wrote that short-term differences in economic interests would manifest themselves overtly through conflict in open forums. "Conflicts of interest derive from the multisectoral nature of the economy," he asserted. "The interests of enterprise management and the workers of the enterprises are in many respects identical, but conflicts of interest may also emerge here, and it is the trade union organizations of the enterprise that are called upon to reconcile them." Differences in interests, he predicted, might further emerge between economic organizations and cultural and social-policy institutions with respect to budgetary allocations, or in connection with the application of the principles of profitability, but "it is possible to bridge these difficulties with the participation of the organizations' representatives."[3]

In a statement on ideological work issued in 1986, the Central Committee of the HSWP acknowledged that the "building of socialism was not free from clashes of interests." Reform was the means of resolving social conflicts and of renewing "socialist society," and the Party would play a "key role" in recognizing this need for renewal and in satisfying it. By recognizing that the working class and other social strata and groups and individuals also had their own specific interests in a socialist society, the statement pointed out that political power had already evolved from the dictatorship of the proletariat into an "all-people's power" exercised through an institutionalized system. In such a system, "the Party leads in ideological and political matters in cooperation with various communities in society."[4]

The acceptance of the existence of plural interests later evolved into the acceptance of the need for dialogue and cooperation between the party and social interests. In 1986 the PPF organized a group of economists and social scientists to draft a reform proposal. The proposal urged a dialogue between Party and government leaders and society in general on an assessment of the situation and an evaluation of the reforms. "An open, accountable, and debated program lends credibility to forthcoming policy," the document asserted. Since the success of the reform depended on the attitudes and actions in the non-economic spheres of the society, the proposal went on, economic reforms should be accompanied by "societal reform." Such societal reform should provide for public participation and pluralistic representation of the political interests of various groups, thereby offering the members of society effective means of social control over a market-oriented economy and governmental behavior.[5] Although the authors of the proposal used the term "societal reform," their argument seemed to imply political reform.

The proposal also offered a means to distinguish among the variety of social organizations. It suggested that social organizations and institutions not be operated solely by the state, but that elements of society should be let to share the responsibility, such as market-oriented organizations, professional associations, movements, churches, and families. According to the proposal, "The independent subjects (the legal entities) of the market economy should be able to represent their own interests, while employees should be represented by trade unions (which should function unambiguously as interest groups and not as organs to facilitate production)." Employers and enterprises should be represented by the Chamber of Commerce, by the National Committee of Agricultural Cooperatives, and similar bodies. "These organizations should abandon their quasi-governmental status and their role in intra-governmental bargaining and should negotiate as equivalent partners [with the government]."[6]

At the founding meeting of the Hungarian Democratic Forum in 1987, the general secretary of the Patriotic People's Front Imre Pozsgay, issued a strongly worded statement in support of civic initiatives and associations, saying that for a consensus to be achieved within society, "people need greater freedom, civic autonomy, and participation in [making] decisions, that is, a situation in which government for the people is replaced by government by and through the consent of the people."[7] Similarly, the Hungarian prime minister, Karoly Grosz, acknowledged in September 1987 that the Party did not have a monopoly on solutions to Hungary's problems and announced that he was ready to exchange ideas with people from different "political currents" and with all who wanted "socialism but held views and offered proposals different from those advocated by the authorities."[8]

Reflecting these lively efforts to articulate the interests and opinions of various social strata in Hungary, some scholars and research institutes started designing the transition toward a mechanism that could resolve open conflict by achieving compromise among political wills. In support of this effort, Bela Pokol argued that it was becoming more and more apparent that there was a point beyond which the economic reforms could not be continued unless the political system underwent some transformation.[9] Deriving his arguments from the studies of several research groups, Pokol urged the political institutionalization of the expression and reconciliation of interests. The political system, he pointed out, should be able to allow the articulation of diverse interests and forge compromises among them. More representative organizations capable of expressing the society's interests should be created; with the abolition of organizational monopolies, the members of the society themselves would have a chance to decide which representational organs to support.[10]

In contrast to their eagerness to move ahead with the notion of pluralism, Hungarian intellectuals and leaders seemed more cautious in directly discussing any limitations on the Party's leadership. Carefully deriving his views from the now generally accepted proposition of the existence of plural interests, Mihaly Bihari, chairman of the political science department of the

University of Budapest, directed his arguments to the reform of the system of representation. He suggested that the function of representation be transferred from the Party to the administrative and representative organs of the state. The representation of interests, their publicly and democratically controlled conflicts and their integration, Bihari claimed, were the functions of the whole political system and should not be monopolized by the Party. If the internal social contradictions and diversity of existing socialism were to be channeled into the legislature, Bihari argued, then the old forms of parliament were no longer sufficient. These reforms would transform rather than challenge the Party's ruling position. Basically, the Party would perform no representational functions; instead, it would be an organization and a movement with a political ruling function, determining the major processes in the development of the society.[11]

Similar to the Hungarian experience, after the Third Plenum of the Eleventh Central Committee in 1978, designing institutional reforms has been a constant theme in China's political life and in Party documents. This reconceptualization can be roughly divided into three phases. The first, from 1979 to 1981, represented the initial thaw; the second was the year 1986, when open discussion of political reform gained momentum; and the third stage started in 1987 after the campaign against bourgeois liberalization and ended in the summer of 1989.

Perplexed by the painful experience of the Cultural Revolution, the Chinese initially focused on two themes in their discussion of political reform. The first was the importance of fighting against feudalism, the typical features of which were said to include the cult of personality and a patriarchal style of leadership. The second theme was the danger of the overconcentration of power in the Party and in individuals within the Party. The suggested solutions included a collective leadership and the separation of Party and government. All these arguments, however, were heavily shadowed by the persistent ideological presumption that all reforms should strengthen the Party's leadership.

In August 1980 Deng Xiaoping spoke on "the reform of the system of party and state leadership." In this speech he vowed to remove the defects in the existing system, such as bureaucratism, overconcentration of power, patriarchal leadership methods, life tenure in leading posts, and privileges of various kinds. The most important point Deng made, though vaguely, was that there were institutional causes of all these defects and that the solution lay in institutional reforms.[12] Deng's speech set the tone for the discussion of institutional reform in the first phase.

Despite Deng's remarks, serious political reform was not on the Party's agenda until late 1985 and early 1986. At that point, as urban economic reform moved in the direction of marketization, it met resistance from the existing administrative structure that had been designed for a planned economy. In June 1986 Deng Xiaoping made two speeches calling for political reform.[13] His goals included revitalizing Party and state institutions, raising efficiency by overcoming bureaucratism, separating the Party and government, and stimulating the enthusiasm of the people by decentralizing power. Although Deng referred mainly to the rationalization of administrative structure, his ambiguous usage of "political reform" suggested broader connotations to some prominent intellectuals. The wave of ideological liberalization in 1986 was characterized by heated debates about political reforms. A distinctive feature of this period was the extent of openness in discussing political issues. Ideological liberalization had resulted in the introduction of concepts, methods, and theories from Western political science, which widened the theoretical perspectives and influenced the thinking of Chinese intellectuals.

With much greater richness in terminology and deeper understanding of the matter, the discussion of political reform in this second stage developed along several lines. The first was the redefinition of the functions of the government vis-à-vis those of society. After more than three decades of communist rule, Chinese were not accustomed to the notion that the power of the government should be restricted but believed that the government was all-powerful and should be able to solve all problems. Against this background, some people spoke frankly of the necessity of a limited government and a strong society.[14] Yan Jiaqi, the director of the Institute of Political Science, cogently argued that there was an area upon which the power of state should not encroach, that is, human rights. The over-concentrated powers of Party and government should therefore be separated.[15]

For the first time, the notion of supervising the state's power came up. Some argued that a system that could effectively supervise and restrict political power was needed. This point contributed to the second theme of the 1986 discussion of political reform—political participation. State affairs, some suggested, should be open to the society, because political democracy could be ensured only by increasing the political participation of the masses and by stepping up supervision to prevent the misuse of political power. The major focus of expanded political participation would be the people's congresses, which should be strengthened at every level, guaranteeing their authority to supervise administrative and judicial agencies. In China's political system, an article in *China Daily* argued, representatives should be chosen in direct general elections, and the electorate should have the right to dismiss and replace them.[16] Because the people exercised their right to participate in state affairs through these representatives, some argued, they must have political sense and skills. Communication between the electorate and their representatives should be strengthened, as should the former's supervision over the latter.[17]

The campaign against bourgeois liberalization in early 1987 interrupted the discussion about political reform. However, as the freeze thawed in the summer of that year, the debate over the same fundamental issues resumed in the third stage, albeit in milder tones. The notion of pluralism, which had been discussed sporadically in 1986, became a matter of consensus in 1987. Although the Chinese had lagged behind their Hungarian counterparts on this issue, they caught up quickly, in part because economic reform heightened socioeconomic differences and hence pushed the issue to the forefront, and in part because of an exchange of ideas with their Hungarian comrades. After a visit to Hungary in 1986, Chen Yizi, the director of the Institute of Economic System Reform, argued in several articles that the Party should not be a player or even a referee in politics but a commissioner who supervises all the referees (social organizations, local and central government agencies, etc.). If people were dissatisfied with social conditions, they could complain to social organizations, and if they were disgruntled over economic conditions, they could complain to economic organizations. Let individuals, enterprises, the market, and society take care of their own business, Chen said; only when difficulties exceeded their capabilities should the government step in, and only when the local government could not handle the problem should the central government intervene. The Party should be the last to be brought into day-to-day business.[18]

On the eve of the Thirteenth Congress of the CCP in 1987, Zhao Ziyang, then Party general secretary, elaborated on this idea before the Central Committee. "Socialist society is not a monolith," he said. "In this society, people of all kinds, of course, share common interests, but their special interests should not be overlooked. The conflicting interests should be reconciled. The government should work to coordinate various kinds of interests and contradictions; the party committees must be even better at the coordinating work."[19] Yu Dehai, who was then in charge of the social survey system in China, pointed out that if there were no normal channels through which to articulate their interests, people would have to employ extreme means such as riots, demonstrations, and strikes. He suggested that intermediate organizations serve as effective channels to express demands, so as to prevent a direct confrontation between government and the masses.[20]

The political report of the Thirteenth Party Congress in 1987 devoted a section to political reforms. For the first time in the Party's history, the congress acknowledged that the Party did not embody a unified social interest but had to reconcile contradictions among a number of interests.[21]

The political report noted that groups might have different interests and views, and they needed opportunities and channels for the exchange of ideas.

After the Thirteenth Party Congress, attention turned toward the development of institutions and procedures to express people's interests and to supervise the power of the Party. People started to realize that the establishment of democratic principles was not enough, because such principles only worked in a system designed for their implementation.[22] Thus, some scholars raised the issue of transformation from "nonprocedural politics" to "procedural politics." According to this argument, democratic politics was procedural politics, creating mechanisms to correct mistakes, and did not depend on good or bad politicians.[23] What was more, under the new circumstances of economic reform, since class struggle was no longer a principal contradiction, the government should protect the minorities' rights to their own opinions.[24] These concepts were not new in the Western political vocabulary, but for a country with a limited tradition of democracy,[25] the transplantation of such ideas and their gradual acceptance by the leaders and masses was of great significance.

The concept of the supervision of political power through checks and balances and through law and institutions became popular as well.[26] In addition to the supervision of state power, the issue of supervision of the Party power was posed. Most theories of Party leadership agreed that, first, Party leadership should not be the direct leadership of Party organizations or Party members and should not be equivalent to the management of state affairs; it should be an indirect leadership and should be separated from state affairs. Second, the Party should not be placed above all other organizations, and there must be effective surveillance of the Party. The leaders should be checked by the Party members, and the Party should be subject to supervision by the society, by other political parties, by public opinion, and by the press. Some suggested that there should be both external and internal checks on the power of the Party. External checks included strengthening the function of the people's congresses and encouraging mass participation; internal checks referred to the normalization and publicization of Party factions.[27]

Finally, a major theme throughout the discussion on political reform that has continued to this day was whether or not to promote democracy at the current stage of development. There was little dispute over the need for democracy in China, but people disagreed on how and how soon democracy should be achieved. While agreeing that democracy was possible only when people's understanding of the process was greatly enhanced, some believed that people would learn how to exercise their democratic rights only through participating in democratic processes.[28] Others believed that although democracy was necessary, it should not be advocated in China at the present stage because the country was economically backward and the people's sense of democracy weak. This theme later developed into the discussion of neo-authoritarianism. The group advocating the notion argued that, in the current period, reform required strong authority, not democracy. According to the neoauthoritarians, the urgency of reform and the enormity of the obstacles to it allowed no delay for consensus formation or compromise. They argued that the most dangerous threat to reform came not from conservatives in the leadership but from social groups adversely affected by inflation, unemployment, and other transitional problems. They called for nondemocratic rule by a reformist elite that would push the reform program through despite any resistance.[29] With the mounting social and political tensions generated by economic reform, the neoauthoritarian approach increasingly became the middle ground for the Chinese leadership, between the conservative resistance to economic reform on one side, and the liberal reformers' push for democratization on the other.[30]

From the notion of absolute Party leadership to the acceptance of the existence of a plurality of interests, restrictions on state power, and most important, limitations on the power of the Party, the outer limits of the official ideological spectrum had shifted a significant distance as the party-state adapted to the challenges created by reform. Not all of these views reflected official perspectives or policies in either Hungary or China. However, their appearance in the official press demonstrated official encouragement and tolerance and in many instances presaged changes in official policy. By introducing the notion of pluralism and its institutionalization and by recognizing the limitations of Party leadership, ideological adaptation had alleviated the need to repair a disintegrating ideological system and shaped the contours of further institutional adaptation.

Ideological adaptation in Hungary and China, as we discussed above, had its limits. The acceptance of the notion of pluralism did not entail the tolerance of a full range of autonomous social or political organizations and their active participation in the decision-making process. Neither China nor Hungary (until 1988) was prepared to accept this degree of pluralism. In 1987, the prime minister, Karoly Grosz, pointed out that the government hoped to establish a dialogue with all those who sought solutions in the interest of "socialist resurgence" but not with those who "from a hostile platform willfully try to discredit our goals and our efforts aimed at achieving those goals."[31] The CC secretary of HSWP in charge of ideological affairs, Janos Berecz, strongly defended the ruling position of the HSWP, saying that although social organizations might share responsibility with the HSWP in the decision-making process, the Party could not be challenged by any institution, including the government.[32] Similarly, the

Chinese leaders firmly rejected the tendency toward "bourgeois liberalization," as they termed the demand for a Western type of political democracy
with free elections and a multiparty system.

Given these constraints, the Party could accept a social order of a more
corporative nature. In such a system, interests are organized but noncompetitive, and the Party would not exercise direct control over the activities of
the interest groups but would still coordinate the articulation of their
demands.

Institutional Adaptation: The Emergence of Corporatism

In both Hungary and China, the reform of political institutions began
together with economic reform and political liberalization, but became more
meaningful only in a later stage of reform. The major goal of institutional
reform was to increase the efficiency and responsiveness of the government
in the face of an increasingly diverse and less easily controlled society. One
component of institutional reform was the effort to grant more autonomy to
mass organizations and to create more channels for consultation and
dialogue, which went hand in hand with the discussion and acceptance of the
notion of pluralism. Apart from being lenient toward the new nonpolitical
social groups, the regimes also tried to transform the functions of the
existing mass organizations, which held legitimate positions in the political
system and had established organizational structures and leaderships, from
official agencies to guardians of the interests of their respective constituencies.

Among all the existing social organizations, the most powerful were the
trade unions. Other organizations either did not embody any aggregated
professional or sectoral interest, such as the Youth League, or else lacked
social status and powerful leaders, like the women's federations. In addition,
in the more diversified ownership and management structure introduced
under reform, the trade unions were given greater authority to represent the
interests of the staff and workers and check the power of a more autonomous management.

The Trade Unions in Hungary

Theoretically, in a workers' state, the interest of the Party, which claims
to be the party of the workers, is closer to the interests of the working class
than to those of any other group. The traditional role of the trade unions in
state socialist societies, however, was to serve as a transmission belt,
providing a two-way channel of communication between the Party and the

workers. It would pass information, ideology, and directives down from the Party to the union members and at the same time pass the views of its members up to the Party. Yet in practice, the downward transmission was the sole function of the trade unions. The unions always pledged themselves to mobilize and organize staff and workers to rally around the Party.

The position of organized labor in Hungary during the reform stood in rather stark contrast to the utilitarian and subservient role played by all other Eastern European trade unions, save in Poland in a different context. The function of the trade unions as defenders of workers' interests had been promoted with greater official tenacity and insistence. The new emphasis on the role of the unions in representing and protecting the interests of the workers was reflected in a labor code enacted in 1967. It stipulated that the collective contract and the enterprise safety regulations could come into force only with the agreement of the trade unions, and that the trade unions had the right to distribute social and cultural funds of the enterprise; to supervise the implementation of regulations pertaining to the living and working conditions of the workers; to veto management decisions; and to be consulted on the hiring, promotion, or dismissal of enterprise leaders.[33] The transmission-belt concept disappeared from the labor code. Although the 1971 trade union congress continued to assert that the unions must play a "dual role," one aspect of which was to transmit the Party's policy to the working class, union representatives practically ignored that function after 1968, concentrating instead on the defense and representation of workers' interests.

The transmission-belt concept itself had changed. The trade unions, according to Sandor Gaspar, secretary general of the National Trade Union Council (NTUC), should not merely transmit policy but actively participate in its creation. "Certainly there is a meaningful distinction," Robinson commented, "between the transmission of policies made solely by outside agencies and the transmission of policies made in genuine collaboration with those officially entitled to represent the workers."[34] There were, however, further differences. In the past, for example, policy transmission meant simply relaying orders regarding workers' obligations to the socialist state. It had come to include the transmission of information and the education of the workers regarding their legal and political rights. The official definition of trade union functions no longer required the unions to be mere junior partners of management in fulfilling production plans. As a result of this new perspective, Hungarian trade unions began to create an image that increasingly reflected a labor viewpoint on significant issues.

It was reported that the trade unions had resorted to their veto powers on a number of occasions. Although there were no systemic data on this matter, it was estimated that the trade unions vetoed enterprise decisions several dozen times at the enterprise level during 1968-1969. Scattered reports revealed that the trade unions had exercised their right of veto by ordering the cessation of work if the safety and health provisions were deemed inadequate. The NTUC secretary claimed that under certain circumstances the trade unions would agree to strike.[35]

The trade unions also became much more critical of the manner in which they and their proposals were being treated by government authorities. In July 1970 several union officials interviewed by Radio Budapest accused Jozsef Bondor, minister of public construction and urban development, of extensive violations of union rights when he suddenly dismissed two high-ranking managers of a cement and lime works at the beginning of June without prior consultations with the appropriate trade union bodies. This infringement of workers' rights aroused such consternation on the part of the enterprise trade union committee that two members promptly resigned in order to demonstrate their "profound condemnation" of the minister's action.[36]

It was obvious that the trade unions had become more assertive. In October 1970 members of the NTUC secretariat, including Gaspar, initiated a meeting with minister of the interior, the minister of justice, and the head of the local council department of the Council of Ministers to air grievances concerning the way state agencies were handling workers' affairs. Although the communiqué issued afterward indicated a degree of compromise on the matter (workers were asked to be a bit more understanding of the problems confronting the average civil servant), the trade union clearly carried the day.[37]

The unions' most salient role was to criticize the income inequalities generated by the economic reform. As Richard Portes observed, "Moonlighting, real estate speculation, country houses at Balaton, high earnings of private artisans and of agricultural cooperatives, 'profiteering,' 'moneygrubbing,' and 'materialism'—all offended the sensibilities of the working class and their representatives."[38] Moreover, the sharp deceleration in the growth of real wages in state industry in 1971-1972 and increasingly visible earnings differentials between enterprises were to the disadvantage of manual workers in the state sector, while peasants, the self-employed, and workers in cooperatives were all doing relatively well. Dissenting from Kadar's alliance policy, which gave equal emphasis to professional qualifications and political reliability, union leaders announced that "some workers might be inadequate in terms of professional training or general culture, but these were qualities that are easily acquirable, while an alert worker's spirit is not."[39]

Trade union leaders effectively conveyed to the Party leadership the discontent of industrial workers. At the November plenum in 1972, under pressure from the trade unions, the HSWP Central Committee decided to suspend economic reform and recentralize the economic system. Other problems, such as the deteriorating world economic situation, which severely affected Hungary's foreign trade, also contributed to the decision. However, the pressure from the trade unions on redressing income inequality was a major consideration. At the plenum Kadar stressed the relative drop in the economic position of industrial workers, argued that equality had to take precedence over efficiency, and criticized petit-bourgeois excesses.[40] The decision to postpone further economic reform was not primarily due to economic reasons but rather reflected a clear priority for the goals of a politically acceptable income distribution and a minimum rate of increase of living standards for all major groups in the population, with special concern for industrial manual workers.[41]

Under the Kadar regime, the NTUC had become an active participant in national economic policy-making, and no important question affecting wage earners could be decided without its involvement. According to NTUC secretary Magda Kovacs, the improvement of living standards was the trade unions' priority. This had inevitably led to differences with various government bodies during the drafting of the five-year plan. Nevertheless, she said, it would be more correct to speak of an alliance rather than of clashes between unions and the government.[42] It was mainly under union pressure that Hungary's planners opted for a firm policy to control inflation by not allowing price increases to exceed 5 percent a year and by promising to freeze the prices of the most essential consumer goods. The unions also sent out more than 10,000 activists to assist the state in inspecting and controlling prices.[43] In the field of social and welfare policy, the unions supported a strategy designed to reduce inequalities, to prevent social tension, and to promote social justice. In practical terms, this meant helping various disadvantaged groups such as large families, partially incapacitated workers, young people starting a family, and pensioners. In 1986 Hungary took its first step to preserve the real value of the lowest pensions and of the pensions of those over the age of seventy.[44]

Official newspapers praised the important role the unions played in Hungary's political system and their participation in economic policy decisions. At the same time, however, in response to the growing activism of their members and their frank criticism, the Party warned the trade unions to take economic realities into account in formulating their policies, since not all justifiable union demands could be satisfied at once. The HSWP reaffirmed once again that the unions' basic political and economic functions had not changed and that their principal task was to organize and mobilize their members for the further "building of socialism" in Hungary.[45]

As discussed in the previous chapter, the first independent Hungarian trade unions were created in the wave of democratic change in 1988. In

May 1988 the Democratic Union of Scientific Workers was established. The Democratic Movie Union was founded in October 1988. Both unions declared that they were independent from the NTUC.[46] These new unions were organized mainly by intellectuals rather than manual industrial workers. As the country entered into a period of dramatic political change shortly after these unions emerged, however, it is difficult to assess their role in the country's political life during the short transition period.

Trade Unions in China

Trade unions in China were organized by both industrial sector and geographic region. In general, the industrial unions were much weaker than the local unions, which had long acted as departments of Party committees at all levels. With the implementation of economic reforms, demands for a more independent role for the trade unions increased in China. In 1982 an editorial in *Gongren Ribao* (Workers' daily) stated:

> While carrying out instructions, the trade unions should pay attention to the workers' wishes and feelings and make them known to the Party. When instructions from above are harmful to the workers' interests and go against their wishes, the trade unions should not blindly carry out such orders but should put forth their views. Then the workers would regard the trade union organization as representing their own interests.[47]

Some trade union cadres even openly advocated that the trade unions should only defend the vital interests of staff and workers and need not care about contributing to the "Four Modernizations."[48]

The constitution of the Tenth All-China Federation of Trade Unions (ACFTU) Congress of 1983 urged the unions, as the guardians of workers' rights and interests, to fight against bureaucratism, crime, and other offenses detrimental to socialism. A spokesman of the ACFTU further said that when the lives of workers were threatened or endangered by unbearable working conditions, unions had the right to evacuate them from their work sites in defiance of orders from the management. He explained that workers had their own special interests on which the bureaucracy might encroach by unlawful practices. Thus, according to ACFTU, the interests of the workers, the Party, and the state were not as identical as the Party would have it.[49]

It was generally acknowledged that one tendency in the past had been to ignore the differences between the government administration and the unions, to overlook the importance of the trade unions' participation in policy-making and management, and to avoid disagreements with the bureaucracy. Despite the growing role of the trade unions, however, the

Party still firmly believed that the trade unions should continue to educate and persuade workers to support the Party's leadership because the Party was the vanguard of the working class, and that they should take into consideration the interests of the state because in a socialist country the working class was the owner of the state's property.[50]

When the political report of the Thirteenth Party Congress stressed the function of social organizations as representatives of people's interests, the trade unions took a more independent stand. In a meeting of the ACFTU in 1988, Ni Zhifu, the chairman of ACFTU, proclaimed that in China trade unions were the products of socioeconomic contradictions and protected the interests of the workers. In the past, because the trade unions had ignored this role, they had to a large extent been divorced from the masses and exhibited more and more official and administrative tendencies. Ni claimed that guarding the workers' interests was the purpose of the existence of the trade unions: "In the preliminary stage of socialism, democracy and the legal system are not perfect, there are abuses in the regular practice of the Party and the society and a great deal of injustice in social distribution. Under such circumstances, workers' democratic rights and self-interest are often encroached upon in various social respects."[51] Ni suggested that the relationship between the trade unions and the government should require democratic participation and social supervision on the part of the trade unions. He also emphasized that trade unions should attract workers to participate in the economic construction of the country, in state and social affairs, in the management of the enterprises, and in the education of workers.

The ACFTU began to articulate its corporative interests more forcefully, lobbying intensively for a trade union law and an enterprises law. The ACFTU succeeded in modifying the language of the enterprise law, inserting clauses to guarantee various rights of the workers against greater power invested with the enterprise managers.[52]

When economic reform gave more power to managers and directors, the Party also endorsed greater union activity as a way to counterbalance the shift. Thus, when the manager of the Wuhan Wool Textile Factory, which was leased out to individual management, decided to fire seven workers, the trade union's investigation proved that six of them were innocent of the accusations; only one worker was finally fired.[53]

Worker strikes—one of the most acute forms of social conflict—had largely become a matter for the trade unions and enterprises rather than the Party. A spokesman of the ACFTU, Yu Qinghe, expressed the union's stand on worker strikes. He asserted that "the main causes for workers' strikes, slow downs, or stoppages are bureaucratism and bad behavior of the enterprise leadership, which has seriously encroached on the legal rights of the workers, especially on issues like distribution, democratic rights, and welfare."[54] For example, in February 1988 at the Xiaoshan Third Textile Factory in Zhejiang Province, 1,500 workers went on strike for two days allegedly because of the unjust distribution of the annual bonus. A strike at the Northwest Medical Equipment Factory involving more than 1,000 workers lasted for three months in early 1988 and resulted in a zero net profit for the factory in the first quarter. The main cause was that the manager of the factory had ignored workers' rights and had been absent from the factory for too long. Yu said that once there was a strike, the trade union would support the legitimate demands of the workers and persuade the enterprise and government to resolve the problem promptly. The trade unions would advocate reconciliation, dialogue, and compromise, not a strike, he added, and thus far no force had been used in settling labor disputes.

His remarks indicated, first, that most labor disputes were considered to be nonpolitical; instead, they reflected economic conflicts between workers and enterprise managers. Second, trade unions were to be neither government agents nor strike organizers but mediators cooperating with government to resolve labor disputes between the management and workers.

As the trade unions had strong political potential because of their position in the national economy, they were allowed to operate only within certain limits. One fear of the Party leadership was that worker alienation might lead to the advocacy of truly independent unions. Such a fear was heightened by the creation of Solidarity in Poland.[55] From time to time, the Party would remind the trade unions that they should maintain unity with state statutes and mobilize workers to fulfill government tasks. In other words, the activities of the trade unions were officially set within a more corporatist structure. As an editorial in *Renmin Ribao* explained, the government should respect the legal status and rights of the trade unions, support the trade unions in protecting the legal interests of the workers, inform the trade unions of important matters, engage in consultation and dialogue with the trade unions on policies involving the workers' interests, and make the trade unions close collaborators and pillars of society.[56]

In China and Hungary alike, then, trade unions were granted greater autonomy to articulate and protect workers' interests. They began to appear as the defenders of the well-being of the working class. Yet this was only a partial shift from their traditional role as departments of the Party, for they continued to perform their new functions under the Party leadership. The trade unions in Hungary were quite active and assertive at the national level in representing the workers' interests, especially on the issues of wages and income inequality. The trade unions in China, in contrast, had just begun to play a role in local disputes and were far from exerting a decisive influence on national policy-making. This may in part have b•en due to the rural orientation of the CCP during the revolution, its relative inexperience in dealing with trade union movements, and hence its uneasiness concerning the potential political power of the trade unions.

Consultation and Dialogue

In addition to granting more autonomy to existing mass organizations, another means to incorporate citizens into the official framework and to increase the responsiveness of the political establishment was to strengthen consultation and dialogue between the Party leadership and social groups. Consultation and dialogue were intended to make public the activities of leading bodies, disseminate information about major events, bring into discussion important issues, consult affected interests before making decisions, and create new ways through which people could express their views.

In China the establishment of such a system of communication was first formally raised in Zhao Ziyang's report to the Thirteenth Party Congress in 1987. Its emphasis on consultation and dialogue indicated that the Party intended to improve its leadership by being more responsive to a wider social audience, recognizing that different interests coexisted among different groups in society. The Party hoped that a system of two-way communication would be developed in which policies would be explained so the masses could better understand them, their demands and complaints could in turn be heard, and then adjustments could be made on both sides. The expansion of this system started with the better use of existing institutions and channels, especially the political consultative conferences and the democratic parties. These organizations were given more opportunities to organize consultations and dialogues and make the results known to the government departments concerned.

There were eight noncommunist parties in China known as "democratic parties."[57] The main forum for the democratic parties to participate in policy-making was the Chinese People's Political Consultative Conference (CPPCC), China's highest multiparty advisory body, founded in 1949 just before the announcement of the People's Republic. Representatives of all the noncommunist parties and groups were invited to participate in the CPPCC. However, its consultative function diminished dramatically after 1957, when all the outspoken figures who believed they had a say in state affairs were punished in the antirightist campaign. From that time, the democratic parties and the CPPCC, like the National People's Congress, became absorbed into the structure of the Communist Party's dictatorship. Their members enjoyed social prestige and material welfare in return for their complete subordination to the Party.

After the introduction of economic reforms in 1978, when the Communist Party began to solicit broad social support for the reform and exploit talent and knowledge from all sectors of the society, it revised its policy toward the democratic parties, proposing long-term coexistence and mutual supervision; treating each other with sincerity and sharing weal and woe (*Changqi gongcun, huxiang jiandu*; *gandan xiangzhao, rongru yugong*). The democratic parties were regularly informed of the conferences and the documents being drafted by the Communist Party. For example, the political report to the Thirteenth Party Congress was discussed among the representatives of democratic parties before its delivery.[58] The parties were also consulted on the drafts of five-year plans, reform policies, and major economic projects. For instance, their views on the "Preliminary Scheme for Price and Wage Reform" were solicited before the plan's implementation.[59] The democratic parties also worked hard requesting more money for education, especially for primary schools, and made an issue of inadequate pay for middle-aged intellectuals.[60]

On one occasion the democratic parties played quite tough. They firmly opposed the state council's proposal for the Three Gorges Dam. The leading opponents were engineers in the Jiusan Society, one of the eight democratic parties, who undertook a feasibility study. Among the targets of their criticism were the cost of village relocation, the rising cost of the dam itself, and their pessimistic forecasts of the economic returns on the project.[61] They were largely responsible for the repeated delays in the construction.

The democratic parties grew in size and influence during the reform period. For example, membership in their Beijing chapters doubled to more than 10,000 between 1979 and 1986. Generally, the democratic parties had limited their membership to intellectuals and people who had been capitalists before the 1949 revolution but who had decided to remain in China. But in the 1980s, as their memberships declined with the deaths of these elderly members, the parties recruited younger people and rejuvenated their leadership. Most of the new members were artists, public health professionals, educators, and scientists.[62]

The new status of the democratic parties provided opportunities for some younger Chinese to pursue political careers outside the Party. They explained that even though they understood that they would not be eligible for the highest political positions still reserved for Party members, they would be able to participate in a wide range of political activities, join the CPPCC at either the national or provincial level, and exercise some influence in the consideration of national policies. At the same time, they would not be subject to the internal discipline or have to cope with the internal politics of the Communist Party.[63] As one member of a democratic party pointed out, "If there is something that needs to be discussed, I now can go directly to the Communist Party, which is a bit more inclined to listen if you are a member of a democratic party."[64]

These democratic parties were hardly political parties in any traditional sense, for they were not able to compete for political power. In fact, some of the principal activities of the democratic parties were the promotion of education, primarily through the establishment of what we may call private schools, and technological consultation for enterprises, making them more like charities or professional firms than political parties. At most, as James Seymour pointed out, the democratic parties acted as interest groups. In addition to some social work, they worked collectively to gain political "goods" for their members and for similarly situated individuals outside the organization.[65]

In Hungary the demand for dialogue between the leadership and the society originated from below. In responding to the difficult economic situation in the 1980s, a group of economists drafted a reform proposal suggesting that the only way to avoid an economic crisis was a public reckoning by the leadership of the seriousness of the situation and the launching of truly radical social and economic reforms through a genuine and frank dialogue with citizens.[66]

There was no formal structure for a multiparty umbrella group and consultative forum in Hungary comparable to the CPPCC in China. The largest mass organization, the People's Patriotic Front, had such a close relationship with the Party that its secretary general had to be a member of the Politburo of the HSWP. In order to carry on a dialogue with citizens, Party leaders engaged in more talks with experts and participated in meetings held by social organizations. Ferenc Havasi, a member of the Politburo who was responsible for the economy as secretary of the Central Committee, was sharply criticized by the economists he met in October 1986.[67] The secretary general of the PPF, Imre Pozsgay, attended the first meeting of the Democratic Forum and delivered a speech encouraging civic initiative in participating in the political life of the country. In late 1988, as independent social organizations mushroomed, political organizations close to the Party or those that had functioned in the past under Party direction, such as the Youth League and the trade unions, adopted more and more independent platforms and increasingly played the role of pressure groups emancipated from Party and government tutelage. The Party broadened its dialogue with them in order to reach a mutually acceptable compromise.

Other approaches to establishing a system of consultation and dialogue included the creation of new channels through which people could express their opinions. The development of opinion polls was one response to this need, as they could collect information on social attitudes and intentions that might influence the making and implementation of decisions and provide a connection between society and the state. In a planned economy, what people thought did not appear to be very important to the planners. It was easy to get the support of the people simply by labeling as "enemies" those who disagreed. Economic reform began to alter this tradition as it redistributed interests, changed the status of various social sectors, and pluralized perceptions and demands of the society. Engaged in a series of difficult and controversial economic reforms and governing an increasingly diverse and less easily controlled society, Party reformers needed a more sophisticated understanding of the views of the people. For example, some policies, such as price reform, required a certain degree of psychological endurance from the society that needed to be carefully gauged in order to determine the most appropriate timing. It was also important to assess and calculate the degree of damage some policies might do to the interests of certain groups. Furthermore, some policies needed follow-up surveys to measure their effects. Public opinion polls were, from the Party's point of view, the "safest" form of consultation. They involved no organized interest groups of any kind but enabled the Party to claim that it was attentive to public opinion.

The development of opinion surveys in Hungary started with the political liberalization of the early 1960s, especially the revival of sociology and the establishment of the Sociology Research Group in 1963. Along with the "alliance policy," the official attitude was that "socialist democracy" required better and more effective knowledge about the needs and desires of the public. Two organizations—the Public Opinion Research Group and the Mass Communications Research Center—were responsible for conducting opinion polls. The surveys initially covered topics like taste in music, use of free time, and views on social issues. After 1968, however, changes in opinions and attitudes toward the New Economic Mechanism became a major subject of study. Polls surveyed the population's expectations for the reforms, their reaction to changes in wage levels, the acceptability of differences in standards of living, and other matters.[68]

One well-known Hungarian economist, Jozsef Bognar, defined the role of public opinion in the relationship between the state and citizen in the following manner:

> When making decisions the government pays increased attention to the interest of groups affected by them. The general intention is to coordinate the social optimum with the various group interests to avoid contradictions arising from the implementation of the decision. . . . The anticipated reaction of public opinion

to decisions to be made is given increased consideration. . . . It follows that influencing public opinion (by the press, television, radio, publications, scientific discussions, etc.) has acquired added importance.[69]

There were, of course, topics that could not be the object of such surveys, such as the power of the Party bureaucracy and the legitimacy of the Party or the government and their potential fallibility.[70]

In China the development of survey research went through a two-stage process. The first was the application of decentralized, methodologically unsophisticated survey research that grew out of the early years of the post-Mao reforms. The second stage started in the mid-1980s, when the reform program faced a series of problems whose solution required a comprehensive understanding of the state of society. More sophisticated public opinion studies that used scientific sampling methods were then employed on a national scale.[71]

The first professional polling office in China was set up in 1985, managed by the institutions that were to provide policy alternatives for decision-makers. Various sectors of the population were interviewed on topics ranging from their attitudes toward reform in general to more specific questions on education, housing, family, and price reform. By June 1989 two major networks were conducting social surveys, one managed by the Center of Rural Economic Development and the other by the Institute of Economic System Reform. From 1985 to 1988, they conducted about sixteen major social investigations. The first large-scale opinion poll, on the topics of price reform and social security, involved eleven cities, sixteen counties, and over a hundred enterprises, including the health, education, commercial, and service sectors. The revival of sociology in China had a significant effect on these polls, from the design of the questionnaires to the computer processing of the results. The method of opinion polling was also adopted by various organizations and government departments. For example, the Youth League and the Federation of Women regularly conducted opinion polls on problems concerning youth and women, such as careers, marriage, and family.

Opinion polls started to move from economic and social spheres to the political sphere in the late 1980s. Some questionnaires began to ask about people's political attitudes toward certain issues, their political beliefs, their reaction to the Party congress, including questions on the prestige of the Party. The average response rate of about 95 percent indicated that people were receptive toward this method of surveying and were not as afraid to express criticism or doubts. Rosen observed that opinion polls also became a means for a variety of social and political forces to pursue policy agendas, as an alternative to more standard means of exercising influence, by demonstrating the unpopularity of the policy with members of the targeted group.[72]

The concept of consultation and dialogue had its limitations. It was a way to listen but not a way to make decisions. As a practical matter, the concept was very selective. The Party would deal only with institutions that it had established or with individual members of the society with whom it wished to deal. It refused to recognize social groups that were not within the status quo framework, such as the independent organizations that emerged during the 1989 protest movement.

Institutional Adaptation: Elections and Legislatures

Representation and responsiveness are key components of a democratic system. In Hanna Pitkin's definition, "political representation" means "acting in the interest of the represented, in a manner responsive to them." Although the ruling ideology in state socialist countries claimed that socialist democracy was more genuine than capitalist democracy, the basic concept of responsiveness was absent from communist practice. In China, for example, the "mass line," as it had been practiced, was more of a method to mobilize the masses to support the Party leadership than to hold the ruling Party accountable to the masses.[73] However, during the course of economic reform and ideological liberalization, the Party leadership started to accept the notion of pluralism and political participation.

Reformers in state socialist countries in the 1980s increasingly turned to the legislature as an arena in which the Party could make room for societal initiatives. The general motive was to improve government efficiency, rationalize authority, and regularize one-party rule. In China and Hungary, however, legislative reforms were carried out in the context of profound economic reform, which gave them more distinctive motivations and content. Legislative reform in Hungary was an adaptive effort by the leadership to address economic distress through moderate institutional changes. The increased political participation within the legislative framework could help to defuse mounting sociopolitical pressures and help the Party and government authorities to share responsibility for decision-making.

The people's congresses in China had completely ceased to function during the Cultural Revolution; the resumption of their operation reflected a desire to institutionalize the political system. This rationale was reinforced by economic reform. With a swift change of policy from class struggle to economic development, an active, lively legislature would heighten enthusiasm and encourage the people's cooperation in modernization efforts.[74]

Moreover, as reform decentralized administrative control over the economy and established contact with the world market, legislation was needed to regulate the booming economic activities that involved foreign ventures as well as domestic transactions.

Electoral Reform

Elections constitute the basic mechanism that determines the accountability and quality of congressional deputies. Simply put, deputies are responsive to those who select them. If they are chosen by the authorities, they are responsive to the authorities. If they are elected by the voters through a competitive process, they tend to feel more obligated to the voters who have chosen them and are therefore compelled to be more responsive to them. In the past practice of state socialism, deputies were designated by the authorities and elected by a ceremonial vote with no competition. Deputies were therefore loyal followers of the Party. This upward loyalty reinforced the rubber-stamp function of the legislature.

As part of the political liberalization then underway, the electoral law of 1966 in Hungary introduced a degree of limited choice from among a range of officially sponsored candidates. The possibility of multiple-candidate races was intended to stimulate popular interest and participation in national affairs and to make each parliamentary deputy directly responsible to a specific constituency. Reformers thought that with the elections of more suitable and expert people, the standards of the Hungarian parliament would be raised, even if everyone was obligated to support the same program.[75]

Unfortunately, the 1967 elections did not fulfill these goals. Out of 349 National Assembly seats, double candidacies occurred in only nine cases, and in all instances the official nominees of the PPF won easily. Out of more than 84,000 local council districts, multiple candidates were nominated in 686 instances, and only 120 unofficial nominees were elected. The general elections of 1971 were likewise disappointing in their outcome. Out of 352 National Assembly districts there were forty-eight double candidacies and one triple candidacy (representing 14 percent of the total number of seats). Out of 68,946 local council districts, there were 3,016 double or triple candidacies (representing 4.3 percent of the total seats).[76] According to Robinson, such results were due to the continuous organizational monopoly of the PPF in the nomination process.[77] The number of double and multiple candidacies for the National Assembly fell to thirty-four in 1975 and only fifteen in 1980. The declining trend in the late 1970s coincided with the stagnation of economic reform and political liberalization.

As the country resumed its course of economic reform, the HSWP Central Committee decided in July 1983 that further changes should be made in Hungary's electoral system. The committee authorized the National Assembly to enact new legislation for the election of deputies to the National Assembly and of members to local councils. Politburo member and Central Committee secretary Mihaly Korom said in a radio interview that "in the present electoral system, elections don't have much political significance" because there was no real electoral choice. In an outspoken newspaper interview at the beginning of 1983, Rezso Nyers called for an increase in the National Assembly's political role and the toleration of alternative views within it. With regard to the reform of the electoral system, he said that its aim was to have as many interests as possible represented in parliament in order to achieve a "pluralism of interests and views."[78]

The electoral law introduced in 1985 made it mandatory that at least two candidates be nominated in each district for elections to the National Assembly and local councils. Seven hundred and sixty-two candidates had been chosen to compete for 352 seats in the National Assembly and 87,334 for the 42,500 seats in the local councils.[79] The PPF nominated two candidates for each seat, but the third and fourth candidates were nominated by voters in 58 of the 352 districts, providing some alternatives to the official choices. About 156 candidates were proposed from the floor at nomination meetings, 71 of whom won enough votes to get on the ballot.

The June 1985 National Assembly election was a series of close contests and occasional upsets, giving it the appearance of a free election. For example, of the 352 contested assembly seats, 196 were won with 60 percent of the vote or less, sometimes with only a plurality in a three- or four-way race. Twenty-five unofficial candidates were elected. Some prominent political figures were defeated: Former premier Jeno Fock lost 44.8 to 54.3 percent, and former interior minister Bela Biszku lost in a run-off, receiving only 26.6 percent of the vote.[80] Ninety-eight of 172 incumbents defended their seats. Fifty-four lost, and twenty were forced into run-off elections.

The electoral law of 1985 also stipulated that a list of at least 10 percent of the total number of deputies (in this case thirty-five) prominent individuals were to be elected on a separate national list for the National Assembly. The candidates running on this national list would be nominated by the PPF National Council on the basis of recommendations made by political and social bodies and special interest groups that were members of the PPF.[81] The seats were not open to competition. But even these candidates lost significant numbers of votes compared to their past records. No one obtained 98-99 percent of the votes, as most of them had in 1980. Instead, they won only 60-70 percent, and some even dropped to barely 50 percent.

Pozsgay was quoted as saying that "for years there has been voting in Hungary, now there will be an election."[82] Voters in most constituencies apparently appreciated the choice of candidates, even if it was as if "between two eggs." In view of this alone, Hungary's new electoral reform could be seen as a step, however minor, in the direction of reform of the political institutions. Nevertheless, the results were not threatening to the regime. No dissidents won, and no incumbent Politburo members were defeated. Although the regime appeared firmly committed to the main features of the electoral reform, restrictions were aimed primarily at preventing dissidents from taking "unscrupulous" advantage of the electoral law. In one exceptional case, a prominent dissident, Laszlo Rajk, won the required minimum of votes at a nomination meeting and might have made the ballot had the authorities not packed subsequent nomination meetings with people instructed to vote against him.[83]

The "Electoral Law of the People's Republic of China for the NPC and Local People's Congresses at All Levels" was adopted by the second session of the Fifth National People's Congress in July 1979, to take effect on 1 January 1980. It contained a number of departures from the 1953 law, including a system of nominating more candidates than vacancies, direct election of delegates to the county people's congresses, and a more open nominating process. Further innovations included the requirement for secret ballots and procedures for recalling delegates.

Reports of county-level elections held during 1979 and 1980, however, showed that all the previous conceptions about the election remained unchanged. It was still widely believed that the candidates should be model workers. There was no direct competition among candidates: Public bulletin boards and broadcasting networks disseminated information concerning the candidates, and campaign materials were read aloud before and after work and in political study meetings. These elections remained a symbolic gesture to show popular support for the regime. They were carried out in a festive atmosphere, with people beating gongs and drums and exploding firecrackers and music broadcast over the loudspeakers. Posters featuring slogans such as "Voters are guaranteed full democratic rights!" and "People's deputies are elected by the people and work for the people!" were pasted everywhere around the polling stations.[84]

There were deviant cases in several universities where competitive elections were held in 1979 and 1980. At Beijing University, for instance, more than twenty candidates who were not nominated by the authorities launched vigorous campaigns for two seats in the Haidian district people's congress in Beijing. There were lively debates over various political and economic issues. Hu Ping, a graduate student of Western philosophy and one of the prominent unofficial candidates, ran on a platform of freedom of speech. He finally defeated the officially sponsored candidate and won the election. (The other seat was void because no one else got more than half of the votes needed.) However, although Hu held the title of people's deputy, he encountered tremendous difficulty in finding a decent job after graduation since most academic units that might have hired him were intimidated by the authorities.

Because of the undesirable results of elections at several universities in 1980, the Party decided to modify the electoral law in 1982. In the 1979 law, parties and groups had been able to promote candidates by various means, including election campaigns. In a 1982 amendment, this was said to be improper. Instead of permitting open campaigns and debate, the amendment prescribed that parties and groups should introduce candidates at official meetings of voters.[85]

Eight years of economic reforms and political liberalization produced increasing demands for strengthening the NPC and brought forward the question of raising the quality of deputies. In his report on the election of county deputies of 1987 to the Fifth Plenary of the Sixth NPC, Chen Pixian (vice-president of the NPC Standing Committee) suggested that the candidates should have the ability to organize social activities and discuss politics. This indicated not only that the deputies had not had such capabilities before but also that they were not seriously expected to have them. Chen proposed three changes in the election procedures. First, all candidates who were nominated by more than ten voters should be listed in the primary list. Second, in certain cases, the candidates could meet the voters and answer their questions. Finally, there must be adherence to the principle of multicandidate elections.[86]

It is unclear how many delegates were nominated through group recommendation nationwide, but in Liaoning Province, 90 percent of the people's congress delegates were so nominated, and these comprised 66 percent of those elected. In the Fujian municipality of Xiamen, all four incumbent vice mayors lost their seats to independently nominated local delegates.[87] In the elections in 1987, the offspring of the top leaders, including the sons of Deng Xiaoping and Chen Yun, were defeated.

Although these quasi-competitive elections offered only a limited range of choices, the people did not hesitate to exercise them. As China's electoral system was indirect, the central institutions were not directly affected. However, in a preliminary way the elections had some impact on the perceptions and performance of the deputies.

The Revitalization of Legislative Institutions

The real impact of the electoral reform should be measured through the changes in the procedures and roles of the legislature. In Hungary the enlargement of the role of the National Assembly was the focus of political attention after the passage of the electoral reform and the 1985 elections. According to Barnabas Racz, the 1985-1986 session of the assembly breathed new air into the stale chambers and invigorated what had previously been a matter of pure formalities. "The expanding horizons of law-making activities," Racz pointed out, "appeared to represent a modest qualitative transformation extending to the outer perimeters of legislative participation."[88]

Compared with past sessions, members' participation on committees and plenary levels was more articulate and assertive. Press accounts of discussions showed a significantly more critical attitude toward government policies, and many suggestions were presented to the plenary session either for immediate consideration or for future deliberation by the government and parliament. In the 1985-1986 plenary session, out of 102 speakers, 24 made definite criticisms, 18 included both critical points and proposals for modifications in policies or laws, while 24 avoided criticizing but made proposals for change.[89] The voting pattern became less unanimous and more diversified. There was also a notable increase in the number of interpellations submitted.[90]

Committee work was strengthened. There were more committee meetings and more substantive debates than previously. While in 1984-1985 there were only sixteen committee meetings, by the end of June 1986, forty-nine meetings had been held, and sixty-four were reported in the following year. The Legal, Administrative, and Judiciary Committee was particularly animated in preparing a tax law. The meetings of the committee were characterized by vigorous discussions about fundamental aspects of the proposed bill, including key principles and their impact upon the taxpayers. The debate also produced the unprecedented result that a part of the committee proposal was voted down in plenum.[91] A substantive modification was submitted on the floor by a deputy. After the minister of finance argued for the rejection of the proposal, the plenum voted overwhelmingly for the motion, handing down what Racz called a defeat to the government for the first time in the history of the socialist legislature in Hungary.[92]

In the September 1987 session of the parliament, deputies sharply questioned the political leadership's responsibility and accountability. The legislature's lengthy session, the extensive committee proceedings, and the sharp debates on the floor were a departure for the Hungarian parliament. Members of parliament began to assert themselves and seek their own roles within the one-party system. There were discussions about constitutional reform; further modification of the electoral rules, the redefinition of the division of labor among the Party, government, and parliament; creation of a second chamber; and a further revision of the assembly's rules. Deputies also began to work in the interest of their constituencies and apply pressure within some committees. For example, many Commerce Committee speakers represented their own particular geographical interests in the discussions of tourism development plans, and their local pride dominated some deliberations.[93] Racz also observed that mass organizations and special interest groups exercised more influence and increased their contact with high-level decision-making agencies.[94]

In China, although legislative reform started in the early 1980s, not until 1988 did the plenary sessions become lively. The Seventh NPC, held in March 1988, was a much more active and democratic congress than the previous ones. The election of the Standing Committee started to involve multiple candidates for each vacancy. Foreign journalists were allowed to listen to the group discussions and report the elections on-site.

Many deputies found they had to change their traditional function of studying and approving government reports and take a more active role in discussing political matters.[95] Debates were exemplified by the struggle for the microphone among governors, mayors, and ordinary deputies; because more people wanted to get the chance to speak, a time limit was imposed on each speech, which had never before been necessary.[96]

The most unusual case was the election of government officials. For the first time, no one received 100 percent of the votes. Even Deng Xiaoping, the paramount leader, received twenty-five negative votes and eight abstentions (out of 2,883) for the position of chairman of the Military Committee. Also for the first time, deputies cast negative votes and abstained in significant numbers. Those who failed to be elected received as many as 1,375 negative votes—certainly a change from the previous convention of unanimity.

The revitalization of the legislative body could also be seen on several occasions when the NPC was able to modify the proposed legislation or the details of the state budget. In 1986 the adoption of a national bankruptcy law was repeatedly delayed by opposition and reservations among members of the NPC, and it was approved only after significant changes were made in the text of the drafted law.

Elections of executive officials by local people's congresses also indicated more conscious participation on the part of the deputies. In Dingxiang County of Shanxi Province, for example, deputies took their responsibilities much more seriously. Earlier, people would talk to each other while voting; now they would not let others see for whom they voted. One deputy told a reporter, "In the past, it did not matter who was elected the head of the county, since he could not make things better or worse. Now, the head of the county makes a lot of difference. It is very relevant to us."[97] Several incumbent town leaders were voted out in this election. In the contests for county and town executive officials in Liaoning Province,

24 incumbent county leaders and 267 incumbent town leaders were defeated.[98] In October 1987 the people's congress of Yilan County, Heilongjiang Province, held an election for the head of the county. Despite intensive mobilization by Party organizations before the voting, the official candidate lost by a margin of three to one to the candidate the delegates had nominated.[99]

The deputies' perception of their own role gradually changed. The Public Opinion Research System conducted a survey of incumbent deputies to the Seventh NPC in 1988. In response to the question, "What kind of function should the deputies to the NPC perform in the national politics of our country?" about 18.4 percent chose the traditional role: "to approve every bill proposed by the government and support the government," whereas 14.3 percent opted "to report people's opinion to the government," and fully 67.2 percent chose "to supervise the government on behalf of ordinary citizens." Among those who believed that the NPC should supervise the government, only 13 percent of the respondents thought that the government had performed its job well, while 53.2 percent of the respondents were not satisfied.[100] When asked on what basis they cast their votes for the chairmen of special committees and for bills, 54.6 percent of deputies based their decisions on their own judgment, whereas 45.6 percent trusted the judgment of the authorities. The rate was somewhat different for bills: 63.7 percent voted on their own judgment, and 36.3 percent followed the authorities.[101]

The change in the role of the people's congresses in political life gradually began with less political matters, in keeping with what Heinz Eulau and Paul Karps describe as "service responsiveness" and "allocation responsiveness." Service and allocation responsiveness refer respectively to the efforts of the representatives to secure particular benefits for individuals or groups in their constituencies and to obtain benefits for their constituencies through pork-barrel exchanges in the appropriations process or through administrative interventions.[102] Compared to the notion of "policy responsiveness"—a situation in which the policy orientation of the representatives and their subsequent decision-making conduct are related to the policy positions of their constituencies—service and allocation responsiveness do not necessarily contradict the Party leadership but may put a check on local bureaucrats and establish close relationships between the deputies and their constituencies.

Efforts by deputies to obtain advantages and benefits for particular constituents were infrequent in the NPC's earlier generations. This slowly changed during reform. Each session of the congress received thousands of motions, which usually concerned individual problems or vague policy recommendations. Bills ranged from the reopening of a Muslim restaurant to the appropriation of funds for Huaibei saltworks.[103] Beginning in 1980 and continuing every year since, the Standing Committee of the NPC organized its members to carry out inspections or spot-checks of local units. After 1986 each of the deputies had fifteen days off each year for their inspection trips. They were issued special cards and were able to visit any place at any time on their own.[104] These tours served both as a link between deputies and their constituencies and as checks on local government. In some places people's deputies had a regular reception day, during which they held meetings with their constituents, listening to their complaints and helping them to solve their problems.[105]

There was no doubt that the NPC remained largely a rubber stamp for the Party. Moreover, the limited function the Party allowed the people's congresses was further impinged on by local power holders. For example, the existing political power structure prevented the normal operation of elections. In the nomination phase of the election process, candidates recommended by the masses were sometimes arbitrarily crossed off the ballot or replaced, cadres were assigned to be candidates from various districts, and candidates equal in number to the offices were proposed. During the elections themselves, some cadres adjusted the ballots to put the names of the candidates in order of official preference.[106]

Comparison

Facing the challenges that arose from the course of economic reform and political liberalization, the leaderships in Hungary and China made considerable efforts toward accommodation. The parties accepted the existence of plural interests and the notion of political reform to make the Party leadership more responsive and accountable. Following these conceptual changes, official mass organizations were given more autonomy to represent their members, and more channels of consultation and dialogue were created to increase the responsiveness of the Party and government. Legislative bodies were invigorated by holding multicandidate elections and increasing the participation and the responsiveness of the deputies.

Comparing the forms of adaptation in Hungary and China, there was an observable difference with regard to the level of institutionalization. In Hungary the trade unions enjoyed a more routinized role in the decision-making process concerning workers' interests than did their counterparts in China. Both the electoral and legislative reforms in Hungary were also more institutionalized. In China, despite the lively atmosphere of the NPC sessions, there were few sustained institutional changes. The significant changes concerned attitudes, not procedures, which were of course much more susceptible to changes in political currents. This is not to say that the reform in the Hungarian National Assembly could resist political reversal, but the institutional stability smoothed the future transition of the political system.

The Chinese emphasized consultation over formal accountability in their political process, unlike the Hungarians. This was congruent with their traditional conviction that consensus could be achieved by consultation rather than by democracy. The Chinese also had the Chinese People's Political Consultative Conference and democratic parties, which provided the institutional basis for elite consultation.

To be sure, the scale and pace of political institutional reform was slower than that of economic reform in each country. To those who take democratization as the benchmark for political reform, the adaptations of the political establishments in the two countries represented only marginal and inadequate changes. Ideological adaptations never allowed a challenge to the principle of Party leadership, and institutional adaptations did not ensure full autonomy for the mass organizations. Electoral competition was restricted; even the relatively advanced Hungarian electoral reform in 1985 exempted a list of thirty-five top officials from competition. The functioning of the legislature was determined largely by the tolerance of the Party leadership and was closely related to the political atmosphere: When the Party leadership was more tolerant and the political atmosphere was more liberal, the legislature was livelier and bolder. The legislative body itself had no control over the political situation.

In assessing this seemingly sluggish development of political reform in reforming state socialist countries, we should keep in mind, first, that the existing institutions themselves possessed great inertia. Political institutions are the stable, recurring, and valued organizations and procedures through which politics takes place. They are developed to assure stability and continuity. By definition they should be able to resist swift changes. Second, rapid economic reform, by redistributing resources and introducing different operational mechanisms, is a dynamic process. If such economic reform coincides with rapid political institutional changes, it could lead to a very unstable situation. Therefore, the slower pace of political reform may not necessarily be a negative factor in the whole transition process in the long term. Moreover, we should also take into account the strength of the conservative resistance to rapid political changes within a state socialist system. The changes that had been achieved thus far were the result of the reform coalitions' efforts.

Despite the limitations, these adaptations had great significance for the future. The first involved the changing roles of the existing official organizations. In a transition period, the most important change may not be the creation of new institutions but the transformation and revitalization of the old ones. As we have seen, they may assume a dual role: They may continue to support the regime but may also assume more extragovernmental functions for their respective constituencies. As a matter of fact, as far as they were shifting to the latter function, it was not important whether they supported or affiliated with the official framework. Under certain circumstances, these official organizations may turn against the establishment, a phenomenon discussed in chapter 7.

Second, these early adaptations show that it is not impossible for the Communist Party to make major concessions regarding its power. With the implementation of reform, the central position along the political spectrum shifted a tremendous distance from what it had been under traditional state socialism. In theory the Party was modifying its leadership. In practice the HSWP eventually accepted the multiparty system in 1989. Although the CCP insisted on its leadership, the content and form of this leadership had been undergoing a quiet evolution. The process of political learning was critical. And the communist elites were learning.

In fact, by 1989 the communist leaderships in both Hungary and China were on the verge of further democratic reforms. But whereas the Hungarian reformers moved from pluralism to a multiparty system, the Chinese backed away from this position after 1989. The determinants of this divergence were many, as we will see in the next chapter.

NOTES

1. Gyorgy Aczel, "Hungarian Cultural Policy and the Hegemony of Marxism," *New Hungarian Quarterly* 12, no. 42 (Summer 1971): 19.

2. William F. Robinson, *The Pattern of Reform in Hungary: A Political, Economic and Cultural Analysis* (New York: Praeger, 1973), pp. 231-73.

3. Rezso Nyers, "Interrelations Between Policy and the Economic Reform in Hungary," *Journal of Comparative Economics* 7 (1983): 217-18.

4. "HSWP Searching for New Ideology," *Radio Free Europe Research (RFER)* 12, no. 48, 4 December 1987, pp. 3-8.

5. Council for Social Policy of the Patriotic People's Front of Hungary, "Change and Reform, 1986," manuscript.

6. Ibid., pp. 57-60.

7. "PPF Daily Publishes Statement of Hungarian Democratic Forum," *RFER* 12, no. 48, 4 December 1987, pp. 13-18.

8. "Regime Still Uneasy About Nonconformist Views," *RFER* 13, no. 2, 15 January 1988, pp. 13-14.

9. Bela Pokol, "Changes in the System of Political Representation in Hungary," in *Economy and Society in Hungary*, eds. Rudolf Andorka and Laszlo Bertalan (Budapest: Karl Marx University of Economic Sciences, Department of Sociology, 1986), pp. 267-286.

10. Ibid.

11. Mihaly Bihari, "The Political System and the Representation of Interests," in *Economy and Society in Hungary*, eds. Rudolf Andorka and Laszlo Bertalan (Budapest: Karl Marx University of Economic Sciences, Department of Sociology, 1986), pp. 287-331.

12. Deng Xiaoping, "On the Reform of the System of Party and State Leadership," *Selected Works of Deng Xiaoping* (Beijing: Foreign Languages Press, 1984), p. 316.

13. *Zhengming*, September 1986, pp. 15-16.

14. Miao Qiming, "Lun shehuizhuji wenming de sanweijiegou" [On the three-dimensional structure of socialist civilization], *Xinhua Wenzhai*, no. 2 (1986): 5-7.

15. From a speech given by Yan Jiaqi at a meeting on political reform held in August 1986 in Beijing.

16. Du Feijin and Xu Cailiao, "Luetan zhengzhi minzhuhua he fazhi" [Brief discussion on political democratization and legal system], *Renmin Ribao* (overseas edition), 11 November 1986, p. 2.

17. Ibid.

18. Chen Yizi, "Zhengzhi tizhi gaige shi jingji tizhi gaige di baozheng" [Political reform is the guarantee for economic reform], *Shijie Jingji Daobao*, 13 July 1987; and "Gaige shi shixian shehuizhuyi xiandaihua de keguan yaoqiu" [Reform is the objective request of the socialist modernization], *Shijie Jingji Daobao*, 10 August 1987.

19. Zhao Ziyang, "On Separating Party from Government," *Beijing Review*, 14-20 December 1987, p. 20.

20. Wei Qun and Duan Yue, "Yinmi wangguo zhong de jige wenti: zoufan zhongguo shehui diaocha xitong" [Several questions in the hidden kingdom: a visit to China's social survey system], *Zhongguo Qingnian*, November 1987, p. 13.

21. *Beijing Review*, 9-16 November 1987, pp. 41-42.

22. Wu Guoguang and Gao Shan, "Cujin women shehuizhuyi minzhu zhidu de zhiduhua" [Promoting the Institutionalization of Our Socialist Democratic Politics], *Hongqi*, no. 21 (1987): 43-48.

23. Yan Jiaqi, "Cong feichengxu zhengzhi zouxiang chengxu zhengzhi" [From non-procedural politics to procedural politics], *Xinhua Wenzhai*, no. 10 (1988): 1-5.

24. Qin Xiaoying, "Shehuizhuyi minzhu ye yinggai baokuo shaoshu yuanze" [Socialist democracy should include the minority principle], *Xinhua Wenzhai*, no. 12 (1988): 12-15.

25. For the limited tradition of democracy in China, see Andrew Nathan, *Chinese Democracy* (New York: Alfred A. Knopf, 1985).

26. For example, see Bao Xinjian, "Shehuizhuyi chuji jieduan minzhu zhengzhi jianshe xinlun" [On the construction of democratic politics in the primary stage of socialism], *Xinhua Wenzhai*, no. 11 (1988): 1-4.

27. Deng Chundong, "Jingnianlai lilunjie guanyu dang de lingdao wenti de zhongyao guandian zongshu" [Review of the major theoretical views on the Party leadership in recent years], *Xinhua Wenzhai*, no. 12 (1988): 8-9.

28. *China Daily*, 30 August 1986, p. 4.

29. See, for example, Wu Jianxiang, "Xin quanwei zhuyi shuping" [On neoauthoritarianism], *Shijie Jingji Daobao*, 16 January 1989; and "Guanyu xinquanwei zhuyi de taolun" [Discussions on neoauthoritarianism], *Xinhua Wenzhai*, no. 4 (1989): 1-9.

30. The former Party general secretary Zhou Ziyang said that he mentioned the theory of neoauthoritarianism to Deng Xiaoping during a visit to Deng. Deng said although he basically agreed with the idea, he prefered another label for this model. Personal conversation with Zhao Ziyang, September 1993, Beijing.

31. "Regime Still Uneasy About Nonconformist Views," *RFER* 13, no. 2, 15 January 1988, pp. 13-14.

32. "Ideological Pluralism Under One-Party Rule?" *RFER* 12, no. 13, 3 April 1987, pp. 8-9.

33. Robinson, *The Pattern of Reform in Hungary*, pp. 239-40.

34. Ibid., p. 329.

35. Ibid., p. 241.

36. Ibid.

37. Ibid., p. 242.

38. Richard Portes, "Hungary: Economic Performance, Policy and Prospects," in Joint Economic Committee, 95th Cong., 1st sess., *East European Economics Post Helsinki* (Washington, D.C.: U.S. Government Printing Office, 1977), p. 785.

39. Robinson, *The Pattern of Reform in Hungary*, pp. 337-38.

40. Portes, "Hungary," pp. 787-88.

41. Ibid., pp. 766-815.

42. "Trade Unions Brace Themselves for Lively 25th Congress," *RFER* 11, no. 10, 7 March 1986, p. 5.

43. "25th Trade Union Congress: Restlessness Below, Platitudes from the Top," *RFER* 11, no. 12, 21 March 1986.

44. Ibid.

45. Ibid.

46. Gabor Revesz, *Perestroika in Eastern Europe: Hungary's Economic Transformation, 1945-1988* (Boulder, Colo.: Westview Press, 1990), p. 130.

47. *Gongren Ribao*, 10 October 1979.

48. Ibid., 15 April 1981.

49. Lee Lai To, *Trade Unions in China: 1949 to the Present* (Singapore: National University of Singapore Press, 1986).

50. "Unions Take on New Role at the Top," *China Daily*, 24 September 1986, p. 4.

51. *Renmin Ribao* (overseas edition), 27 July 1988, p. 1.

52. Anita Chan, "Revolution or Corporatism? Workers and Trade Unions in Post-Mao China," *Australia Journal of Chinese Affairs*, no. 29 (January 1993): 31-61.

53. *Renmin Ribao* (overseas edition), 25 December 1987.

54. Ibid., October 26, 1988, p. 1.

55. Jeanne L. Wilson, "'The Polish Lesson': China and Poland 1980-1990," *Studies in Comparative Communism* 23, no.3/4 (Autumn/Winter 1990): 259-79.

56. "Jiaquai gonghui gaige bufa" [Speed up reform of the trade unions], *Renmin Ribao* (overseas edition), 22 October 1988, p. 1.

57. For the names of these parties, please see note 20 in chapter 2.

58. *Renmin Ribao* (overseas edition), 6 September 1987, p. 1.

59. Ibid., 19 September 1988, p. 1.

60. "Middle-aged" usually refers to those between thirty-five and fifty. These people constituted the backbone in research institutes and universities, yet their salaries were about the same as those for blue-collar workers and became even lower during economic reform.

61. James D. Seymour, *China's Satellite Parties* (New York: M. E. Sharpe, 1987), p. 78.

62. *China Daily*, 2 November 1986, p. 4.

63. Harry Harding, *China's Second Revolution* (Washington, D.C.: The Brookings Institution, 1987), p. 350, n. 32.

64. Seymour, *China's Satellite Parties*, p. 76.

65. Ibid., p. 90.

66. Council for Social Policy of the Patriotic People's Front of Hungary, "Change and Reform, 1986."

67. Paul Lendvai, *Hungary: The Art of Survival* (London: I. B. Tauris, 1988), pp. 113-14.

68. Robert Blumstock, "Public Opinion in Hungary," in *Public Opinion in European Socialist Systems*, eds. Walter D. Conor and Zvi Y. Gitelman (New York: Praeger, 1977), pp. 132-66.

69. Ibid.

70. Ibid.

71. Stanley Rosen, "Public Opinion and Reform in the People's Republic of China," *Studies in Comparative Communism* 22, no. 2/3 (Summer/Autumn 1989): 153-70.

72. Ibid.

73. Liu Zhiguang and Wang Suli, "Cong qunzhong shehui zouxian gongmin shehui" [From mass society to citizen society], *Xinhua Wenzhai*, no. 11 (1988): 9-12.

74. Kevin O'Brien, "China's National People's Congress: Reform and Its Limits," *Legislative Studies Quarterly* 13, no. 3 (August 1988): 343-74.

75. Robinson, *The Pattern of Reform in Hungary*, p. 207.

76. The increase in National Assembly seats was due to an increase in the population since 1967. The decrease in local council seats was due to the merger of a number of districts.

77. Ibid., pp. 206-12.

78. "Cautious Liberalization of Electoral Law Permitted," *RFER* 8, no. 32, 12 August 1983.

79. "On the Eve of the 1985 National Elections," *RFER* 10, no. 26, 28 June 1985.

80. Werner Hahn, "Electoral Choice in the Soviet Bloc," *Problems of Communism* 36 (March-April 1987): 36-37.

81. "Hungary Unveils Draft Electoral Law and Submits It to Public Debate," *RFER* 8, no. 40, 7 October 1983.

82. "On the Eve of the 1985 National Elections."

83. Ibid.

84. Tian Sansong, "Election of Deputies to a County People's Congress," *Beijing Review*, 25 February 1980, pp. 11-19.

85. *Renmin Ribao*, 16 December 1982.

86. *Renmin Ribao*, (overseas edition), 3 April 1987, p. 1.

87. Pierre Robert, "Let 2,970 Flowers Blossom: The Seventh NPC," *China News Analysis*, 15 May 1988, p. 5.

88. Barnabas Racz, "Political Participation and the Expanding Role of the Hungarian Legislature," *East European Quarterly* 22, no. 4 (January 1989): 465.

89. Ibid., p. 467.

90. Ibid., pp. 459-93.

91. Ibid., pp. 475-76.

92. Ibid., pp. 459-93.

93. Barnabas Racz, "The Parliamentary Infrastructure and Political Reforms in Hungary," *Soviet Studies* 41, no. 1 (January 1989): 48-49.

94. Ibid., p. 58.

95. *Renmin Ribao* (overseas edition), 4 April 1988, p. 2.

96. *Renmin Ribao* (overseas edition), 6 April 1988, p. 2.

97. Ibid., 28 November 1987, p. 4.

98. Ibid., 13 February 1988, p. 4.

99. Guang Hui and Duan Yao, "Minzhu de gushi" [Story of democracy], *Zhongguo Qingnian*, July 1988, pp. 6-8.

100. Tianjian Shi, "Role Culture of Deputies to the Seventh National People's Congress, 1988," Paper prepared for the annual meeting of the Association for Asian Studies, Washington, D.C., March 1989.

101. Ibid.

102. Heinz Eulau and Paul D. Karps, "The Puzzle of Representation: Specifying Components of Responsiveness," *Legislative Studies Quarterly* 2, no. 3 (August 1977): 233-54.

103. Lu Yun, "China Speeds Up Democratization," *Beijing Review*, 20 April 1987, p. 18.

104. Yang Xiaobing, "NPC: Its Position and Role," *Beijing Review*, 30 March 1987, p. 20.

105. *Renmin Ribao* (overseas edition), 26 October 1988, p. 4.

106. Barrett McCormick, "Leninist Implementation: The Election Campaign," in *Policy Implementation in Post-Mao China*, ed. David M. Lampton (Berkeley: University of California Press, 1987), pp. 383-413.

CHAPTER 7

COALITION AND CONFRONTATION

As noted in the introduction, Przeworski has suggested that the outcomes of the transition to democracy depend on the kind of coalition formed by reformers and hard-liners within the regime and moderates and radicals within the opposition, which may produce either repression, democracy, or liberalization without democracy. In following sections, I explore the evolution of events in Hungary and China in 1989 in the context of the interactions among conservatives and reformers in the Party leadership and moderates and radicals in the protest movement.

Compromise and Negotiation: The Case of Hungary

Although the HSWP initially insisted on preserving its leading role, it ultimately adopted a much more tolerant attitude toward opposition groups in Hungary. The year 1987 was the turning point. The inauguration of *glasnost* in the Soviet Union under the leadership of Mikhail Gorbachev removed the threat of Soviet military intervention. The more conservative members of the Hungarian leadership therefore lost powerful backing for their adherence to a Leninist system, and more liberal leaders gained greater leeway with which to pursue institutional changes. Without this brake from abroad, a process of radicalization in both the establishment and opposition could move forward. The balance of power started to tilt more and more toward liberal reformers within the leadership and toward radical factions within the opposition.

In 1987 the Hungarian leadership was composed of three major groups. Ironically, Kadar, the longtime patron of economic reform in Hungary, represented the conservative forces. His lengthy tenure in power had made him reluctant to pursue further changes in either the political or economic structures, and he had become a symbol of the immobility of the regime.

The prime minister, Karoly Grosz, was the leading figure among the moderate reformers. He was willing to pursue far-reaching economic reform but insisted upon upholding the Party's superior status in political life. He considered himself to be part of the center position between what he called "limitless democracy" and some sort of traditional state socialism. "I am not a reformist and I am not a fundamentalist," he claimed, "I am a communist. It follows from this that I am a realist."[1] He favored a limited degree of pluralism that kept a one-party system in which the HSWP would retain a leading role.[2]

The radical reformers headed by Imre Pozsgay and Rezso Nyers favored both radical economic reform and wide-ranging political reform. Pozsgay announced that the state socialist system as it existed in the Soviet Union and Eastern Europe was unreformable, and that only a shift in structure could solve the crisis of state socialism.[3] He also rejected the idea that the Communist Party should be guaranteed a leading role in a multiparty system, arguing that it should compete with other parties in an open political contest.[4] Nyers's position was relatively milder than Pozsgay's. He believed in the necessity of reform within the Party but did not think that the Party had to compete in free elections.[5] As a member of the Social Democratic Party before it merged with the Communist Party in 1948, Nyers increasingly emphasized his social democratic values and the social democratic tradition of the Party.[6]

The radical reformers sought to strengthen their position by looking outside the leadership circles and supporting societal initiatives for reform. For example, as mentioned earlier, Pozsgay attended the founding meeting of the Hungarian Democratic Forum, an independent political movement to promote democratization and economic reform later developed into the most important political opposition group. Pozsgay issued a strongly worded statement in support of these kinds of civic initiatives and associations. His speech was later considered the beginning of an informal alliance between reformers in the leadership and the moderate organized forces of political society.[7]

By May 1988 the moderate reformers led by Grosz and the radical reformers headed by Pozsgay and Nyers had formed a coalition of convenience. At a special Party conference, they removed Kadar from the Politburo and Secretariat, as well as from the leadership of the Party, creating for him instead the honorary but powerless post of Party president.[8] Grosz replaced him as the Party general secretary.

As the newly formed interest groups began to challenge the Party's authority, the post-Kadar Party leadership faced the daunting task of reconciling political pluralism with a one-party system. Although the Party conference of 1988 endorsed the development of "socialist pluralism" built around the Party's leading role, there was no consensus over how to implement such a concept. With the rapid changes in the political spectrum, Grosz, who had been a moderate reformer in the alliance to remove Kadar, appeared to represent a more conservative agenda in the post-Kadar leadership. He charged that behind the loud demands for democracy and reform were counterrevolutionary forces, whose true intention was to turn the pressure for change into an uncontrollable situation. He openly spoke of the necessity to confront these hostile forces.[9]

Representing the radical reformers, Pozsgay took a different stand. He proposed that independent political parties might have a place within an "institutionalized system of socialist pluralism."[10] In November 1988 Kalman Kulcsar, the justice minister, announced that the government would introduce a bill to legalize political parties other than the Communist Party.[11] The first step of the new program was to draft laws that would legalize independent political groups and public demonstrations. By providing legal channels for protest and opposition, the radical reformers within the Party hoped to minimize the disruptive effect of discontent among workers in the coming economic reform. "My idea," said a top Party official helping to direct the process, "is to make sure that political dissatisfaction does not get ahead of political development."[12]

In a further move to rally social support, Pozsgay declared in early 1989 that the 1956 incident was a "popular uprising," contradicting the official verdict of the event. This gained him tremendous popularity. Under pressure from both above and below, the Central Committee began to reconsider the events of 1956. On 29 March, following his return from visit to Moscow, Grosz reported that he and Soviet president Gorbachev had reviewed the history of the 1956 invasion of Hungary and that Gorbachev had spoken against foreign intervention in Warsaw Pact nations. On 6 June Imre Nagy, the former premier hanged in 1958 following the 1956 uprising, was reburied as a national hero.

As the reformist group within the Party leadership ascended, numerous reform circles among rank-and-file Party members emerged. A national congress of reform circles of the HSWP was held on 2-3 September, 1989. Taking part were 357 delegates representing 158 reform circles and Party cells.[13] The appearance of these organized reformist forces at all levels of the Party hierachy indicated the existence of progressive forces within the Party, and their organization provided favorable conditions for the enlargement of a political society.

With the support of reformers within the Party, groups of eminent intellectuals openly advanced various programs for political reform.

Frustration over economic stagnation drove intellectuals to seek a systemic political solution in the belief that only political democracy could lead to genuine market reform. The economists published "Reform and Change," the journalists published "The Reform of Public Forums," and the democratic opposition put forward a "Social Contract." These manifestos called for further economic reform, the right to assembly, freedom of the press, and parliamentarism.[14] Following the lead of the Hungarian Democratic Forum, all kinds of political clubs, circles, and associations mushroomed. Among them were independent trade unions, youth organizations, and parties that had been banned after 1949, such as the Independent Smallholders Party (ISP). Together, they formed a sizable political society demanding a voice in the country's political life.

Moreover, during this high tide of political pluralization, the official mass organizations, one by one, turned against the establishment, asserting more forcefully their independence from the Party. Some even became instrumental in the struggle against the Party. Official labor union leaders publicly declared that there was a conflict between Party and government policies and labor interests, calling for the restoration of "the classic function of labor unions, the defense and representation of the members' interests." The Union of Postal Workers insisted that their relationship with the government should be a "partnership of equals." The National Conference of Railroad Workers published a long list of grievances that ranged from declining incomes and unfair taxes to a government economic policy that allegedly considered the living standards of working people to be of only secondary importance.[15]

As the official representative of the labor movement, the NTUC was at first hostile toward the newly emerged nonofficial labor unions but later became resigned to their existence and finally offered to cooperate with them, aware that it was in danger of becoming irrelevant as its members began to go over to other organizations. The NTUC decided to join the nonofficial unions in a campaign against antistrike legislation the government had proposed. The NTUC indignantly reasserted the workers' right to strike, including the right to a solidarity strike. The voice of protest from the official labor unions was as loud as, if not louder than, that from the nonofficial organizations.[16]

Other auxiliary organizations of the Party defected as well. In December 1988 the Council of Agricultural Cooperatives called an urgent national conference to discuss ways to protect the cooperatives' interests, protesting the price scissors between agricultural and industrial products. When university teachers threatened to go on strike unless they received immediate salary increases, the Youth League at colleges and universities declared full support for the teachers' demands and announced their willingness to join the strike.[17]

In May 1989 the Party accelerated its shift toward liberalization. At a closed session of the Central Committee, Kadar was removed from his honorary post as Party president and expelled from the Central Committee. At the same meeting, the radical reformers put Grosz on the defensive by proposing both radical economic and political programs. The conference decided to restore a multiparty system.[18] By late June a four-member collective party presidency of Nyers, Grosz, Nemeth, and Pozsgay replaced the one-person leadership of Grosz. Thus, the reformers held a majority in the HSWP top leadership. The reformers obviously calculated that the Party, or at least their faction within in it, would retain a dominant role in this multiparty system. Had not the international atmosphere so quickly become charged with democratization during the latter half of the year, their assumption might have been correct.

Of the major opposition parties, the largest was the Hungarian Democratic Forum, formed primarily by "populist" intellectuals. It focused principally on the issues of national identity, social inequality, and the interests of the underprivileged.[19] It advocated a mixed economy and free elections in a multiparty system. It was relatively moderate compared with the Alliance of Young Democrats, a party dominated by college students and young professionals between sixteen and thirty-five, and the Alliance of Free Democrats, an urban-based party of political dissidents and intellectuals. These latter two parties favored Western-style democracy, a return to a European identity, and rapid economic change.

Despite the differences in their political agendas, nine major opposition groups formed the Opposition Roundtable in March 1989 and agreed on a relatively moderate platform to present during negotiations with the regime. The members of the roundtable demonstrated solidarity by refusing to enter into talks with the government separately. After extensive negotiations and compromises on both sides, the HSWP and the opposition groups reached an agreement to hold discussions on the political transition to a democratic system in Hungary. As part of this agreement, the HSWP managed to include the official mass organizations (the PPF, the trade unions, the National Council of Hungarian Women, and the Communist Youth League) as a third side in the negotiations. The agreement stipulated that the third side was expected to represent an unified opinion, just like the Opposition Roundtable.[20]

Fifty chief delegates and 500 experts representing the HSWP, the nine opposition organizations, and the six official mass organizations met in June 1989. The negotiations on political issues revolved around constitutional reform, legislation to govern parties and financial subsidies to the political parties, the electoral law, principles for the modification of the penal law, information policies, and guarantees of a nonviolent transition. The economic negotiations covered such topics as inflation, the debt burden, social policy, property reform, the land question and collective farms, state budgetary reform, and competition and antimonopoly legislation.

While the negotiations on political issues were both lively and fruitful, the economic discussions did not produce results. It seemed that politicians on all sides were more interested in designing a political framework than in solving economic problems. This may have reflected a belief common at the time that once political change had been achieved, economic development would necessarily follow. One notable aspect of the economic talks was that the HSWP and the Opposition Roundtable seemed to agree more with each other about economic reform than with the third side. The official mass organizations were willing to preserve the existing economic system, whereas even the HSWP was unable to accept such a line. The mass organizations thus had a keener sense of the impending social costs of radical economic reform.

On 18 September the negotiators reached an agreement on the gradual political transition to democracy. Two radical opposition parties, the Federation of Young Democrats and the Alliance of Free Democrats, refused to sign the agreement on the grounds that the Opposition Roundtable had made too many compromises on political principles. But despite this rift within the opposition movement, the informal alliance between the political opposition demanding democracy and the reform communists willing to pursue radical reform had successfully neutralized the previously omnipotent party apparatus and established a democratic system in Hungary.

At a special congress in Budapest in October 1989, the Hungarian Socialist Workers' Party voted to transform itself into the Hungarian Socialist Party (HSP) and adopted a new program renouncing Marxism in favor of European democratic socialism.[21] On 18 October the Hungarian National Assembly voted to delete references to the HSP's "leading role" in society, to allow the free formation and functioning of other political parties, and to rename the country, from the "People's Republic of Hungary" to the "Republic of Hungary."[22] The parliament also ordered the ruling party to start dismantling its cells in the workplace.

The first free election for the National Assembly was held in March 1990. The Hungarian Democratic Forum took nearly 43 percent of the vote, giving it about 165 of the 386 contested seats in the new parliament. The Alliance of Free Democrats finished second with 24 percent of the vote and 92 seats. The Socialist Party, the former HSWP, won just 8.3 percent and 33 seats. Its leaders said it would become a leftist opposition force in parliament.[23]

Confrontation: The Case of China

In the spring of 1989, despite widespread social grievances over inflation and corruption, the political environment in China was relatively relaxed compared with previous periods. After the Thirteenth Party Congress, reformers in the leadership had promised to speed up political reform and had established a central office to supervise the process. Although official tolerance of the opposition movement was limited, liberal and prodemocracy forces did control several institutes, newspapers, and journals. They had planned a big drive for political reforms that year to coincide with three anniversaries: the seventieth anniversary of the May Fourth Movement, which had advocated the principles of democracy and science, the bicentennial of the French Revolution, which had highlighted the concepts of human rights and freedom, and the fortieth anniversary of the People's Republic. And yet this open atmosphere did not lead to further political reform but instead to events that destroyed any chances for such reform in the following years.

On 15 April 1989, Hu Yaobang died of a heart attack while attending an enlarged Politburo meeting. As a liberal reformer who had been dismissed as the Party general secretary for sympathizing with the student demonstrations in 1987, Hu had won respect from the students. Seeing Hu's death as an opportunity to pay tribute to him and, more important, as a pretext for voicing their discontent with the slow pace of political reform, college students in Beijing started to gather in Tiananmen Square by the thousands. They demanded the renunciation of the 1987 campaign against bourgeois liberalization (during which Hu had been dismissed), freedom of the press and of demonstration, and an end to government corruption. Despite their persistent protests in Tiananmen Square and in front of the Central Committee headquarters, the students' demand to meet with government officials was ignored.

In late April Zhao Ziyang, the Party general secretary and a reformist leader, was on an official visit to North Korea. During his absence from the Politburo, the conservatives prevailed and decided to resort to the traditional mechanisms of control. In an effort to intimidate the students, on 26 April *Renmin Ribao* published a harsh editorial calling the student movement an instance of social turmoil. According to precedent, such an editorial signaled an official crackdown. But instead of being intimidated and withdrawing, the students launched a counterdemonstration, demanding a retraction of the editorial. Millions of Beijing citizens cheered the students as they passed in the streets. For the first time in the PRC's history, the people ignored a threat issued by the Party; the Party leadership discovered that it could not secure compliance as easily as it had in the past. The conservatives, however, believed that the editorial represented the bottom line because its retraction would have serious political consequences for the officials responsible for issuing it.[24] Thus, the strongly worded warning pushed both sides into a more rigid position.

In order to remedy the deteriorating situation, Zhao, back from Korea, proposed to "keep calm, exercise reason and restraint, maintain order, and seek a solution through democracy and law."[25] With his support, newspapers were allowed to report the ongoing events relatively freely for a short period in May. Indeed, journalists considered the first half of May the most liberal period in the history of the People's Republic. Zhao also suggested comprehensive consultation and dialogue to increase understanding between the government and society. For a few days in May, then, top leaders held talks with students and workers. Although these meetings were mainly intended to calm down the movement rather than to engage in sincere dialogue, they could have been the start of a process of compromise between the government and the people. In fact Zhao's approach pacified the demonstrators, and many students started to go back to their campuses.

Fearing a loss of momentum, Chai Ling, a student from Beijing Normal University, and some of her fellow student activists decided to adopt a radical strategy: a hunger strike and the occupation of Tiananmen Square during Gorbachev's visit to Beijing. This action was later endorsed by Capital Autonomous University Student Federation, an independent student organization that had emerged in late April. The objectives of the hunger strike were to ask for the retraction of the 26 April editorial and for equal and open dialogue with Party leaders. Although some moderate student leaders were skeptical about the idea at first, they were finally persuaded to join in. The hunger strike radicalized the protest movement and made the demonstration far more emotional. The sensational nature of the hunger strike was exemplified by Chai Ling's statement: "Between life and death, we want to see the face of the government. Between life and death, we want to see the expression of the people. Between life and death, we want to see if the nation still has a conscience or not."[26]

The hunger strike turned the Sino-Soviet summit, intended to be a victory for Chinese diplomacy, into an absolute disaster for China's leaders. As a fascinated world watched via satellite, the Chinese leadership seemed barely able to meet the schedule for its Soviet visitors. Because of the student occupation of the Tiananmen Square, major events had to be postponed or relocated. The welcoming ceremony could not be held in Tiananmen Square, and the participants in the meeting at the Great Hall of the People had to enter through back doors. At the same time, it seemed imprudent for the leaders to use force to clear the square during Gorbachev's visit.

The students' stand against government corruption attracted widespread sympathy from various sectors. Leaders of democratic parties, managers of state factories, Party members in government agencies, and staff members of government research institutes all called on the government to hold talks with the students. Crowds of citizens came to Tiananmen Square to show their solidarity with the students, and many of them openly identified their work units. Supporting the student movement became a way of expressing popular frustration over government policies. Even thieves declared that they would temporarily stop stealing in support of the students' demands.[27]

Faced with tremendous pressure for dialogue from all sectors of society, the Party reluctantly agreed to talk with the students and had the meeting broadcast on national television on 18 May. The meeting was characterized by paternalistic lectures by premier Li Peng and a confrontational posture by the student leaders, dramatized by Wuer Kaixi's impudent interruption of Li's remarks and later by Wuer's physical collapse, apparently due to weakness from his fast. Radical tendencies among the rank and file prevented the students' representatives from making any compromises in their dialogue with the government.[28]

Reformers among the leaders repeatedly appealed to the students for cooperation. Understanding the potentially disastrous result of confrontation, Yan Mingfu, head of the Party's United Front Department and a member of the Central Committee Secretariat, tried several times to persuade student representatives to withdraw from the square. On 13 May Yan went to Tiananmen Square and asked the students to stop the protest and give the reformist leadership some time. Otherwise, he warned, the outcome would be far more devastating than the students could ever imagine. On 16 May he returned to the square and conceded to certain minor demands, acknowledging that the student movement was patriotic and offering to initiate a genuine dialogue immediately. But he excluded the possibility of recognizing the legitimacy of the autonomous student organizations or repudiating the 26 April editorial. Believing that the Party reformers were just as corrupt as other leaders and fearful of being manipulated by the reformers to gain advantage in the power struggle within the leadership, the students rejected Yan's appeal. The confrontation had started down the path of no return.

On the morning of 19 May, seeing that the students could not be persuaded by rational argument, Zhao decided as a last resort to try a plea from the heart. In an emotional speech in the square, he told the students that they were still young and should not be preoccupied with the success or failure of a single event. What he meant to say, as he later recalled, was that the older generation would pass away, the future of China was in the hands of the younger generation, and there was no reason to waste lives and blood in unnecessary sacrifice.[29] Yet given the overwhelmingly radical mood in the square, his plea was simply too weak and too late.

Moderate elements in the protest movement similarly tried to avoid confrontation by urging students to withdraw from the square, but they, too, failed. Some student leaders, such as Wang Dan, Wuer Kaixi, and Wang Chaohua, were inclined to accept Yan's offer in order to avoid bloodshed. On 14 May several prominent scholars and writers, who were sympathetic to the students but feared that radical acts would only lead to harsh repression, also appealed for an end to the hunger strike, saying that democracy could not be created in the course of one day.

But the hunger strike had reached an emotional high tide. Students ignored the appeal from the moderate intellectuals and voted several times to continue the protest until the government backed down. At the time, it seemed that the whole capital city was behind the hunger strikers, creating a euphoric sense that the people's power displayed on the square was invincible. People simply refused to believe that the government would dare to use force. On 17 May twelve intellectuals signed a radical statement criticizing Deng Xiaoping as a decrepit dictator; emotions rose even higher. On 2 June a pop singer from Taiwan and three intellectuals staged another hunger strike on the square. Although they declared that they were seeking peaceful solutions to lead to a democratic system, the act only inflamed the movement.[30]

The emotional nature of the hunger strike made it impossible for the moderate student leaders not to ally themselves with the radicals. As Wuer Kaixi explained, the decision-making mechanism in the square did not involve majority rule but rather was "one in which 99.9 percent follow 0.1 percent—if a single hunger striker refuses to leave the square, then the other several thousand will not leave either."[31] Moderate student leaders were either voted out or else forced to stay with their radical colleagues. The alliance of moderates and radicals in the protest movement, by rejecting the conciliatory gestures of the reformers in the leadership, led to the confrontation between the two blocs that ended in bloodshed.

On 19 May, aware that martial law was about to be declared, the hunger strikers declared that they would end their protest. But the occupation of Tiananmen Square continued. The student organizations were plagued by internal dissention and unstable leadership. In addition to the Capital Autonomous University Student Federation, the Beijing Students' Dialogue Delegation, the Hunger Strike Group, and later, the Headquarters for Defending Tiananmen Square, as well as autonomous student unions from various universities and colleges, all contended for leadership of the movement.[32] The interaction among these groups became a process of competitive radicalization. Moderate leaders were replaced by more radical ones almost daily. On 23 May, when Wuer Kaixi announced that the students should withdraw, he immediately lost favor with his followers.[33] The withdrawal was postponed several times, with the latest date set for 20 June, because Tiananmen Square had become "a symbol of democracy in China, and we [protestors] couldn't abandon it."[34]

In addition to student groups, other organizations, such as the Capital Autonomous Workers' Union and the Autonomous Association of Intellectuals, were active in the square.[35] Without all these autonomous organizations, the movement could not have lasted as long as it did. But these organizations were merely the products, rather than the organizers, of events.[36] On the surface the movement appeared to be organized and controlled, such that violence and criminal activities rarely occurred. Beneath the surface, however, the lack of organization was reflected in the student leaders' inability to demobilize the demonstrations when it would have been desirable to do so. The highly moralistic and personal attacks on Party and state leaders fueled an emotional fever that was impossible to calm.[37] The inability to demobilize the mass movement in turn led to the final bloody confrontation with the hard-liners.

The exhausting occupation of Tiananmen Square and the extensive participation by all sectors of society outstripped any noncoercive mechanisms of control the Party could possibly marshal. The escalated confrontation obviously weakened the position of the reformers in the leadership and strengthened that of the conservatives, for it proved that a moderate solution was not going to work. The more intransigent the students became, the weaker the reformers' position became. Moreover, the protesters' rigidity pushed some reformers to stand together with the conservatives, because they did not want to see the collapse of their own regime either. For example, Wan Li, then chairman of the National People's Congress, who had long been considered a liberal reformer within the leadership, was on a visit to the United States when martial law was declared. People had hoped that he would stand behind Zhao after he came back in late May. Instead, he chose to support the regime.

Deng Xiaoping, father of China's economic reform, was the most influential figure in this political confrontation. He firmly supported market-oriented economic reform, but he was also determined to use all possible means to maintain political stability. During the events of 1989, he stood with the conservatives. Finally the Party decided to resort to force, the only effective means left to suppress the rebellion. On 19 May martial law was declared, and Zhao Ziyang was deprived of his power. After a number of failed attempts to uphold martial law without using force, the army opened fire on unarmed citizens in the evening of 3 June and morning of June 4, resulting in the deaths of several hundred people. After the shooting, the

government launched a campaign of terror, arresting thousands of participants in the demonstrations and executing dozens of so-called counter-
revolutionaries without due process.[38]

Comparison

Clearly, the kind of coalition formed between the protest movement and
the political establishment led to the contrast in outcomes in Hungary and
China. In Hungary liberalization of the Soviet politics after Gorbachev came
to power in 1985 significantly weakened the conservative forces in the
political leadership. Hungary, therefore, experienced rapid liberalization in
politics in the late 1980s. The radical and moderate reformers first formed
an alliance to oust the increasingly conservative Kadar. The radical
reformers then allied with the moderate forces in the opposition movement,
neutralized the new conservative forces in the political leadership, and
brought the country onto a democratic path. The opposition movement, for
its part, managed to maintain its own unity and was able to present a
relatively moderate program, aiming at negotiating an agreement with the
establishment rather than waging a revolution against it. This was a typical
case of an alliance between reformers in the regime and moderates in the
opposition, with reformers neutralizing the hard-liners and moderates
controlling the radicals.

China was quite a different story. The student demonstration demanding
rapid political reforms was in itself a radical form of protest, which
indicated that the radical tendencies had dominated the movement from the
beginning. The reformers among the leaders repeatedly reached out to the
protesters, trying to persuade the students to withdraw from the square so
that the situation could be kept in check. The emotional appeal of the hunger
strikes, however, forced the moderates in the opposition to maintain their
alliance with the radicals rather than cooperate with the reformers in the
leadership. The students' intransigence in the end not only provided
conservatives with a pretext to remove from the leadership some reformers
who opposed violent repression, but also forced other reformers to side with
the regime rather than with the students. When a relatively unified regime
became pitted against a radicalized opposition, it was the side with coercive
capabilities—the regime—that won.

The question, then, is why a coalition between reformers in the
leadership and moderates in the opposition formed in Hungary but not in
China. There are several reasons why this was so. The first concerns the
relative strength of conservatives and reformers in the two political
establishments. In both countries the reformers enjoyed considerable power

in the regime, based on the success of their reform policies. For a time, the reformist Party leaders in China, who were sympathetic to many of the students' demands, were able to paralyze the state's repressive capability. As many scholars have pointed out, one reason the student movement could generate such momentum and persist for so long was the inaction and division within the Party leadership.[39] Similarly, the predominance of reformers in the Hungarian leadership in 1989 led the regime to compromise and negotiate with the opposition and establish a democratic system.

But the conservatives in the two countries had significantly different levels of power. In essence, the conservatives in Hungary were much weaker than their counterparts in China. The power of the Hungarian conservatives rested primarily upon the backing of the Soviet Union. The rapid removal of the Soviet conservative constraints after 1985 drastically changed the balance of the political establishment in Hungary in favor of the reformers. In China, in contrast, the power of the conservatives was rooted deep in the Party and state bureaucracy. The revolutionary veterans, although retired from their political posts, were still alive and influential. The changes in the Soviet Union had no impact on the balance of power within China's political establishment. The tragic outcome of the Tiananmen incident demonstrated that conservatives were still able to prevail over the reformers in the Party.

That the most important source of conservative strength was more foreign rather than indigenous to Hungary was a considerable factor in the tactics of the reformers there. It was easy for the reformers in the Party leadership to point to the Soviet Union as an ultimate constraint on reform and to reach a consensus with the protest movement on the need to avoid any actions that might provoke a Soviet intervention. This initial tactical consensus later provided the basis for a broader coalition between reformers and moderates on the need for peaceful political reform.

In China, by comparison, the main conservative force was domestic. Its willingness to accept or reject reform was much more ambiguous than were the attitudes of the Soviet leadership. Therefore, it was hard to gauge the balance between reformers and conservatives, especially when personal relations among factions were much more complicated than those between Hungarian leaders and Soviet conservative forces. This ambiguity was confusing to the opposition. For example, participants of the protest movement at times had illusions that fundamental change was within reach, as when rumors circulated that the NPC was going to repeal martial law and that the army had refused to follow orders; at other times they believed that the communist regime was unchangeable and that any compromise would be tantamount to surrender. Neither perception encouraged the formation of a coalition between moderates in the opposition and reformers in the Party.

A second explanation concerns the degree of compatibility between the objectives of the establishment and those of the opposition. Although the reformers in the Chinese Party leadership were willing to pursue political reform, they were not prepared to accept the legitimacy of a political opposition and a multiparty system, as were their counterparts in Hungary. Conversely, the Chinese protest movement presented a much more radical challenge to the establishment, in form if not in content, than did the Hungarian opposition. The protestors' demands—the retraction of an editorial and a dialogue with the government—in fact were far less radical than the ones raised by the Hungarian opposition for a multiparty system. In Hungary, however, the demands were presented during behind-the-scenes negotiations; in China they were voiced through mass rallies, the physical occupation of public spaces, and large-scale hunger strikes. In other words, the radicalization of the Hungarian political spectrum was controlled and balanced on both sides, whereas in China the radicalization of the opposition movement became uncontrollable and was not matched by the strength or flexibility of the reformers within the leadership.

The differences in strategy and structure between the opposition movements provide a third explanation for the diverse outcomes in the two societies. The Hungarian opposition movement was obviously more organized. It did not take to the streets to press for political reform. Instead, it insisted on holding talks with the establishment inside government offices. The underdevelopment of China's political society meant that the opposition lacked a secure institutional base, without which the protest movement could not present itself as a serious contender at the negotiating table or a credible partner in future cooperation.[40] Chinese dissidents therefore resorted mainly to individual protests or temporary mass demonstrations. These spurts of movement were both hard to sustain and hard to control. The leaders found it difficult to persuade their followers to reach compromises with the government, to form a coalition with reformers within the Party, or to halt their protests when they had become counterproductive. The excitement of mass demonstrations also tended to generate radical and utopian ideas, rather than pragmatic strategies for gradual political reform, which further reduced the chances for compromise with the state. In these ways the Chinese protest movement became consistently more radical and less compromising than its Hungarian counterpart. And as long as the government prevents the opposition movement from developing any institutional base, the movement will remain but a movement.

The role of the official mass organizations during the political confrontation also differed between Hungary and China. In the late 1980s, the Hungarian mass organizations one by one declared their independence from the Party. During the protest movement, groups of Chinese demonstrators, including workers and citizens who crowded into the streets, were organized by their work units. Staff members from various factories and state agencies joined in the demonstrations with banners indicating their place of work. When the political balance between state and society shifted in society's favor, the roles of official organizations thus could become flexible. The desertion of the official mass organizations in both countries further isolated the hard-liners within the regimes and added to the pressure for political change.

However, there was a difference between the Chinese and Hungarian cases. The Hungarian organizations were more intent upon promoting their institutional interests, such as declaring independence from the government and protecting their members' rights. In contrast, during the protest movement in 1989, the official Chinese organizations were brave enough to take a different line from that of the government, but only in the form of offering their moral support for the students. In other words, the desertion of the official mass organizations in Hungary was an institutional desertion, whereas in China it was a moral one. In Hungary it created pressure on the regime to seek an institutional solution. In contrast, the prostudent positions taken by certain official institutions and mass organizations were event-specific, and could therefore easily be reversed.[41]

Finally, we have to take into consideration the different contexts within which the confrontation occurred. The alliance between reformers and moderates in Hungary was formed in normal times, with compromises made on both sides. In contrast, the outbreak of the protest movement on Tiananmen Square created a crisis situation. In a time of crisis, the reformers were in a particularly vulnerable position, because they had to convince the conservatives that the crisis was not the result of their reform policies and that it could be contained. Because of their weak position in the leadership, the reformers basically asked the students to retreat so as to end the crisis, rather than making sincere efforts to form an alliance with the students for further political reform. This provided the moderate student leaders with little incentive to ally with the reformers in the Party. The escalation of the crisis situation further polarized the sides, forcing various factions to make decisive choices. Most of them chose to stay with their own camps. This again made it hard to form a coalition.

In summary, the successful coalition between the reformers in the leadership and moderates in the opposition in Hungary was due to the reliance of the conservatives on foreign support that proved unreliable, the compatibility between the objectives of the reformers and the opposition, the relatively restrained strategies adopted by the opposition, and the ability of all the contending political forces to conduct pragmatic negotiations in an institutionalized setting. The emergence of this coalition led to a peaceful transition to democracy. Such a coalition never formed in China because of the relative strength of the indigenous conservative forces in the leadership, the incompatibility between the aims of the reformers and the opposition, the radical moral and emotional orientation of the protest movement, and the intransigence of the hard-liners and the radical opposition alike. The combination of these factors led to the tragic end of the 1989 protest movement.

NOTES

1. Foreign Broadcast Information Service, *Daily Report: Eastern Europe* (*FBIS-EEU*), 31 May 1989, p. 18.

2. *Radio Free Europe Report* (*RFER*) 14, no. 12, part 1 of 4, 23 March 1989, pp. 9-13.

3. *FBIS-EEU*-89-102, 30 May 1989, p. 30.

4. *FBIS-EEU*-88-240, 14 December 1988, p. 48.

5. *RFER* 14, no. 40, part 3 of 4, 6 October 1989, p. 5.

6. *FBIS-EEU*-88-247, 23 December 1988, pp. 12-13, and *FBIS-EEU*-89-134, 14 July 1989, p. 23.

7. Laszlo Bruszt, trans. by George K. Horvath, "1989: The Negotiated Revolution in Hungary," *Social Research* 57, no. 2 (Summer 1990): 365-87.

8. "Hungary: Change of Leadership," Foreign and Commonwealth Office, London, August 1988.

9. Sandor Agocs, "The Collapse of Communist Ideology in Hungary: November 1988 to February 1989," *East European Quarterly* 27, no. 2 (June 1993): 187-211.

10. Ibid.

11. *New York Times*, 11 November 1988, A16.

12. Ibid., 5 December 1988, A19.

13. "HSWP Reform Circles Call for a New, Radically Reformed Party To Be Set Up," *RFER* 14, no. 40, 6 October 1989.

14. Miklos Haraszti, "The Beginning of Civil Society: The Independent Peace Movement and the Danube Movement in Hungary," in *In Search of Civil Society: Independent Peace Movements in the Soviet Bloc*, ed. Vladimir Tismaneanu (New York: Routledge, 1990), pp. 71-73.

15. Agocs, "The Collapse of Communist Ideology in Hungary," pp. 196-200.

16. Ibid.

17. Ibid.

18. *New York Times*, 9 May 1989, A10.

19. Andras Bozoki, "Intellectuals and Democratization," *Hungarian Quarterly* 34, no. 132 (Winter 1993): 93-106.

20. Andras Bozoki, "Hungary's Road to Systemic Change: The Opposition Roundtable," *East European Politics and Society* 7, no. 2 (Spring 1993): 276-308.

21. *New York Times*, 8 October 1989, A1 and A12.

22. *Washington Post*, 19 October 1989, A35.

23. *Washington Post*, 9 April 1990, A1, A14.

24. Zhao Ziyang made this point in a conversation with the author in September 1993. He did not specify whose political reputations were at stake.

25. *Renmin Ribao* (overseas edition), 5 May 1989, p. 1.

26. Han Minzhu and Hua Sheng, eds., *Cries for Democracy: Writings and Speeches from the 1989 Chinese Democracy Movement* (Princeton, N. J.: Princeton University Press, 1990), p. 198.

27. Zhang Boli, "Cong jueshi dao fushi," [Hunger strike from beginning to the end], *Zhongguo Zhi Chun*, no. 127 (March-April 1994): 72-76; and no. 128 (May 1994): 45-48.

28. Reflecting on the developments of 1989, numerous participants in the demonstrations have subsequently suggested that in their later stages the student movements in China, especially the one in 1989, were beyond the control of the student leaders. For example, one student representative recalled that the thing that scared him most during the protests was not the government but the anger of his fellow students, who would have killed anyone they believed compromised democratic goals. *Zhongguo Zhi Chun*, no. 86 (July 1990): 6-10.

29. Personal conversation with Zhao, Beijing, September 1993.

30. Han Minzhu and Hua Sheng, *Cries for Democracy*, pp. 349-54.

31. Marsha L. Wagner, "The Strategies of the Student Democracy Movement in Beijing," in *Tiananmen: China's Struggle for Democracy, Its Prelude, Development, Aftermath, and Impact*, eds. Winston Yang and Marsha Wagner (Baltimore: University of Maryland Press, 1990).

32. For a detailed account of the organizations and their leaders, see Zhang Boli, pp. 45-48.

33. Ibid.

34. Wagner, "The Strategies of the Student Democracy Movement in Beijing," p. 72.

35. Andrew G. Walder, and Gong Xiaoxia, "Workers in the Tiananmen Protests: The Politics of the Beijing Workers' Autonomous Federation," *Australian Journal of Chinese Affairs*, no. 29 (January 1993): 1-29.

36. Andrew Walder, "The Political Sociology of the Beijing Upheaval of 1989," *Problems of Communism* 38 (September-October 1989): 30-40.

37. Dorothy Solinger, "Democracy with Chinese Characteristics," *World Policy Journal* 6, no. 4 (Fall 1989): 628.

38. There are numerous books about the events in 1989. See, for example, Michel Oksenberg, Lawrence Sullivan, and Marc Lambert, eds., *Beijing Spring, 1989: Confrontation and Conflict* (New York: M. E. Sharpe, 1990); Liu Binyan, with Ruan Ming and Xu Gang, trans. by Henry L. Epstein, *Tell the World: What Happened in China and Why* (New York: Random House, 1989); *Time* Magazine, *Massacre in Beijing: China's Struggle for Democracy* (New York: Time Books, 1989); Mok Chiu Yu and J. Frank Harrison, *Voices from Tiananmen Square: Beijing Spring and the Democracy Movement* (New York: Black Rose Books, 1990); George Hicks, ed., *The Broken Mirror: China After Tiananmen* (London: Longman, 1990); and Tony Saich, ed., *The Chinese People's Movement: Perspectives on Spring 1989* (New York: M. E. Sharpe, 1990).

39. Walder, "The Political Sociology of the Beijing Upheaval of 1989," pp. 30-40; and Andrew Nathan, "Chinese Democracy in 1989: Continuity and Change," *Problems of Communism* 38 (September/October 1989): 16-29.

40. In a conversation with the author in 1993, Zhao Ziyang commented that the 1989 student movement changed its leaders almost daily in the square, and most of the student leaders in 1989 were basically self-appointed and unable to command the crowd. This comment revealed that Zhao did not consider the students a potential party in a coalition or negotiation. However, since Zhao did not believe that the student movement was capable of overthrowing the government, he insisted, then and now, that the crisis should and could have been solved through peaceful means.

41. David Strand, "Protest in Beijing: Civil Society and Public Sphere in China," *Problems of Communism* 39 (May-June 1990): 1-19.

CHAPTER 8

DEVELOPMENTS IN HUNGARY AND CHINA AFTER 1989

Although they had previously followed similar trajectories, in 1989 China and Hungary embarked on two very different paths. The Chinese Communist Party survived the protests in Tiananmen Square. For a short period, conservatives gained the upper hand in the leadership. Out of fear of further popular uprising, the regime tightened its political control and retreated from political reform. Economic reform also came to a halt with strong recentralization pressures from the center. In Hungary the Hungarian Socialist Party, the renamed HSWP, lost the 1990 election and went into opposition. The new government, controlled by liberal reformers, then proceeded with marketization and privatization schemes at a much faster pace.

Nor did the story end in 1989-1990. The Communist Party remained in power in China and even began to regain popular support, despite predictions that it would collapse soon after the Tiananmen crisis. The Hungarian Socialist Party returned to power in the election of 1994, coinciding with the general revival of former communist parties elsewhere in Eastern Europe. In the economic sphere, China has shown greater dynamism, with a high growth rate and improving living standards. Hungary, in contrast, has experienced an economic downward spiral and plunged into recession.

The unanticipated vitality of the communists in both countries and the contrast between economic performances under different political systems again raise the basic question of the relationship between economics and politics. Clearly, rapid economic growth helped the Communist Party prolong its rule in China, and the economic contraction brought the former communists back to power in Hungary. The question remains, however, of whether an authoritarian regime is more capable of guiding economic transition than a democratizing state.

One explanation for the gap in economic performance is that the new democratic government in Hungary undertook a radical marketization reform program, while the communist regime in China continued its gradual and organic approach to economic reform. The difference between the reform strategies in the two countries lies not in their direction, which is essentially the same, but in the priority assigned to privatization, the attention paid to the social costs of reform, the speed with which bureaucratic coordination was replaced by market forces, and the extent to which the state continued to lead the economic transition.

In Hungary the new government put tremendous faith in the self-regulating mechanisms of markets and pursued a radical economic transition program, while neglecting both the social costs of these reforms and the role of the state in the economy. The Chinese government, in contrast, has been cautious about privatization and much more sensitive to social grievances, and has maintained a relatively effective role in nurturing the growth of markets and in promoting economic development.

Further questions remain. To what extent are reform strategies related to the type of political system? Does a democratizing regime tend to adopt radical reform strategies? Similarly, does an authoritarian government usually take more cautious measures in its economic transition? Is it true that an authoritarian system provides more effective government regulation of the economy than a democratic regime? Not enough time has passed since 1989 to draw any definite conclusions. However, a brief comparison of the post-1989 development in Hungary and China may help us gain more insight into the complex and uncertain transition from state socialism.

Governing Coalitions and Reform Strategies

The type of political system—authoritarian or democratic—does not in itself determine whether a society adopts a radical or gradual approach to reform. Rather, the adoption of one strategy or another reflects the basic orientation of the political elite in power and the overall political atmosphere. It is, therefore, a product of a particular governing coalition in a given political environment.

The Radical Reform Coalition in Hungary

When the HSWP signed the agreement with the Opposition Roundtable to establish a multiparty democracy in September 1989, it did not expect defeat in the coming election. But the swiftly rising tide of liberalization in Eastern Europe in the last months of 1989 generated an overwhelming anticommunist fever that doomed the reform communists in Hungary. The opposition parties won the 1990 general election by setting their pledge of radical yet relatively painless Westernization against the record of the ruling party. The story of the 1990 election, as Jason McDonald pointed out, was the story of how the promise of capitalism defeated the reality of Leninist socialism.[1] The reform communists, who had been on center stage in Hungary for more than two decades, were marginalized in the new political scene. The opposition parties now found themselves at the center of the political arena, committed to a rapid transition to democracy, markets, and a Western European identity.

After winning the election in 1990, the Hungarian Democratic Forum (HDF), which gained a plurality of seats in parliament (165 out of 386), forged a ruling coalition with the Independent Smallholders Party (ISP) and the Christian Democratic Party (CDP), which came in third (with 44 seats) and sixth (with 21 seats) respectively in the election. The ISP and the CDP were considered relatively conservative parties ("conservative" here means promarket and socially conservative), the ISP having populist and rural values and the CDP strong Christian values.[2] Like all the other postcommunist regimes in Eastern Europe, this government pledged to make a rapid and painless transition to markets and the West. The new government therefore initiated a radical reform program that envisioned a free market economy, based on private ownership, and fully integrated into Western Europe. A program of privatization was seriously pursued. Imports were dramatically liberalized, prices were freed, and budgetary subsidies were drastically slashed.[3] But in terms of economic performance, the record of Hungary's postcommunist democratic government during the transition to a market economy was unimpressive, to say the least. After 1989 Hungary plunged into an economic recession. Its GDP dropped by 18 percent between 1989 and 1993, and gross industrial output fell by 25 percent.[4] Agricultural production fell by 16.6 percent in 1991 and another 6.7 percent in 1992.[5]

The question arising from the post-1989 Hungarian experience is: To what extent is this troubled economic transition merely a coincidence, as opposed to the result of political democratization. Some scholars argue that the state socialist countries of Eastern Europe, Hungary included, were overindustrialized and excessively subsidized, which made the transition extremely difficult.[6] Others suggest that the collapse of the CMEA trading framework and the decline in demand from the former Soviet Union were the main causes of the recession.[7]

Yet most economists seem to agree that one further cause of economic difficulty was the disruption of the economic coordination mechanisms in the course of reform. The elimination of the old bureaucratic planning apparatus was not followed immediately by the creation of effective market mechanisms, which many economists now admit cannot be formed overnight. The absence of new means to govern economic behavior, the lack of a comprehensive legal system, and the shortage of economic information left many economic actors reluctant to make decisions.[8]

The rapid removal of bureaucratic coordination and the failure to understand that market mechanisms develop slowly was not purely a miscalculation of economic policy. It has its political origins. Excited by the triumph of the liberal political opposition over communism, Hungary, like the rest of Eastern Europe, suffered from a popular "politics in command" syndrome, which believed that democracy could create a painless transition to capitalism and Westernization. This overenthusiastic sentiment dramatically radicalized reform strategies. Because the toppling of the communist regimes had seemed so quick and easy, Hungarian elites believed that dispensing with the rest of the state socialism and building a liberal political and economic order would also be quick and easy.[9] There was enormous pressure to rush through the transition.

Long frustrated by the political and ideological restrictions on further economic reforms, liberal intellectuals were the principal proponents of this radicalization of economic policy after 1989. Western economic theories, which held that the predominance of private ownership and the restriction of the redistributory role of the state budget are necessary conditions for a market economy, gained popular support among economists and politicians alike. Few were aware of the political and social costs of the transition to markets.

To be sure, there were economists who warned that suddenly opening up the economy and massive privatization might produce disastrous consequences. However, these opinions could not be published at a time when the political stage was dominated by a unidirectional revolutionary swing away from socialism and the state.[10] The prevailing conception of the transition maintained that the state regulatory apparatus and state-owned enterprises should be liquidated and the domestic market opened to foreign competition. Private ownership and foreign competition would then force Hungarian companies to restructure and become more efficient. All in all, the overriding opinion was that by abolishing the remnants of the state regulatory mechanism, a free market could automatically be established within two to three years.[11]

In the subsequent debates over the relative superiority of contending reform strategies—especially gradualism versus shock therapy defenders of shock therapy have argued that Hungary has adopted a gradualist reform approach and fared no better than those who have proceeded more rapidly.[12] It is true that Hungary did not implement privatization and marketization as quickly or decisively as Poland or the Czech Republic. Still, after 1989, Hungary's preference for radical economic reform was no different than the others. Although implemented somewhat more slowly, the policy of complete marketization imposed high social and economic costs. For example, when price liberalization was coupled with liberalization of foreign trade, many enterprises had to cut or completely cease production.[13]

Moreover, Hungary also adopted a policy of radical privatization. It is true that the privatization program turned out to be a much slower and more difficult process than the postcommunist politicians had anticipated. By the end of 1993, only about $3-4 billion of the state's assets had been transferred into private hands in an economy where the total state assets were estimated at $80-120 billion. Most of the units sold were small businesses. Large state enterprises remained in the hands of state agencies and continued to lose money.[14] Much of the privatization turned out to be spurious, involving, for example, change of legal ownership without actual property transfer, the proliferation of cross-ownership between state-owned economic units and banks, and the subdivision of state enterprises into smaller units over which the state retained control. What has happened has been a property redistribution among members of the surviving old and emerging new elite.[15] Although privatization did not go very far, as an officially established principle of economic transition, it nonetheless created confusion over property rights and generated grievances over the perceived injustice in redistributing the property, which in turn led to a decline in productivity. Introducing uncertainties with regard to the future of enterprises—whether they would be privatized and how—also had a negative effect on investment and even led to disinvestment.

Attempts to privatize assets rapidly gave rise to numerous claims to public property from every direction and further obscured the property structure.[16] For example, the postcommunist government declared that its policy was to provide compensation for property the communists had seized or forcibly collectivized. The Smallholders Party, a partner to the HDF in the coalition government, advocated a radical redistribution of rural assets back to the "original" owners and their heirs. The sum total of land claims covered 31 percent of the cultivated land and 81.8 percent of the land owned communally by the co-ops. The farmers who had worked the land for the past forty years resisted returning the land to those who had owned it half a century before.[17] As the compensation laws were debated in the parliament during 1991 and 1992, farmers in the cooperatives were confused and bitter over the lingering uncertainties. The uncertainty no doubt contributed to the decline of agricultural production.

Another radical measure was the passage of a strict bankruptcy law in 1992, in an effort to harden the budget constraints and force out inefficient enterprises. However, the stringent rules it established set in motion a mass of bankruptcy filings that affected a large number of enterprises. According to official reports, 12 percent of the firms with more than 300 employees filed for bankruptcy, as did 11 percent of the firms with fewer than 300 employees. Many believed this was the single most important reason for the fall in GDP by 3-5 percent in 1992.[18]

This market utopianism, on one side, raised popular expectations to unrealistic heights and on the other led to radical reform policies that ignored the widespread popular dependence on a comprehensive state welfare program. After 1989 Hungary was plagued by high rates of inflation and unemployment. The inflation rate was 35 percent in 1991 and about 23 percent in 1993.[19] The level of unemployment rose from less than 0.5 percent in 1990 to 13 percent in 1993.[20] Out of a somewhat naive faith in the magic of the markets, the Hungarian government simply allowed inflation and unemployment to go unchecked. Declining living standards also contributed to recession by curbing demand.

In summary, the Hungarian government from 1990 to 1994 was controlled by a radical coalition that was operating in a triumphant political atmosphere generated by the democratic breakthrough. Although in many respects, reform proceeded more slowly in Hungary than in neighboring countries, it remained radical with regard to the extent of privatization and marketization and in its insensitivity to the social costs of such reforms.

The Moderate Developmental Coalition in China

The bloody repression of the 1989 protest movement and the subsequent international repercussions bolstered the somewhat reluctant alliance between reformers and conservatives in China. The reformers realized that further political reform would be very destabilizing, and they should focus on economic reform. After a short period of attempting to stall economic reform, the conservatives, too, reached the conclusion that economic reform must continue if they wanted to maintain stability while withholding political rights from the citizens. The key figure in preserving the coalition was Deng Xiaoping, who had ordered the repression of the Tiananmen movement, but who also insisted on turning China into a strong power through economic reform and opening.

Since 1989, this coalition has taken a developmental authoritarian approach to reform, focusing on further marketization and economic development on one hand and a tightening of political control on the other. In contrast to the hesitant and ambivalent policies of the past, the new approach wholly accepts the pursuit of a market economy. Democratization, previously tolerated and even encouraged as a topic of debate, is no longer part of public discourse. Yet the tightening political control is effective only in the sense of preventing organized protest. The regime is unable to control the beliefs and private behavior of the population.

Several distinctive features characterize this post-1989 leadership coalition. First, there now seems to be a general consensus on reform policies among the political elite, which is not deeply divided on any significant issues. No leadership faction, reformist or conservative, favors a return to central planning, the elimination of foreign or private ventures, or the revival of class struggle. The remaining disagreement is largely over the speed of reform rather than on the desirability of reform itself. While the conservatives have accepted the profound changes that economic reform has brought to China, the reformers have also moderated their economic reform strategies. After so many years of economic reform, people have developed a better understanding of its limits and costs. Economic reform has entered a stage in which the main issues no longer involve fundamental principles but the technical solutions to specific problems. Moreover, no leadership faction presently favors rapid or thoroughgoing political reform. Thus, it is now increasingly difficult to label any particular leader as either a reformer or a conservative, except for a few well-known elderly conservative ideologues who are outside the center of power. For example, Vice Premier Zhu Rongji, who is generally considered a reformer, has favored strong state regulation of the economy and a slower rate of economic growth—two policy preferences often associated with the conservatives.

Some observers suggest that there has emerged an assertive military faction in the Chinese leadership, as shown during the crisis in the Taiwan Strait in the spring of 1996. This faction may have produced a less conciliatory approach toward Taiwan and the United States, but it has not changed the basic orientation of domestic policy and is even a part of the current alliance that centers on development. Unless there is large-scale social unrest, the military is not likely to alter the developmental direction of the country.

Second, ideological disagreement is no longer the most important line of division among the leadership. With the new consensus on economic development, ideological opposition to market reform seems less and less relevant. The Fourteenth Party Congress in 1992 declared that China will introduce a "socialist market economy," a change from its previous program of a "planned commodity economy." This indicated the determination of the communist regime in China to move all the way toward a market economy. The Third Plenum of the Fourteenth Party Congress in late 1993 drafted a more detailed program for the development of such a socialist market economy. The plenum's decision shifted the focus of enterprise reform from simply expanding managerial autonomy to deeper issues related to property rights, asset management, corporatization, and corporate governance, and raised the possibility of partial privatization. Although there are divisions within the coalition over the extent to which the Party should emphasize ideological education, the disagreements basically have little effect on economic policies.

Third, related to the developmental orientation and the diminishing importance of ideology to political leaders, a broad generational change has occurred within the political elite. For the first time in its history, China is about to be governed by professional bureaucrats rather than by revolutionaries or political generalists. The emergence of this new generation provides technocratic support for the developmental coalition. As this generation lacks the personal ties that split the previous generation into different factions, the rise and fall of individual leaders or factions will not affect the principal directions of the country.

Finally, this leadership coalition is receiving broader societal support. The resurgence of China's economic reform program in 1992 led urban Chinese to enjoy an expansion of their economic (if not political) freedom and an increase in prosperity. This helped to restore the government's legitimacy that had been so undermined by the Tiananmen crisis. Economic difficulties and political turbulence in Russia and other former communist countries following the collapse of the Soviet Union further persuaded many Chinese that a more gradual approach to political and economic reform was appropriate. Indeed, it led many thoughtful Chinese to question whether the antigovernment demonstrations of 1989, although clearly well intentioned, had been the most appropriate way of promoting gradual reform. Moreover, not only does the general population seem to share the developmental objectives pursued by the leadership, but the moderates in the opposition movement have also shown increasing support for the government.[21] According to Przeworski's model of the impact of political coalitions on policy outcomes, if the moderates within the opposition join an alliance with reformers and hard-liners in the leadership, the result will be liberalization without democratization.[22] This scenario has increasingly become the reality in China and will reduce the likelihood of rapid political reform.

The reform coalition has recognized the importance of developing market institutions. Since the revival of economic reform in 1992, it has abolished most of the remnants of central planning, relaxed remaining price controls, and granted foreign investors significant access to the Chinese domestic market. It has also undertaken tax reform and unified exchange rates. At the same time, the reform has encouraged the growth of the nonstate sector, with its various forms of ownership.[23] This sector accounted for more than 52 percent of China's industrial output and more than 57 percent of nonagricultural employment in 1993.[24] However, as Barry Naughton has pointed out, since 1993 the Chinese leaders have been preoccupied with controlling the negative side effects of reform. They have brought down the inflation rate from 17 percent in 1993 to below 10 percent in 1996.[25] The Chinese leaders have also been particularly sensitive to unemployment. By postponing the reform of large state enterprises, they have kept the unemployment rate to around 5.5 percent.

Following this developmental authoritarian approach, China has achieved astonishing economic growth. In sharp contrast to the recessions in other postcommunist economies, China experienced an average growth rate of more than 10 percent from 1992 to 1995. Consumer goods are in abundance. Popular consumption patterns have gradually shifted from the satisfaction of basic needs to the acquisition of consumer goods and the enjoyment of popular entertainment.

The reform coalition that emerged after the trauma of the Tiananmen incident has been very cautious. The ruling elites understood that they needed to restore their authority by raising the living standards of the people. At the same time, they had to ensure that the social costs of the reform were kept to minimum, so as to avoid triggering another round of large-scale social unrest. And they have been relatively successful.

The Role of the State in Transition

Traditional state socialism featured an omnipresent state controlling the economy. The transition away from this model implies that the state must reduce its role in managing the economy and instead let market mechanisms coordinate economic activities. But market institutions and a legal framework do not spring up spontaneously. The state needs to plan its withdrawal from the economy and, indeed, may even need to limit its withdrawal.

Efficient market institutions take time to grow. They need the state to plant the seeds, as well as to provide a favorable environment for them to take root. During the economic transition, the state must introduce laws and assure their enforcement, adopt rational fiscal and monetary policies, and establish supervision over the financial sector and natural monopolies. The state should initiate and actively assist the development of the new institutions required by a market economy, such as a network of development banks, investment funds, and other financial intermediaries. The state should also help to reduce the uncertainty surrounding the transition. It may form a kind of risk-sharing partnership with private investors by providing guarantees to the financial institutions that extend credit to these investors, and it may give tax concessions or other subsidies to the private investor.[26] Most important, the government should be responsible for providing a safety net to minimize the social costs of the transition.

The Impotent State in Hungary

From the record of its economic performance, it is clear that the state did not do an effective job in Hungary. The problems in the agricultural sector, discussed in the previous section, reflect the state's inability to clarify property relations. Another example occurred in the construction industry. According to Janos Kornai, the construction industry was trapped in limbo. The property market was not operating: There was no mortgage or credit system, the network of real estate agencies was rudimentary, and there was widespread confusion about the structure of rents. At the same time, there was no effective urban planning or social policy.[27] As a result, construction has been chronically sluggish.[28]

The state's failure to provide effective economic guidance has been described as the phenomenon of "state desertion." This has resulted in enterprises being set adrift in uncharted seas with a real possibility of many disappearing into an "economic black hole."[29] There are several factors that may have contributed to the state's substandard performance. First, some scholars suggest that the ruling coalition in 1990 also contained populist elements and suspicion of Western capitalism. As a result, although the regime in general favored a promarket reform, the economic transition in Hungary lacked a comprehensive strategy, and the government lacked a strong political will to implement its policies.[30] The second factor was the new faith in the invisible hand of the market. The disgust with the all-embracing power of the state under the communist regime led to a general mistrust of state power and a naive confidence in the ability of the market to regulate the economy. The third factor was the confusion over the roles and rules of state bureaucracies as the result of the rapid democratization of the political system. The popular demand to purge the old communist elite, though not actively pursued by the Hungarian government, demoralized many experts in the bureaucracy. They either took a wait-and-see attitude or grabbed whatever they could before leaving government service. As a result, political institutions have lost the authority, capability, and motivation to guide the development of a normal market system.

Furthermore, policymakers underestimated the people's dependence on the state welfare system that was among the first to be cut in the course of the market reform. Although people preferred political freedom, they also retained a strong commitment to economic egalitarianism. In a 1992 survey, more than 70 percent of the Hungarians supported a guaranteed income and jobs, government policies to reduce income differences, and extensive social benefits.[31] Many people didn't like the old political system but enjoyed their social programs, full employment, and more equal distribution of income. These socialist values had a deeper hold in the population than the reformers had anticipated. When the state failed to provide satisfactory welfare programs, social grievances increased.

In short, the state did not perform well in the economic transition in Hungary. Without an effective leadership and with both the old and new elites more interested in grabbing resources through privatization schemes than in using them for the economic development of the country, the Hungarian economy was unable to grow.

Developmental State in China

The relative success of Chinese economic reform since the early 1990s has come about because the leadership has not dismantled the state's ability to regulate the economy, as the Hungarian reformers have done, but rather has created incentives for government at all levels to promote economic development. These incentives include both financial and political measures —allowing local governments to retain revenues generated by economic development and by setting economic performance as the principal criterion for promotion or even retention in office. As a result, the existing political institutions have used their resources to promote development.[32] Typical examples include the local governments' rush to create development zones in their jurisdictions to attract foreign investment and their establishment of government-owned township and village enterprises to promote local industrialization.

This new orientation toward development has started to change both the function of the Party and the composition of the elite, especially at the lowest levels. Some grass-roots Party and government officials have become the new bosses of business corporations; conversely, some successful private entrepreneurs have been incorporated into ranks of the political elite. The new economic elites who prefer to stay outside of government are being regularly consulted by local cadres on major community issues. The rich and the powerful are now either identical or are becoming intertwined. Together, they supervise community affairs through formal (Party and government) and informal (clan and religious) organizations.

The more vigorous promotion of the system of "villagers' self-governance" since the early 1990s has brought about competitive elections at the village level. Although it is still a primitive form of democracy and under close Party supervision, according to statistics from the Ministry of Civil Affairs, about 20 percent of incumbent village leaders have been voted out of office in these elections nationwide.[33] Looking ahead, these village elections may gradually become even more competitive and institutionalized should the Party conclude that they provide an effective mechanism for ensuring the responsiveness and accountability of rural elites.

Economic development may cause social tensions if local governments impose heavy tax burdens on the peasants to finance the take-off. A typical case was the previously mentioned peasant riot in Renshou County, Sichuan Province, in 1993—a reaction to the attempt by county leaders to collect extra taxes to build a highway to create a more favorable investment climate. However, where the level of development has reached a higher stage, local government no longer needs to collect extra levies, but can provide more generous welfare measures for its population, thus ensuring social stability.

Because of the consensus on development, the population now has a greater tolerance for official corruption, as long as it is not rampant and can bring local development. Conversely, people are less tolerant of corruption where there is little economic progress, where it benefits individual officials rather than the community as a whole.

In short, a developmental elite will continue to dominate China for the immediate future, determining the politics of the nation in post-Deng era. Top leaders (including military leaders) will maintain their consensus on the primacy of development, forming coalitions on specific developmental strategies and programs. Mid- and lower-level officials will be promoted or dismissed according to their records in promoting development. Social tensions (frustration over official corruption, income inequality, and unfair levies) will be generated and in turn alleviated by different stages of development.

Unfinished Transition

Economic distress in Hungary claimed its victim in the May 1994 elections. Four years after being voted out of office, the former reform communist party, the Hungarian Socialist Party, staged a comeback, winning 209 seats in the 386-seat parliament. The Alliance of Free Democrats came in second, with 70 seats. The incumbent Democratic Forum won only 37 seats.[34] This was a complete reversal of the outcome of the 1990 elections. Still, it was a rather mild reaction to Hungary's economic difficulties, especially when compared with the "Weimarization" scenario some scholars predicted, referring to the Weimar period in Germany in the 1930s when Hitler rose to power through democratic elections during a serious economic recession.[35]

Yet the victory of the former reformist communist party did not mean a reversal of the transition. After all, it was they who started the reform process in Hungary. But their return tells a great deal about the dilemmas and uncertainties of the transition period. People voted for the HSP out of serious discontent over the costs of rapid economic reform. The return of the communists indicated that although there is no longer belief in socialism, there is still nostalgia for the past. The swing back to the former communist party revealed a profound dissatisfaction with the pain and chaos produced by the radical transition to capitalism and a yearning for the secure and stable environment that the HSP had promised.

The Hungarian experience has shown that the initial democratic breakthrough generated two trends that proved counterproductive to a smooth and successful transition from state socialism. One was a wave of euphoria that radicalized the country's economic reform strategy. This led to a neglect of the role of the state in guiding the transition and to an indifference to the persistent dependency on the old social welfare policies of state socialism. The other trend was the dismantling of the state bureaucracy's economic regulatory mechanisms and confusion among bureaucrats as to their new role.

In the past several years, many Hungarian elites have abandoned their somewhat doctrinaire belief in neoclassical Western economic theories.[36] They have concluded that the best remedy for economic recession is to use the state to promote growth and ensure a less painful transition from socialism.[37] Some early evidence suggests that the democratic system in Hungary is able to do this: the economy showed signs of recovery in 1994 and 1995. But the extent to which Hungary's new socialist government can accomplish these objectives over the long term remains to be seen. The potential problem is that if this change of parties within the democratic framework fails to produce a less chaotic transition, the voters may come to prefer a more authoritarian solution.

Rapid economic development in China begins to reshape the social structure. The most obvious change in Chinese society since the Tiananmen incident has been the huge business boom. Money has become the central theme in daily life, and it now seems outmoded and pretentious not to pursue it. The boom has created an affluent middle class, made up of private entrepreneurs, stockholders, the managerial staff of companies in the nonstate sectors, stars of popular entertainment, and corrupt government officials. Whether this ever-growing middle class will demand further political reform remains uncertain. At this point it seems to favor political stability over democracy.

It is more likely that the growth of the middle class will promote the further development of a civil society. The organizations of civil society will continue for some time to perform a dual function, simultaneously semi-official and semisocietal. They may therefore resemble the traditional gentry class in China or the corporatist institutions of the West rather than organizations fully independent from the state. As such, their relationship with the state will be symbiotic rather than antagonistic.

In contrast to the affluent middle class, the intellectuals who were pioneers in promoting democracy in the 1980s have been marginalized by the new economic orientation of society. Their demands for democracy have less appeal to a society that is preoccupied with the search for wealth and leisure. They may even find themselves short on the means of survival if they rely merely on their meager state salaries. Many university professors and professional writers have therefore become involved in business activities. For example, there are about 500 companies organized by university professors in Shanghai, and about 1,500 professors in Tianjin have started their own businesses.[38] Academic research and even political discourse have far less allure than money.

While the role of intellectuals in promoting democracy has dramatically declined, some have found a new role in promoting an ideology that is presently far more popular: Nationalism. Communism no longer has a hold on the general population, and the appeal of democracy has waned markedly since the early 1990s. Yet a wave of nationalism has swept over China in the past several years, associated with pride in the country's growing economic strength as well as a reaction to Western criticism of China's human rights record, which appears to many Chinese to be an ill-intentioned and uninformed attack. This nationalism has provided much-needed support for the Communist Party, insofar as it acts as the guardian of China's national interests against foreign pressure.

At the same time, China is facing some serious challenges. The absence of accepted norms to govern the new market economy has resulted in the creation of a corrupt market system—an anomic framework in which market transactions are undertaken through irregular or unsanctioned means, such as the abuse of official positions, manipulation of personal connections, bribery, or use of violence by criminal organizations. In addition, some enterprises and households have exploited land, production facilities, and capital to an extreme extent, regardless of the impact on future production. This pattern of behavior, which Chinese economists describe as "exploitative management," results from the unclear definition of property rights and a lack of confidence that the reform policies will be sustained.

According to statistics from the Chinese Bureau of Industry and Commerce, the rate of major economic crime (defined as involving 50,000 yuan or more) in 1993 almost doubled compared to 1992. Other than smuggling, most of the cases involved trading in counterfeit products.[39] The lack of respect for property extends to intellectual as well as physical property. The old system involved no concept of patents, copyrights, or trademarks. Any intellectual innovation or discovery was supposed to be shared with others for free. As a result, there have been many instances of falsely labeled products and piracy of intellectual property during the reform period. It has been estimated that China cost the United States $827 million in potential American exports, as a result of the piracy of books, CDs, and computer programs.[40] The violation of patents and copyrights has caused repeated protests from abroad and threats from the United States to impose trade sanctions.

Despite the leadership's caution in pursuing further reform, some sectors of society have still suffered heavy blows. Especially in Northeast China, a stronghold of the state-owned economy, there have been numerous reports of labor unrest, as workers protest the closure of enterprises, demand managerial rights, and seek continued welfare benefits.[41] Farmers have been angered by the unfair taxes collected by local authorities, and confrontations have been spreading in the countryside. In 1993 about 850 unsanctioned demonstrations, over 6,000 strikes (including slowdowns), and 200 violent riots rocked China.[42]

But scattered pockets of social unrest are not likely to develop into a resurgence of the movement to promote political development in post-Deng China. The dissident movement lost its popular base after 1989. An all-out economic reform drive since 1989 has pacified most of the population and reoriented their political energy toward material and business concerns. To most Chinese, democracy seems to be an improbable solution to socioeconomic problems.

Comparison

What does this brief review of the experiences in Hungary and China after 1989 tell us about the transition from state socialism? First, the events of 1989 set different baselines for each of the two countries. The brutal suppression of the protest movement in China served to prolong the coalition between the reformers and conservatives within the Chinese leadership, which ensured a much more balanced reform strategy. In Hungary, in contrast, the victory of the opposition party radicalized economic policy. The overzealous reformers took a great leap forward to a free market system, which did much damage to Hungary's economy.

Second, reform strategies do make a difference. The experiences of Hungary and China suggest that systemic changes should be gradual and evolutionary, and require that the state play a strong and effective role. After 1989 the Hungarian reformers tried to implement radical marketization and privatization, while simultaneously dismantling the central authority of the state. This double shock proved costly. After several years of severe economic recession, the Hungarian voters chose a party that promised a more balanced approach to transition. In this regard, China's approach, which has often been criticized as half-hearted and incomplete, seems to be wiser, although the Chinese leadership chose it not necessarily out of wisdom, but out of political necessity. The Chinese strategy, in essence, is to nurture and redirect the economy to overcome its weakness through an ongoing adjustment process. Economist Barry Naughton has vividly described this method as "growing out of the plan."[43]

Third, a powerful state and institutional stability are essential for a successful economic transition. Yet this is not a choice between democracy and authoritarianism. The problem with Hungary and other postcommunist regimes after 1989 is not that they established a democratic polity but that they were carried away by this breakthrough and adopted excessively radical economic and political reforms. They were too eager to disable the existing state mechanism and failed to replace it with new economic regulatory mechanisms. The result was, in effect, an incompetent state and thus economic recession.

In contrast, the Chinese leadership has a near-obsession with maintaining stability and preserving its own control. But this obsession has provided institutional continuity and effective leadership during the economic transition. Although the central government in China has lost some of its power over local authorities and although policy implementation and law enforcement are imperfect, in general central control remains in place. At the same time, local governments are using their greater autonomy to promote economic development. Thus, compared to Hungary, the Chinese state has become a champion of economic development rather than an obstacle to it.

China has so far established the best record of economic development among all the former communist countries. But the transition is far from complete. The long-term relationship between political and economic transition will continue to unfold. After some initial confusion, it may be possible for a newly democratic government to take a more practical and effective approach to economic transition. By the same token, although an authoritarian system may promote a relatively smooth and successful economic transition in the early years, it may ultimately be undone by its failure to undertake the political reform that its economic success requires.

NOTES

1. Jason McDonald, "Transition to Utopia: A Reinterpretation of Economics, Ideas, and Politics in Hungary, 1984-1990," *East European Politics and Societies* 7, no. 2 (Spring 1993): 203-39.

2. Patrick H. O'Neil, "Hungary's Hesitant Transition," *Current History* 95 (March 1996): 135-39; and Geoffrey Evans and Stephen Whitefield, "Social and Ideological Cleavage Formation in Post-Communist Hungary," *Europe-Asia Studies* 47, no. 7 (1995): 1177-1204.

3. Gabor Bakos, "Hungarian Transition After Three Years," *Europe-Asia Studies* 46, no. 7 (1994): 1189-1214; and World Bank, *Hungary: Structural Reforms for Sustainable Growth* (Washington, D. C. : World Bank, 1995).

4. World Bank, ibid.

5. OECD, *OECD Economic Surveys, Hungary 1995* (Paris: OECD, 1996), p. 6; and Peter Agocs and Sandor Agocs, "'The Change Was but an Unfulfilled Promise': Agriculture and the Rural Population in Post-Communist Hungary," *East European Politics and Societies* 8, no. 1 (Winter 1994): 32-57.

6. Jeffery Sachs and Wing Thye Woo, "Structural Factors in the Economic Reforms of China, Eastern Europe, and the Former Soviet Union," *Economic Policy* 18, no. 1 (1994): 102-45.

7. David M. Newbery, "Transformation in Mature Versus Emerging Economies: Why Has Hungary Been Less Successful Than China?" *China Economic Review* 4, no. 2 (1993): 107.

8. Janos Kornai, "Transformational Recession: The Main Causes," *Journal of Comparative Economics* 19 (1994): 39-63.

9. Valerie Bunce and Maria Csanadi, "Uncertainty in the Transition: Post-Communism in Hungary," *East European Politics and Societies* 7, no. 2 (Spring 1993): 240-75.

10. Bakos, "Hungarian Transition After Three Years," p. 1190.

11. Ibid.

12. Sachs and Woo, "Structural Factors in the Economic Reforms of China, Eastern Europe, and the Former Soviet Union," pp. 119-121.

13. Kornai, "Transformational Recession," pp. 44-45.

14. "The Hungarian State Sector's Dismal Performance," *RFE/RL Research Report* 3, no. 15, 15 April 1994, pp. 22-26.

15. Yudit Kiss, "Privatization Paradoxes in East Central Europe," *East European Politics and Societies* 8, no.1 (Winter 1994): 22-52; Peter Mihalyi, "Plunder—Squander —Plunder: The Strange Demise of State Ownership," *Hungarian Quarterly* 34, no. 130 (Summer 1993): 62-75; and Eva Voszka, "Spontaneous Privatization in Hungary," in *Transition to a Market Economy*, eds. John Earle, Roman Flydwarz, and Andrzej Rapaczyuski (New York: St. Martins Press, 1993), pp. 89-107.

16. Kazimeirz Poznanski, "Restructuring of Property Rights in Poland: A Study in Evolutionary Economics," *East European Politics and Societies* 7, no. 3 (Fall 1993): 395-421.

17. Agocs and Agocs, "'The Change Was but an Unfulfilled Promise,'" p. 43.

18. Jan Adam, "The Transition to a Market Economy in Hungary," *Europe-Asia Studies* 47, no. 6 (1995): 989-1006.

19. "Hungary Makes Slow but Steady Progress," *RFE/RL Research Report* 1, no. 1, 3 January 1992, p. 89; and "Hungary: Political Fragmentation and Economic Recession," *RFE/RL Research Report* 3, no. 1, 7 January 1994, pp. 76-80.

20. World Bank, *Hungary*; MTI (Budapest), 26 March 1991, in *Foreign Broadcast Information Service, Daily Report: Eastern Europe (FBIS-EEU)*-91-060, 28 March 1991, p. 27.

21. The ongoing debates in *Zhongguo Zhi Chun* and *Beijing Zhi Chun*, periodicals published by overseas prodemocracy groups, have revealed that some active participants of the 1989 protest movement have become increasingly critical of the objectives, strategies, and consequences of the movement. These people also tend to take a more cooperative stand in dealing with the Chinese government.

22. Adam Przeworski, *Democracy and the Market: Political and Economic Reforms in Eastern Europe and Latin America* (New York: Cambridge University Press, 1991), pp. 66-79.

23. This category includes three types of enterprises: collectives, which are affiliated with a district or town government or a neighborhood or village; individual businesses that hire fewer than seven people; and other types of ownership, including private business (with more than seven employees), foreign ventures, and joint-stock companies.

24. Peter Harrold and Rajiv Lall, "China: Reform and Development in 1992-93," World Bank Discussion Papers, China and Mongolia Department, no. 215.

25. Barry Naughton, "The Dangers of Economic Complacency," *Current History* 95 (September 1996): 260-65.

26. Kornai, "Transformational Recession," pp. 60-62.

27. Ibid.

28. OECD, *OECD Economic Surveys, Hungary 1995*.

29. Istvan Abel and John Bonin, "State Desertion and Convertibility: The Case of Hungary," in *Hungary: An Economy in Transition*, eds. Istvan P. Szekely and David M. Newbery (New York: Cambridge University Press, 1993), pp. 329-41.

30. O'Neil, "Hungary's Hesitant Transition," pp. 135-39.

31. Barnabas Racz, "The Socialist-Left Opposition in Post-communist Hungary," *Europe-Asia Studies* 45, no. 4 (1993): 647-70.

32. Andrew Walder, "China's Transitional Economy: Interpreting Its Significance," *China Quarterly*, no. 144 (1995): 963-79.

33. Personal interview with the officials from the Ministry of Civil Affairs, Beijing, October 1995.

34. *New York Times*, May 30, 1994, A3.

35. Kornai, "Transformational Recession," p. 60.

36. Ibid.

37. Ibid.

38. Wang Zhaojun, "Rongjie: zhongguo shehui de fei zhezhihua" [Melting: the depoliticization of Chinese society], *Zhongguo Zhi Chun*, no. 127 (March-April 1994): 59-62.

39. *Shijie Ribao* (World Journal), 5 March 1994, A13.

40. Gregory Stanko and Nisha Mody, "Chinese Pirates Sail the Potomac," *New York Times*, 5 May 1994, A21.

41. *Zheng Ming*, April 1994, pp. 30-31.

42. Ibid., p. 21.

43. Barry Naughton, *Growing Out of the Plan* (New York: Cambridge University Press, 1995).

CHAPTER 9

CONCLUSION

At the onset of this book, I raised questions about the mechanisms inherent in a state socialist system that promote or hinder its transformation, the factors that determine the courses and outcomes of transitions from state socialism, and more broadly, the relationship between economics and politics in such transitions. Now it is time to summarize some answers based on this comparative study of reform in Hungary and China.

The transition from a centrally planned economy to a market-oriented one is a complicated process that both consumes and generates political energies. It is a project that no country or party has yet fully mastered. Reflecting the close interlacing of the economic and political systems in state socialist countries, the processes of economic reform and political liberalization are intricately intertwined. The reform experiences of Hungary and China suggest several observations about the mechanisms of transition and the relationship between economic reform and political change.

Political Mechanisms

Political Leadership: Reformers versus Conservatives

The central factors that determine the beginning, course, and outcomes of transition lie within the leadership. The initial conditions within the two countries were different: The political and economic systems in Hungary were more institutionalized, bureaucratized, centralized, and largely dominated by the Soviet Union, whereas in China, these systems were more mobilizational, highly indoctrinated, less institutionalized, and more isolated from the outside world. Nevertheless, we have observed the existence of a relatively cohesive reform elite involved in launching and promoting reform programs in both societies.

The leadership of a reforming state socialist regime is not a monolith but contains different groups with a wide spectrum of political values and policy orientations. The driving force behind the reform programs in both China and Hungary was a reform coalition within the leadership that enjoyed the backing of powerful individual leaders. The figures who played the decisive roles in implementing reform were Janos Kadar in Hungary and Deng Xiaoping in China, both pragmatic leaders with political insight. Kadar did not design or initiate the reform program, but he acted as a political lightning rod and protector for the reformist group within the Party. Deng was the principal decisionmaker for the reform in China and the master coordinator of the reform coalition within the leadership.

Economic reform and political liberalization in Hungary and China were initiated in response to the deterioration of regime legitimacy and economic performance. Traumatic national crises in 1956 in Hungary and between 1966 and 1976 in China presented the reformist groups within both leaderships with the motivation to conduct comprehensive reforms. The reformers mobilized support inside and outside the leadership and neutralized more conservative rivals. In each case the emergence of the reformist leadership increased the flexibility of the political establishment, enabling it to undertake the transformation of the political and economic systems.

A reformist leadership was critical not only in launching the reform but also in continuing to adapt it further. Without the backing of Kadar and without the promotion of key reform leaders like Nyers and Pozsgay, institutional reform would probably not have gone far in Hungary. And without Deng's patronage and Hu Yaobang's and Zhao Ziyang's deliberate encouragement, political change in China would not have been as broad and profound.

While the reform coalition was the engine of reform, conservatives served as the brakes. Since reform was undertaken within the context of state socialism, there was strong opposition from conservative forces, the guardians of orthodoxy. Throughout the course of reform, although the reform coalition managed to push its policies forward, conservatives maintained a strong presence in both countries and at times were able to stall reform temporarily. The conservative presence was reflected not only in the formation of conservative factions within the political establishment but also in the actions of the same powerful leaders who promoted reform in the first place. Their conservative orientation also set the range and speed of reform. Whenever there was a political need to yield to conservative pressure, Kadar did not hesitate to abandon such major reformers as Rezso Nyers, Jeno Fock, and Matyas Timar in the early 1970s, just as Deng dismissed his reformist aides Hu Yaobang in 1987 and Zhao Ziyang in 1989.

The structures of the political establishments in Hungary and China presented different frameworks within which reformers and conservatives maintained their power balance. In Hungary the Soviet Union played a major role as the conservative guardian of socialism. Even so, the distance of the Soviet conservatives from Budapest made it easier for the Hungarian reformers to undertake a considerable degree of economic and political liberalization. By the late 1980s, the rise of a reformist leadership in the Soviet Union weakened most of the conservative tier of the political establishment in Hungary and greatly increased its flexibility. This rapid removal of the Soviet brakes tipped the balance between reformers and conservatives and activated a radical transition process to democracy in Hungary.

In China, in contrast, a generation of elderly leaders acted as protectors of socialism. Their constant presence in Beijing limited the flexibility of the reformist factions, and yet there was much more uncertainty in China about how much political reform the conservatives would ultimately accept. In 1989 the protest movement underestimated the conservatives' strength and followed unrealistic strategies that plunged the country into crisis. This situation handicapped the reformers and favored the conservative forces, which possessed the coercive power that ended the crisis.

Liberalization Without Democratization: The "Two-Front Struggle"

One distinctive characteristic of the transition in Hungary and China was the elite preference for liberalization without democratization because it posed a less obvious challenge to their power. As market-oriented economic reform is ideologically incompatible with orthodox Marxism and operationally incompatible with a tightly controlled political system, its implementation required preliminary political reform to loosen ideological controls over the formation of economic policy and to relax political controls over society. In the initial stage, however, what was necessary was liberalization, not democratization. The insistence on the principle of Party leadership imposed a severe constraint on further political liberalization in both countries. Thus, the system changed from totalitarianism to an enlightened authoritarianism.

But liberalization without democratization can be explosive, especially if policies fail. If, as the "negativist" school predicts, reform produces grievances, then direct challenges to the regime will increase. As the nature of both economic and political reform was to give society more autonomy,

the popular pressures generated by economic reform and political liberalization would persistently threaten the limits that the Party leadership was
willing to accept. Committed to reforms on one hand and to the Party
leadership on the other, reformist leaders in both countries were constantly
conducting a "two-front struggle," that is, fighting the conservatives in the
political establishment to pursue the reform program and fighting the
radicals in society to defend the Party's legitimacy.

During the process of economic and political liberalization, the reformist
leadership had to maintain a steady course between the conservative
mechanisms in the political system and the radical impulses liberated by
reform initiatives. The leadership wanted to conduct a radical economic
reform but did not want it to go so far as to subvert the ideological
foundation of the regime. It wanted to relax ideological controls to
encourage intellectual initiative but did not want the intellectuals to be so
free as to challenge the Party authority. It wanted to encourage more
autonomous social groups to share the responsibilities of the Party and
government but did not want these groups to be so autonomous as to share
power. The leadership wanted to invigorate the legislatures to rationalize
government operations but did not want the legislature to be so powerful as
to obstruct the will of the Party.

Facing the challenges generated by the economic reform and political
liberalization, the Party leaderships in China and Hungary initially attempted
to construct a more corporatist society, in which interest groups would be
authorized but noncompetitive, and the Party would maintain its leading
position. However, the corporatist solutions favored by Party leaders did not
satisfy societal demands for political reform, which constantly went beyond
the limits the Party sought to impose. This was in part because the visible
hand of the state in the economic transition encouraged people to believe
that the state was solely responsible for their socioeconomic grievances, and
that the solutions to these grievances therefore lay in rapid political reform.
The intellectuals' high expectations for radical political reform along
Western lines also tended to push the demands for political change beyond
a corporatist structure.

The "two-front struggle" resulted in a distinctive cyclical pattern in
China, characterized by the alternation between the emergence of a societal
challenge and its subsequent repression by the political establishment. Thus,
the Democracy Wall Movement of 1978, with its proliferation of political
groups and publications, was followed by the arrest of its leaders and a ban
on its publications in 1979; the regime launched a campaign against spiritual
pollution in 1983 in response to the widespread public withdrawal from the
uniformity of ideological hegemony; the student demonstrations for greater
democracy and freedom in 1986 and 1987 were followed by an official

campaign against bourgeois liberalization and the forced resignation of the liberal-minded Party general secretary; and the 1989 student movement that ended in a bloody massacre.

In Hungary only one instance of action followed by reaction occurred, in the early 1970s, when discontent over income inequality led to economic retrenchment. This, however, had nothing to do with a democratic opposition but was a response to the conservative tendency of the society against huge income differentials. The two-front struggle did not cause serious fluctuations in Hungarian political life, despite continuing conflict between the protest movement and the regime. This contrast may be explained by the different pattern of interaction between the opposition and the political establishment in the two countries.

Interactions Between the Opposition and the Political Establishment

There were some basic dissimilarities between the protest movements in the two societies. First, the Hungarian dissidents were better organized and were able to publish their periodicals despite police harassment. Lacking an institutional base to undertake a patient, detailed, and prolonged struggle for democracy, dissidents in China had to issue their demands mainly through demonstrations and political campaigns. Second, because of this lack of an organizational base, the Chinese dissidents tended to sustain the momentum of their demonstrations or campaigns as long as possible in the hope of achieving a point of no return that would reduce the likelihood of subsequent repression. This strategy often exceeded the limits of official tolerance and led to crackdowns, as in the case of the 1989 protest movement.

In contrast, the 1956 incident had taught opposition groups in Hungary to be more realistically aware of the conservative Soviet presence and therefore to exercise greater self-restraint. The Hungarian opposition had also learned that they had to be very cautious about how far they could push their demands before Hungary lost its bargaining position with the Soviet Union. The political opposition and the Party leadership in Hungary thus reached a tacit agreement to pursue incremental changes so as not to bring about another Soviet invasion. In China the protest movement and the reformist leaders failed to understand how not to provoke the old revolutionary generation. The ambiguity about the balance between reformers and conservatives encouraged the protest movement periodically and perhaps imprudently to probe the limits of their tolerance.

There was also a lack of popular support for a radical protest movement in Hungarian society. Hungarians had long been politically apathetic, in part because of the loss of faith in communism and in part because of the existence of the second economy, which channeled the society's energy into economic betterment instead of political issues. Having been enmeshed in a highly politicized environment during the Cultural Revolution and lacking opportunities to acquire wealth, China's urban population was keenly interested in politics. This interest provided the basis for the emergence of a radical protest movement. The political establishment often had to employ extreme measures to squelch the opposition. The radical tendency of the opposition and the repressive measures taken by the regime only served to reinforce one another: As the regime attempted to suppress the opposition, the opposition became all the more rebellious and radical. Since there were few outlets for the expression of social demands and grievances, this discontent rose to dangerous levels. In turn, since the societal challenge was so radical, it tended to exceed the establishment's capacity to accommodate it, thus provoking harsh repression from the authorities. Breaking this unproductive circle will require the development of more rational, moderate, and conciliatory social forces for democracy, as well as a more adaptive political leadership.

The different outcomes in 1989 in Hungary and China have highlighted the crucial importance of the interaction between social challenges and establishment responses in determining the course and outcome of the transition. In Hungary the political opposition did not launch any massive challenge to the regime after 1956. Instead, it was devoted to establishing more independent organizations and cooperating with the leadership whenever possible. In China, in contrast, despite the prudent organization of the demonstrations in 1989, the student movement did not at the outset have a set of clear, obtainable goals. The ambiguity of the demands made them less likely to be met and suggested to the Party leadership that indeed they might have no limit. Later, although the movement reduced its goals simply to the retraction of the 26 April editorial, the movement continued to use extreme tactics of protest, such as hunger strikes and the occupation of Tiananmen Square. The massive movement became more and more emotional and uncontrolled, preventing the student representatives from making any compromises in the dialogue with the government. The two very different cases demonstrated that smooth transition relies on the cooperation of the moderate forces on both sides.

Economic Mechanisms

Reform invigorated the economic system in the two countries by pluralizing the ownership structure and introducing market relations. In doing so, it also strengthened the autonomy of the society vis-à-vis the state.

However, such changes were not without serious costs and left many uncertainties that would dog the progress toward a normally functioning market system as well as the process of political transition.

Societal Autonomy and the Role of the State

Market-oriented economic reform was the key factor in turning the totalitarian state socialist system into an authoritarian one. The state started to play a lesser role in the economy and in people's everyday lives. Economic reform inevitably increased the range of opportunities and choices for the population, as people no longer depended solely on the government for the supply of goods and services. Economic reform also broke the state monopoly of wealth and resources, which in turn provided more space for social groups to exert influence over a variety of affairs, from education to cultural activities. At the same time, rising living standards contributed to the growth of a middle class that may increasingly value participation in decisions that affect their lives. In fact, the growing influence of the new rich in China has forced the local government to take a more corporatist approach to bring these new forces into politics. Although greater societal autonomy and a growing middle class do not necessarily lead to the establishment of democracy, they do foster further change in that direction.

Yet the challenge in a successful economic transition lies in defining the proper role of the state. The state's declining control of the economy means not only greater societal autonomy but also reductions in protection and welfare programs that the population took for granted. The government must carefully nurture market mechanisms to replace the previous functions of the state. Economic reform therefore should be a process of state extrication, not state desertion. As Karl Polanyi has forcefully argued, even the capitalist market was not established spontaneously but with strong state intervention. Society, according to Polanyi, is unable to protect itself from the destructive forces of the market, which may eventually lead to the ruin of the market itself.[1] Even more than the creation of a capitalist market, the transition from plan to market needs a strong state to guide it.

The extrication of the state from the economy produced social frustration in both countries. As the state attempted to shed the all-embracing economic responsibilities of the past, society continued to hold it accountable for many things for which it had previously been responsible. State employees were all too used to the state welfare system that guaranteed their employment, health care, and retirement pensions. They resisted any attempts to—as they saw it—undermine their welfare. The social contract that the paternalistic state and society had entered into prior to the reform period continued to present formidable barriers to successful economic transition, especially in the reconfiguration of the cumbersome state enterprises.

The fine line between state extrication and desertion also created uncertainties in the process of economic transition. Observers detected a loosening and tightening cycle in China's economic decentralization process: Whenever the state granted the local authority and enterprises more autonomy, the situation would quickly get out of hand, especially with regard to overextended investment. But if the central government exercised more control, the economic environment would become dead, economic actors simply losing their incentive. It was by this zigzag path that the state searched for the appropriate mix of market autonomy and control.

As some scholars have pointed out, in postcommunist Hungary the state has abandoned its responsibilities much faster than it has been able to force enterprises to compete and to create a safety net to protect the population from undue economic hardship. The postcommunist government assigned greater importance to market mechanisms that have not adequately developed and minimized the role of the state in leading the economic transition, while at the same time slashing the state welfare system for the general population. Economic recession and the decline of living standards brought parties with moderate reform programs back to the center stage, and policymakers have increasingly acknowledged the proper role of the state in the future transitions.

Social Costs of Economic Reform

The experiences of Hungary and China demonstrate that economic reform, no matter how gradually or partially implemented, involves profound social costs. Economic reform caused inflation so severe that many families found that their real incomes declined relative to rising prices. It also produced inequality by creating a fast-growing sector of the economy, the nonstate sector, whose employees earned much more than workers in the traditional state sector. The coexistence of a multisector economy, multiple channels of distribution, and an inadequate legal system all encouraged corruption. Although the overall standard of living improved significantly, the psychological shocks brought on by inflation, inequality, and corruption diminished popular optimism regarding reform.

The social costs associated with economic transition are potentially dangerous because they may generate instability that disrupts the whole transition process. In China and Hungary, the impact of these costs was exacerbated by the low tolerance of the people for such phenomena and their high expectations for ever-rising and fairly equal living standards. Long accustomed to socialist egalitarianism, the people considered visible inequalities among the population a violation of social justice. Yet once the reform began, they expected to see their incomes grow at a rapid rate.

As the reformers had risen to power by promising higher living standards for the entire population, the tremendous social costs of reform made their position vulnerable: Social grievances can shake the foundation of any incumbent regime. This prevented the regime from implementing unpopular yet necessary reform policies and sometimes even brought economic reform to a halt. For example, protest against income inequality was one of the major causes for the suspension of economic reform in Hungary in the early 1970s. And the grievances over inflation repeatedly forced the Beijing government to postpone its price reform. As one Chinese economist put it, "Whenever it comes to a confrontation between hard interests [of the population] and hard reform measures [of the regime], it is always the hard interests that win."[2] Such a situation led to political crisis for the CCP in 1989 and contributed to the return of the former communists to power in Hungary. By the same token, reduced social costs have buttressed legitimacy of the Party in China since the early 1990s.

Ideological Mechanisms

During the process of ideological liberalization that presaged economic and political reform, many concepts of orthodox doctrine were discredited so as to prepare for the systemic changes to come. In both countries the reformers initiated ideological liberalization gingerly, taking with great pains, as shown in the cautious redefinition of certain concepts and heated debates over the wording of particular policy lines, many of which seem trivial today. Now, there seems little chance of a return to the highly doctrinized social environment in general and policy-making process in particular.

Ideological liberalization generated two forces that challenged the establishment. One was mass alienation, as manifested in the crisis of faith and the collapse of moral order. Although the leadership insisted that ideological liberalization was not a repudiation of Marxism, Marxism nonetheless lost its appeal among the population. With the old dogmas gone and no alternative value system to replace them, an ideological vacuum existed. There was a widespread crisis of faith and a decline in public morality, and the regime found itself unable to rationalize its legitimacy or to convince the population to put up with the hardships induced by reform. The other force that challenged the communist leadership was the desire for democracy among intellectuals. The freer access to information and to Western liberal democratic ideas highlighted the contrast between the repressive nature of state socialism and a somewhat idealized version of the democratic system in the West. Many intellectuals therefore wanted faster and more comprehensive Westernization.

Widespread mass alienation and the drive for democracy either helped the opposition movement to topple the communist system (as was the case in Hungary) or considerably eroded the governing ability of the regime (as was the case in China). But they did not help to create a normal market system or stable democratic institutions. Instead, mass alienation continued to undermine the effectiveness of both the economic reform program and democratic practice. Having become alienated from the official framework, the population did not reenter it after the establishment of democratic procedures and free markets.

The transition from orthodox Marxism to an ideological vacuum created a sense of normlessness, a belief that socially unapproved means were necessary to achieve one's goals. This normlessness was reinforced by economic hardship. When people suddenly lost their sense of economic security in this transition period, they began to regard norms and values as being even less binding than they had been under state socialism. This pervasive sense of normlessness contributed to the development of a corrupt market system, characterized by widespread extortion and graft on the part of government officials, fraud by entrepreneurs, and extensive irresponsibility toward public property and affairs. There was also a rapid rise in crime. Accompanying the abandonment of communist doctrine was a cynicism toward any values and principles, including those inherent in democracy. Together with a desire for freedom went a sense of irresponsibility. Along with the opposition to the old political system emerged a defiance toward any kind of authority. None of this would encourage the emergence of a stable democracy.

Transition After 1989

In 1989 the confluence of three mechanisms (political, economic, and ideological) produced critical transition junctures in both Hungary and China. As the countries passed these junctures, either by turning toward democracy or by suppressing the protest movements, the transitional spectrum changed. Democratic breakthrough and bloody suppression generated different dynamics in Hungary and China.

Political alignments shifted. In Hungary the political stage was dominated by democrats who were previously in the opposition. The focus was no longer on achieving democracy but on its consolidation. A sense of triumph led to the confidence in rapid transition to capitalism and the West. In China political distress thwarted any radical initiatives. As a result, a developmental coalition of reformers and conservatives formed.

Economic development varied. Overconfidence in the legitimacy of a democratic system led to the adoption of some radical economic reform policies that not only caused the decline of economic growth but also produced severe social grievances. So far, the democratic system in Hungary has survived its disappointing economic performance. Yet the consolidation of democracy depends to a large extent on the success of economic transition. The leadership coalition in China pursued an all-out development agenda. Subsequent economic growth in China pacified its somewhat restive population. The emphasis on economic development directed many people's energies toward business ventures. The larger the proportion of the population with a stake in preserving economic prosperity, the less social support for radical political changes there will be. Without radical disruption of the economic transition, there may be a chance of moderate and gradual transition to a more open and democratic political system.

Orthodox Marxist ideology is no longer a restraint on transition. It is nonexistent in Hungary and becoming more and more irrelevant in China. Yet both countries need to develop a more cohesive ideology that provides norms and guidelines for society. This may be particularly critical for China, where the Tiananmen massacre slashed the democratic dreams of many intellectuals. Seeing the troubled economies in other former communist countries, however, Chinese intellectuals are increasingly questioning the appropriateness of liberal democracy in China, at least in its current stage of development. The rising Chinese nationalism may fill the ideological void. However, as nationalism is very volatile, it adds an uncertain element in the mix of factors that will affect China's future development.

After the events of 1989 in the communist world, Ralf Dahrendorf predicted that the construction of a democratic constitution would take several months, that of market institutions a couple of years, and that of civility and a sense of citizenship several generations.[3] Yet all three transitions from state socialism are far from complete. And it is fair to conclude that all good things do not go together. During the transition period, we have seen (in the case of China) economic reform without democratization, and now we see (in Hungary) democratization without successful economic performance. As these two divergent systems evolve, we may find that the authoritarian solution produces better economic results but falls prey to the contradiction of liberalization without democracy, whereas the democratic system remains vulnerable to the grievances produced by suboptimal economic performance.

NOTES

1. Karl Polanyi, *The Great Transformation* (New York: Rinehart, 1944).

2. Personal conversation with a Chinese economist, Honolulu, Hawaii, August 1989.

3. Ralf Dahrendorf, *Reflections on the Revolution in Europe* (New York: Random House, 1990), pp. 105-107.

BIBLIOGRAPHY

Abel, Istvan, and John Bonin. "State Desertion and Convertibility: The Case of Hungary." In *Hungary: An Economy in Transition*, eds. Istvan P. Szekely and David M. Newbery. New York: Cambridge University Press, 1993, pp. 329-41.

Aczel, Gyorgy. "The Dimensions of Social Change." *New Hungarian Quarterly* 26, no. 100 (Winter 1985): 24-33.

_____. "A New System of Values." *New Hungarian Quarterly* 21, no. 77 (Spring 1980): 10-20.

_____. "Hungarian Cultural Policy and the Hegemony of Marxism." *New Hungarian Quarterly* 12, no. 42 (Summer 1971): 3-22.

Adam, Jan. "The Transition to a Market Economy in Hungary." *Europe-Asia Studies* 47, no. 6 (1995): 989-1006.

Agocs, Peter, and Sandor Agocs. "'The Change Was But an Unfulfilled Promise': Agriculture and the Rural Population in Post-Communist Hungary." *East European Politics and Societies* 8, no. 1 (Winter 1994): 32-57.

Agocs, Sandor. "The Collapse of Communist Ideology in Hungary: November 1988 to February 1989." *East European Quarterly* 27, no. 2 (June 1993): 187-211.

Almond, Gabriel, and Sidney Verba. *The Civic Culture*. Princeton, N.J.: Princeton University Press, 1963.

Andorka, Rudolf. "Institutional Changes and Intellectual Trends in Some Hungarian Social Sciences." *East European Politics and Societies* 7, no. 1 (Winter 1993): 74-108.

Andorka, Rudolf, and Laszlo Bertalan, eds. *Economy and Society in Hungary*. Budapest: Karl Marx University of Economic Sciences, Department of Sociology, 1986.

Arato, Andrew. "Civil Society against the State: Poland 1980-1981," *Telos*, no. 47 (Spring 1981): 23-47.

_____. "Empire vs. Civil Society," *Telos*, no. 50 (Winter 1981-82): 19-48.

Bakos, Gabor. "Hungarian Transition after Three Years." *Europe-Asia Studies* 46, no. 7 (1994): 1189-1214.

Balassa, Bela. "The Firm in the New Economic Mechanism." *New Hungarian Quarterly* 12, no. 44 (Winter 1971): 63-68.

_____. "The Hungarian Economic Reform, 1968-82." *Banca Nazionale del Lavoro Quarterly Review* no. 145 (1983): 163-84.

_____. *The Hungarian Experience in Economic Planning: A Theoretical and Empirical Study*. New Haven: Yale University Press, 1959.

Bao Xinjian. "Shehuizhuyi chuji jieduan minzhu zhengzhi jianshe xinlun" [On the construction of democratic politics in the primary stage of socialism]. *Xinhua Wenzhai*, no. 11 (1988): 1-4.

Barnett, A. Doak, and Ralph N. Clough, eds. *Modernizing China: Post-Mao Reform and Development*. Boulder, Colo.: Westview Press, 1986.

Batt, Judy. *Economic Reform and Political Change in Eastern Europe: A Comparison of the Czechoslovak and Hungarian Experiences*. London: Macmillan, 1988.

Bauer, Tamas. "Perfecting or Reforming the Economic Mechanism?" *Eastern European Economics* 26, no. 2 (Winter 1987-88): 5-34.

Baum, Richard, ed. *Reform and Reaction in Post-Mao China: The Road to Tiananmen*. New York: Routledge, 1991.

_____ "Modernization and Legal Reform in Post-Mao China: The Rebirth of Socialist Legality." *Studies in Comparative Communism* 19, no. 2 (Summer 1986): 69-103.

Bell, Daniel. "Ideology and Soviet Politics." *Slavic Review* 24, no. 4 (December 1965): 591-611.

Benewick, Robert, and Paul Wingrove, eds. *Reforming the Revolution: China in Transition*. Chicago: The Dorsey Press, 1988.

Benke, Valeria. "Socialist Democracy and Freedom of Opinion." *New Hungarian Quarterly* 20, no. 74 (Summer 1979): 6-12.

Berecz, Janos. "Socialism and Reform." *New Hungarian Quarterly* 28, no. 107 (Autumn 1987): 78-87.

Berend, Ivan. *The Hungarian Economic Reforms: 1953-1988*. Cambridge: Cambridge University Press, 1990.

Berend, Ivan, and Gyorgy Ranki. *The Hungarian Economy in the Twentieth Century*. London: Croom Helm, 1985.

Bermeo, Nancy. "Democracy and the Lessons of Dictatorship." *Comparative Politics* 24, no. 3 (April 1992): 273-91.

Bihari, Mihaly. "The Political System and the Representation of Interests." In *Economy and Society in Hungary*, eds. Rudolf Andorka and Laszlo Bertalan. Budapest: Karl Marx University of Economic Sciences, Department of Sociology, 1986, pp. 287-331.

Bihari, Otto. "The Development of Socialist Democracy in Hungarian Political Institutions." *New Hungarian Quarterly* 12, no. 42 (Summer 1971): 76-84.

Blejer, Mario I., and Fabrizio Coricelli. *The Making of Economic Reform in Eastern Europe: Conversations with Leading Reformers in Poland, Hungary, and the Czech Republic.* Brookfield, V. T.: Edward Elgar, 1995.

Blumstock, Robert. "Public Opinion in Hungary." In *Public Opinion in European Socialist Systems*, eds. Walter D. Conor and Zvi Y. Gitelman. New York: Praeger, 1977, pp. 132-66.

Bognar, Jozsef. "Economic Reform, Development and Stability in the Hungarian Economy." *New Hungarian Quarterly* 13, no. 46 (Summer 1972): 29-43.

_____. "Economic Reform and International Economic Policy." *New Hungarian Quarterly* 9, no. 32 (Winter 1968): 78-94.

_____. "Overall Direction and Operation of the Economy." *New Hungarian Quarterly* 7, no. 21 (Spring 1966): 3-32.

Bognar, Jozsef et al. "New Developments in the Hungarian Economy." *New Hungarian Quarterly* 6, no. 20 (Winter 1965): 3-27.

Boka, Laszlo. "Impatient Youth." *New Hungarian Quarterly* 5, no. 16 (Winter 1964): 3-15.

_____. "In An Atmosphere of Humanity." *New Hungarian Quarterly* 3, no. 9 (January-March 1963): 3-13.

Bornstein, Morris. "Ideology and the Soviet Economy." In *Comparative Economic Systems*, ed. Jan S. Prybyla. New York: Meredith Corporation, 1969, pp. 81-88.

Bozoki, Andras. "Intellectuals and Democratization." *Hungarian Quarterly* 34, no. 132 (Winter 1993): 93-106.

_____. "Hungary's Road to Systemic Change: The Opposition Roundtable." *East European Politics and Societies* 7, no. 2 (Spring 1993): 276-308.

Brugger, Bill, ed. *Chinese Marxism in Flux, 1978-84.* New York: M. E. Sharpe, 1985.

Brus, Wlodzimierz. "Socialism—Feasible and Viable?" *New Left Review* 154 (September/October 1985): 43-62.

_____. "Political Pluralism and Markets in Communist Systems." In *Pluralism in the Soviet Union*, ed. Susan G. Soloman. New York: St. Martin's Press, 1982, pp. 108-130.

_____. *Socialist Ownership and Political System.* Trans. R. A. Clarke. London & Boston: Routledge & Kegan Paul, 1975.

Bruszt, Laszlo. "1989: The Negotiated Revolution in Hungary." *Social Research* 57, no. 2 (Summer 1990): 365-87.

_____. "Without Us But for Us? Political Orientation in Hungary in the Period of Late Paternalism." *Social Research* 55, no. 1-2 (Spring/Summer 1988): 43-76.

Bugajski, Janusz, and Maxine Pollack. *East European Fault Lines: Dissent, Opposition, and Social Activism.* Boulder, Colo.: Westview Press, 1989.

Bunce, Valerie, and Maria Csanadi. "Uncertainty in the Transition: Post-Communism in Hungary." *East European Politics and Society* 7, no. 2 (Spring 1993): 240-75.

Burawoy, Michael, and Janos Lukacs. *The Radiant Past: Ideology and Reality in Hungary's Road to Capitalism.* Chicago: The University of Chicago Press, 1992.

Burns, John P. "China's Governance: Political Reform in a Turbulent Environment." *China Quarterly*, no. 119 (September 1989): 481-517.

_____. "Reforming China's Bureaucracy, 1979-82." *Asian Survey* 23, no. 6 (June 1983): 692-722.

Cao Changqing. "Kangzheng de shengyin: minban kanwu." [Voice of protest: unofficial periodicals]. *Beijing Zhi Chun*, no. 7/8 (December 1993.12/January 1994): 23-27.

Chan, Anita. "Revolution or Corporatism? Workers and Trade Unions in Post-Mao China." *Australian Journal of Chinese Affairs*, no. 29 (January 1993): 31-61.

Chan, Peter P. F. *China: Modernization and its Economic Laws.* Hong Kong: The Hong Kong Economist Newspaper, 1982.

Chang, Chen-pang. "The Chinese Communists' Ideological Dilemmas." *Issues and Studies* 23, no. 6 (March 1985): 14-26.

Chang, Mau-kuei Michael. "Toward a Theoretical Understanding of Communist China in the Post-Mao Era: The Problem of Ideology and Revolution from the Top." *Issues and Studies* 23, no. 6 (June 1987): 80-97.

Chen, Yizi. "Zhengzhi tizhi gaige shi jingji tizhi gaige di baozhen" [Political reform is the guarantee for economic reform]. *Shijie Jingji Daobao.* 13 July 1987.

_____. "Gaige shi shixian shehuizhuyi xiandaihua de keguan yaoqiu" [Reform is the objective request of the socialist modernization]. *Shijie Jingji Daobao.* 10 August 1987.

Collier, David, ed. *The New Authoritarianism in Latin America.* Princeton, N.J.: Princeton University Press, 1979.

Comisso, Ellen, and Paul Marer. "The Economics and Politics of Reform in Hungary." *International Organization* 40, no. 2 (Spring 1986): 421-54.

Comprehensive Problems Group of the Institute of Development. "Nongmin, shichang, he zhidu zhuanxing: baochandaohu banian hou nongcun fazhan mianlin de shenceng gaige" [Peasants, the market, and innovation in the institution: On the deep structural reform in rural areas after eight years of fixing output for each household]. *Jingji Yanjiu*, no. 1 (1987).

Connolly, William, ed. *Legitimacy and the State.* Oxford: Basil Blackwell, 1984.

Connor, Walter D., and Zvi Y. Gitelman. *Public Opinion in European Socialist Systems*. New York: Praeger, 1977.

Csikos-Nagy, Bela. "Socialist Economic Theory and the New Mechanism." *New Hungarian Quarterly* 8, no. 28 (Winter 1967): 37-52.

Dahl, Robert A. "Pluralism Revisited." *Comparative Politics* 10, no. 2 (January 1978): 191-203.

_____. *Polyarchy: Participation and Opposition*. New Haven: Yale University Press, 1971.

_____. *Preface to Democratic Theory*. Chicago: University of Chicago Press, 1956.

Dahrendorf, Ralf. *Reflections on the Revolution in Europe*. New York: Random House, 1990.

_____. *Class and Class Conflict in Industrial Society*. Stanford, Calif.: Stanford University Press, 1959.

Davies, James C. "Toward a Theory of Revolution." *American Sociological Review* 27 (1962): 5-18.

Deng Chundong. "Jingnianlai lilunjie guanyu dang de lingdao wenti de zhongyao guandian zongshu" [Review of the major theoretical views on the Party leadership in recent years]. *Xinhua Wenzhai*, no. 12 (1988): 8-9.

Deng Xiaoping. *Selected Works of Deng Xiaoping*. Beijing: Foreign Languages Press, 1984.

Diamond, Larry. "Beyond Authoritarianism and Totalitarianism: Strategies for Democratization." *Washington Quarterly* 12, no. 1 (Winter 1989): 141-63.

Diamond, Larry, Juan Linz, and Seymour Martin Lipset. "Building and Sustaining Democratic Government in Developing Countries: Some Tentative Findings." *World Affairs* 150, no. 1 (Summer 1987): 5-19.

Dittmer, Lowell. "Ideology and Organization in Post-Mao China." *Asian Survey* 24, no. 3 (March 1984): 349-69.

Dobb, M. "Modern Western Theories of Economic Growth." *Acta Oeconomica* 1 (1966): 379-84.

Dong Furen. "Suoyouzhi gaige yu jingji yunxing jizhi gaige" [Ownership reform and economic operation mechanism reform]. *Xinhua Wenzhai*, no. 4 (1986): 58-65.

Du Feijin, and Xu Cailiao. "Luetan zhengzhi minzhuhua he fazhi" [Brief discussion on political democratization and legal system]. *Renmin Ribao*. (overseas edition), 11 November 1986, p. 2.

Ehrlich, Stanislaw. *Pluralism: On and Off Course*. New York: Pergamon Press, 1982.

Ekiert, Grzegorz. "Peculiarities of Post-Communist Politics: The Case of Poland." *Studies in Comparative Communism* 25, no. 4 (December 1992): 341-61.

_____. "Democratization Processes in East Central Europe: A Theoretical Reconsideration." *British Journal of Political Science* 21, no. 3 (1991): 285-313.

Eulau, Heinz, and Paul D. Karps. "The Puzzle of Representation: Specifying Components of Responsiveness." *Legislative Studies Quarterly* 2, no. 3 (August 1977): 233-54.

Evans, Geoffrey, and Stephen Whitefield. "Social and Ideological Cleavage Formation in Post-Communist Hungary." *Europe-Asia Studies* 47, no. 7 (1995):1177-1204.

Falkenheim, Victor C., ed. *Citizens and Groups in Contemporary China*. Ann Arbor: Center for Chinese Studies, The University of Michigan, 1987.

_____. "The Limits of Political Reform." *Current History* 86 (September 1987): 261-265, 279-81.

Falus-Szikra, K. "Distribution According to Work and the Reform in Hungary." *Acta Oeconomica* 33, no. 1-2 (1984): 1-16.

_____. "Some Human Factors of Innovation in Hungary." *Acta Oeconomica* 28, no. 1-2 (1982): 19-36.

_____. "Wage Differentials in Hungary." *Acta Oeconomica* 25, no. 1-2 (1980): 163-72.

_____. "Some Questions of the Interpretation of Distribution according to Work." *Acta Oeconomica* 17, no. 3-4 (1976): 257-68.

Felkay, Andrew. *Hungary and the USSR, 1956-1988: Kadar's Political Leadership*. New York: Greenwood Press, 1989.

Fellner, W. "Schools of Thought in the Mainstream of American Economics." *Acta Oeconomica* 18, no. 3-4 (1977): 247-61.

Flakierski, Henryk. "Economic Reform and Income Distribution in Hungary." *Cambridge Journal of Economics* 3, no. 1 (1979): 15-32.

Frentzel-Zagorska, Janina. "Civil Society in Poland and Hungary." *Soviet Studies* 42, no. 4 (1990): 759-77.

Friedman, Milton. *Capitalism and Freedom*. Chicago: University of Chicago Press, 1962.

Gabor, Istvan. "The Second (Secondary) Economy." *Acta Oeconomica* 22, no. 3-4 (1979): 291-311.

Gao Fang. "Lun shehuizhuji duodangzhi" [On multiparty system in socialist countries]. *Zhengzhixue Yanjiu*, July 1987, pp. 4-11.

Gao Youqian. "Dui suoyouzhi wenti de shehuixue toushi" [A sociological perspective of the issue of ownership]. *Xinhua Wenzhai*, no. 10 (1988): 14-17.

Garside, Roger. *Coming Alive: China After Mao*. New York: McGraw-Hill, 1981.

Gati, Charles. 1971. "Hungary: The Politics of Reform." *Current History* 70 (May 1971): 290-94, 308.

Gold, Thomas. "Party-State versus Society in China." In *Building a Nation-State: China after Forty Years*, ed. Joyce Kallgren. Berkeley: Institute of East Asian Studies, University of California, 1990, pp. 125-51.

Goldman, Marshall I. *Gorbachev's Challenge: Economic Reform in the Age of High Technology*. New York: W. W. Norton, 1987.

Goldman, Merle. "Dissident Intellectuals in the People's Republic of China." In *Citizens and Groups in Contemporary China*, ed. Victor C. Falkenheim. Ann Arbor: Center for Chinese Studies, The University of Michigan, 1987, pp. 159-88.

_____. *China's Intellectuals: Advise and Dissent*. Cambridge: Harvard University Press, 1981.

Goldman, Merle, with Timothy Cheek and Carol Lee Hamrin, eds. *China's Intellectuals and the State: In Search of a New Relationship*. Cambridge: Harvard University Press, 1987.

Gomulka, Stanislaw. *Growth, Innovation and Reform in Eastern Europe*. Madison: The University of Wisconsin Press, 1986.

Goodman, David S. G., ed. *Groups and Politics in the People's Republic of China*. New York: M. E. Sharpe, 1984.

_____. *Beijing Street Voices: The Poetry and Politics of China's Democratic Movement*. London: Marion Boyars Publishers, 1981.

Gorlice, Josef. "Introduction to the Hungarian Democratic Opposition." *Berkeley Journal of Sociology: A Critical Review* 31 (1986): 117-65.

Granick, David. *Enterprise Guidance in Eastern Europe: A Comparison of Four Socialist Economies*. Princeton, N.J.: Princeton University Press, 1975.

Griffin, Keith, ed. *Institutional Reform and Economic Development in the Chinese Countryside*. London: Macmillan, 1984.

Guang Hui, and Duan Yao. "Minzhu de gushi" [Story of democracy]. *Zhongguo Qingnian*, July 1988, pp. 6-8.

Gurr, Ted Robert. *Why Men Rebel*. Princeton, N.J.: Princeton University Press, 1970.

Habermas, Jurgen. Trans. by Thomas Burger. *The Structural Transformation of the Public Sphere: An Inquiry into a Category of Bourgeois Society*. Cambridge: The MIT Press, 1989.

Hahn, Werner. "Electoral Choice in the Soviet Bloc." *Problems of Communism* 36 (March-April 1987): 29-39.

Halpern, Nina P. "China's Industrial Economic Reforms: The Question of Strategy." *Asian Survey* 25, no. 10 (October 1985): 998-1012.

Hamrin, Carol Lee, and Timothy Cheek, eds. *China's Establishment Intellectuals*. New York: M. E. Sharpe, 1986.

Han Minzhu, and Hua Sheng, eds. *Cries for Democracy: Writings and Speeches from the 1989 Chinese Democracy Movement*. Princeton, N.J.: Princeton University Press, 1990.

Hankiss, Elemer. *East European Alternatives*. New York: Oxford University Press, 1990.

_____. "Demobilization, Self-Mobilization and Quasi-Mobilization in Hungary, 1948-1987." *East European Politics and Societies* 3, no. 1 (Winter 1989): 105-151.

_____. "The 'Second Society': Is There an Alternative Social Model Emerging in Contemporary Hungary?" *Social Research* 55, no. 1-2 (1988): 13-42.

Haraszti, Miklos. *A Worker in a Worker's State*. Trans. by Michael Wright. New York: Universe Books, 1978.

Harding, Harry. *China's Second Revolution: Reform After Mao*. Washington, D.C.: The Brookings Institution, 1987.

_____. *Organizing China: The Problem of Bureaucracy, 1949-1976*. Stanford, Calif.: Stanford University Press, 1981.

Hare, P. G. "The Beginning of Institutional Reform in Hungary." *Soviet Studies* 35, no. 3 (July 1983): 313-30.

Hare, P. G., and P. T. Wanless, "Polish and Hungarian Economic Reforms —A Comparison." *Soviet Studies* 33, no. 4 (October 1981): 491-517.

Harrold, Peter, and Rajiv Lall, "China: Reform and Development in 1992-93." World Bank Discussion Papers, China and Mongolia Department, no. 215.

Hasegawa, Tsuyoshi. "The Connection Between Political and Economic Reform in Communist Regimes." In *Dismantling Communism: Common Causes and Regional Variations*, eds. Gilbert Rozman et al. Baltimore: The Johns Hopkins University Press, 1992, pp. 59-117.

Havas, Zs. "The Role of the Institute For Economic and Market Research Under the New Economic Management." *Acta Oeconomica* 3, no. 2 (1968): 228-32.

Hayek, Friedrich A. *The Road to Serfdom*. Chicago: University of Chicago Press, 1944.

Hedlund, Stefan, "Exit, Voice and Loyalty—Soviet Style." *Coexistence* 26 (1989): 179-208.

Heldman, Dan C. "Ideology, Science, and the Party." *Problems of Communism* 16 (January/February 1967): 67-72.

Hewett, Ed A. "The Hungarian Economy: Lessons of the 1970s and Prospects for the 1980s." *East European Economic Assessment*. Part I. Joint Economic Committee, 97th Cong., 1st sess. Washington, D.C.: U.S. Government Printing Office, 1981, pp. 483-524.

_____. *Reforming the Soviet Economy*. Washington, D.C.: The Brookings Institution, 1988.

Hicks, George, ed. *The Broken Mirror: China After Tiananmen*. London: Longman, 1990.

Hintze, Otto. "Economics and Politics in the Age of Modern Capitalism." In *The Historical Essays of Otto Hintze*. New York: Oxford University Press, 1975.

Hirschman, Albert. "Exit, Voice and the Fate of the German Democratic Republic: An Essay in Conceptural History." *World Politics* 45, no. 1 (1993): 173-202.

_____. *Exit, Voice, and Loyalty: Responses to Decline in Firms, Organizations, and States*. Cambridge: Harvard University Press, 1970.

Hockenos, Paul. *Free to Hate: The Rise of the Right in Post-Communist Eastern Europe*. New York: Routledge, 1993.

Howe, Christopher, and Kenneth R. Walker. *The Foundations of the Chinese Planned Economy: A Documentary Survey, 1953-65*. London: Macmillan, 1989.

Hsu, Immanuel C. Y. *China Without Mao: The Search for a New Order*. Oxford: Oxford University Press, 1982.

Hsu, Robert C. "Conceptions of the Market in Post-Mao China." *Modern China* 11, no. 4 (October 1985): 436-60.

Hu Kehong, Zheng Bin, and Li Yongfeng, "Guanyu guojia qunali zhiyue jizhi de bijiao yanjiu" [Comparative study of the checking mechanism of the state power]. *Xinhua Wenzhai*, no. 8 (1986): 8-15.

Hu Qiaomu. "Dangqian sixiang zhanxian de ruogan wenti" [Some questions on the present idelogical front]. *Hongqi*, no. 23 (1981): 1-15.

_____. "Observe Economic Laws, Speed Up the Four Modernizations." *Peking Review*, 10 November 1978, pp. 7-12.

Hua Sheng et al. "Weiguan jingji jichu de chungxin gouzao" [Reformation of micro economic basis]. *Jingji Yanjiu*, no. 3 (1986): 21-28.

Huntington, Samuel P. *The Third Wave: Democratization in the Late Twentieth Century*. Norman: University of Oklahoma Press, 1991.

_____. "One Soul at a Time: Political Science and Political Reform." *American Political Science Review* 82, no. 1 (March 1988): 3-10.

_____. "The Change to Change: Modernization, Development, and Politics." *Comparative Politics* 3, no. 3 (April 1971): 283-322.

_____. *Political Order in Changing Societies*. New Haven: Yale University Press, 1968.

Huntington, Samuel P., and Jorge I. Dominguez. "Political Development." In *Handbook of Political Science: Macropolitical Theory*, eds. Fred I. Greenstein and Nelson W. Polsby. Reading, Mass.: Addison-Wesley, 1975.

Huo Da. "Wan Jia You Le" [The sadness and happiness of thousands of households]. *Xinhua Wenzhai*, no. 3 (1987): 120-40.

Janos, Andrew C. *The Politics of Backwardness in Hungary: 1825-1945*. Princeton, N.J.: Princeton University Press, 1982.

Jiang Zemin. "Renzhen xiaochu shehui fenpei bugong xianxiang" [Seriously fight against the phenomenon of unfairness of social distribution]. *Xinhua Wenzhai*, no. 7-8 (1989): 55-58.

Jin Pei. "Yi gongping cujin xiaolu, yi xiaolu shixian gongping" [Use justice to promote efficiency, use efficiency to realize justice]. *Jingji Yanjiu*, no. 7 (1986): 78-82.

Jowitt, Kennth. *New World Disorder: The Leninist Extinction.* Berkeley: University of California Press, 1992.

Judt, Tony. "The Dilemmas of Dissidence: The Politics of Opposition in East-Central Europe." In *Crisis and Reform in Eastern Europe*, eds. Ferenc Feher and Andrew Arato. New Brunswick, N.J.: Transaction, 1991, pp. 253-301.

Keane, John, ed. *Civil Society and the State: New European Perspectives.* London: Verso, 1988.

Kelliher, Daniel. *Peasant Power in China: The Era of Rural Reform, 1979-1989.* New Haven: Yale University Press, 1992.

Kemenes, Egon. "The Enterprise and the National Economy." *New Hungarian Quarterly* 10, no. 36 (Autumn 1969): 61-76.

Kiss, Yudit. "Privatization Paradoxes in East Central Europe." *East European Politics and Societies* 8, no. 1 (Winter 1994): 122-52.

Kornai, Janos. "Transformational Recession: The Main Causes." *Journal of Comparative Economics* 19 (1994): 39-63.

_____. *The Socialist System: The Political Economy of Communism.* Princeton, N.J.: Princeton University Press, 1992.

_____. *The Road to a Free Economy: Shifting from a Socialist System.* New York: W. W. Norton, 1990.

_____. *Contradictions and Dilemmas: Studies on the Socialist Economy and Society.* Cambridge: The MIT Press, 1986.

_____. "The Hungarian Reform Process: Visions, Hopes, and Reality." *Journal of Economic Literature* 24, no. 3-4 (December 1986): 1687-1737.

_____. "The Dilemmas of a Socialist Economy: The Hungarian Experience." *Cambridge Journal of Economics* 4, no. 2 (1980): 147-57.

Kornhauser, William. *The Politics of Mass Society.* New York: The Free Press, 1959.

Kovrig, Bennett. *Communism in Hungary: From Kun to Kadar.* Stanford, Calif.: Hoover Institute Press, 1979.

_____. *The Hungarian People's Republic.* Baltimore: The Johns Hopkins University Press, 1970.

Kramer, Joseph C., and John T. Danylyk. "Economic Reform in Eastern Europe: Hungary at the Forefront." *East European Economic Assessment.* Part I. Joint Economic Committee, 97th Cong., 1st sess. Washington, D.C.: U.S. Government Printing Office, 1981, pp. 549-70.

Laki, M. "Competitive Situation and Product Pattern of Hungarian Enterprises on the Market of Consumer Goods." *Acta Oeconomica* 14, no. 2-3 (1975): 251-67.

Laky, T. "The Hidden Mechanisms of Recentralization in Hungary." *Acta Oeconomica* 24, no. 1-2 (1980): 95-109.

Lambilliotte, Maurice. "Humanism and Socialism." *New Hungarian Quarterly* 3, no. 9 (January-March 1963): 14-21.

Lampton, David M., ed. *Policy Implementation in Post-Mao China.* Berkeley: University of California Press, 1987.

Lardy, Nicholas. "The Role of Foreign Trade and Investment in China's Economic Transiformation." *China Quarterly*, no. 144 (December 1995): 1065-1082.

Laszlo, Leslie. "Religion and Nationality in Hungary." In *Religion and Nationalism in Soviet and East European Politics*, ed. Pedro Ramet. Durham and London: Duke University Press, 1989, pp. 286-98.

Lee, Chung H., and Helmut Reisen, eds. *From Reform to Growth: China and Other Countries in Transition in Asia and Central and Eastern Europe.* Paris: OECD, 1994.

Lee, Hong Yung. "Ideology, State and Society in China." *Journal of International Affairs* 39, no. 2 (Winter 1986): 77-90.

Lee, Peter Nan-shong. "Enterprise Autonomy Policy in Post-Mao China: A case study of policy-making, 1978-83." *China Quarterly*, no. 105 (March 1986): 45-71.

Lendvai, Parl. *Hungary: The Art of Survival.* London: I. B. Tauris, 1988.

Lerner, Daniel. *The Passing of Traditional Society.* New York: The Free Press, 1958.

Li Chungguang, "Zhengzhi wenti yingdang ziyou taolun" [Political issues are subject to free discussion]. *Xinhua Wenzhai*, no. 10 (1986): 19-20.

Li Shaomin. "Tongxian ziyou zhi lu" [A path to freedom]. *Zhongguo Zi Chun* 56 (January 1988): 36-39.

Li, Yunqi. "China's Inflation." *Asian Survey* 29, no. 7 (July 1989): 655-68.

Lieberthal, Kenneth, ed. *Bureaucracy, Politics, and Decision Making in Post-Mao China.* Berkeley: University of California Press, 1992.

Lin, Yu-Sheng. *The Crisis of Chinese Consciousness: Radical Antitraditionalism in the May Fourth Era.* Madison: The University of Wisconsin Press, 1979.

Lin Zili. "Shehuizhuyi jingji tiaojie lilun tantao" [Explore the theory of socialist economic coordination]. *Jingji Yanjiu*, no. 11 (1980): 19-32.

Lindblom, Charles. *Politics and Market.* New York: Basic Books, 1977.

Ling Zhijun, "Qiantan bashiniandai de zhongguo baoye" [On the Chinese newspapers in the 80s]. *Renmin Ribao* (overseas edition), 21 June 1986, p. 2.

Link, Perry, ed. *Unofficial China.* Boulder, Colo.: Westview Press, 1988.

_____. "Intellectuals and Cultural Policy After Mao." In *Modernizing China: Post-Mao Reform and Development*, eds. A. Doak Barnett and Ralph N. Clough. Boulder, Colo.: Westview Press, 1986, pp. 81-102.

_____, ed. *Stubborn Weeds: Popular and Controversial Chinese Literature after the Cultural Revolution*. Bloomington: Indiana University Press, 1983.

Lipset, Seymour M. "Some Social Requisites of Democracy." *American Political Science Review* 53 (1959): 69-105.

Liu Binyan, with Ruan Ming and Xu Gang. Trans. by Henry L. Epstein. *Tell the World: What Happened in China and Why*. New York: Random House, 1989.

_____. "Dierzhong zhongcheng" [The second kind of loyalty]. *Fazhi Wenxue*, May 1985.

_____. "People or Monsters?" In *People or Monsters?* ed. Perry Link. Bloomington: Indiana University Press, 1983.

Liu Chengrui, Hu Naiwu, and Yu Guanghua, "Jijua he shichang xiangjiehe shi woguo jingji guanli gaige the jiben tujing" [The integration of planning and market is the basic path for our reform of economic management]. *Jingji Yanjiu*, no. 7 (1979): 37-46.

Liu Guoguang. "Guanyu suojouzhi guanxi gaige de ruogan wenti" [Several questions on ownership reform]. *Xinhua Wenzhai*, no. 3 (1986): 66-69.

_____. "Luelun jihua tiaojie yu shichang tiaojie de jige wenti" [On some questions of plan coordination and market coordination]. *Jingji Yanjiu*, no. 10 (1980): 3-11.

Liu Guoguang and Wang Ruisun. "Restructuring of the Economy" In *China's Socialist Modernization*, ed. Yu Guangyuan. Beijing: Foreign Languages Press, 1984.

Liu Jiazhen. "Woguo liyong waizi de huigu yu zhanwang" [Retrospect and prospect of the utilization of foreign investment in our country]. *Renmin Ribao*. 28 February 1990, p. 2.

Liu Zhiguang and Wang Suli. "Cong qunzhong shehui zouxian gongmin shehui" [From mass society to citizen society]. *Xinhua Wenzhai*, no. 11 (1988): 9-12.

Lomax, Bill. "The Hungarian Revolution of 1956 and the Origins of the Kadar Regime." *Studies in Comparative Communism* 18, no. 2-3 (Summer/Autumn 1985): 87-113.

_____. "Hungary: The Quest for Legitamacy." In *Eastern Europe: Political Crisis and Legitimation*, ed. Paul G. Lewis. London and Sydney: Croom Helm, 1984.

Lowenthal, Richard. "The Ruling Party in a Mature Society." In *Social Consequences of Modernization in Communist Societies*, ed. Mark D. Field. Baltimore: The Johns Hopkins University Press, 1976, pp. 81-118.

Lu Tao and Wang Bing. "SOS, linghun de jinji hujiao" [Emergency call from souls]. *Zhongguo Qingnian*, July 1988, pp. 28-29.

Lu Yun. "China Speeds Up Democratization." *Beijing Review*, 20 April 1987, p. 18.

Maroti, Lajos. "The Building of Socialism on a Higher Level." *New Hungarian Quarterly* 12, no. 44 (Winter 1971): 3-25.

Martin, Helmut. *Cult and Canon: The Origins and Development of State Maoism*. New York: M. E. Sharpe, 1982.

Marx, Karl. "A Contribution to the Critique of Political Economy." In *The Marx-Engels Reader*. 2nd ed. ed. Robert Tucker. New York: W. W. Norton, 1978, pp. 3-6.

McCord, William. *The Springtime of Freedom: Evolution of Developing Societies*. New York: Oxford University Press, 1965.

McCormick, Barrett L. "Leninist Implementation: The Election Campaign." In *Policy Implementation in Post-Mao China*, ed. David M. Lampton. Berkeley: University of California Press, 1987, pp. 383-413.

McDonald, Jason. "Transition to Utopia: A Reinterpretation of Economics, Ideas, and Politics in Hungary, 1984 to 1990." *East European Politics and Societies* 7, no. 2 (1993): 203-239.

Meaney, Connie Squires. "Market Reform and Disintegrative Corruption in Urban China." In *Reform and Reaction in Post-Mao China: The Road to Tiananmen*, ed. Richard Baum. New York: Routledge, 1991, pp. 124-42.

_____. "Market Reform in a Leninist System: Some Trends in the Distribution of Power, Status, and Money in Urban China." *Studies in Comparative Communism* 22, no. 2/3 (Summer/Autumn 1989): 203-20.

Mesa-Lago, Carmelo, and Carl Beck, eds. *Comparative Socialist Systems: Essays on Politics and Economics*. Pittsburgh: University of Pittsburgh Center for International Studies, 1975.

Meyer, Alfred G. "The Functions of Ideology in the Soviet Political System." *Soviet Studies* 18, no. 1 (January 1966): 273-85.

Miao Qiming. "Lun shehuizhuji wenming de sanweijiegou" [On the three-dimensional structure of socialist civilization]. *Xinhua Wenzhai*, no. 2 (1986): 5-7.

Mihalyi, Peter. "Plunder—Squander—Plunder: The Strange Demise of State Ownership." *Hungarian Quarterly* 34, no. 130 (Summer 1993): 62-75.

Mizsei, Kalman. "Totalitarianism, Reforms, Second Economy: Logics of Changes in the East European Economic Systems." Manuscript, 1986.

Moody, Peter R. Jr. *Chinese Politics After Mao: Development and Liberalization 1976-1983*. New York: Praeger, 1983.

Myers, James T. "China—The 'Germ' of Modernization." *Asian Survey* 25, no. 10 (October 1985): 981-997.

Nathan, Andrew J. *China's Crisis*. New York: Columbia University Press, 1990.

_____. "Chinese Democracy in 1989: Continuity and Change." *Problems of Communism* 38 (September/October 1989): 16-29.

_____. *Chinese Democracy*. New York: Alfred A. Knopf, 1985.

Naughton, Barry. *Growing Out of the Plan*. New York: Cambridge University Press, 1995.

_____. "The Dangers of Economic Complacency." *Current History* 95 (September 1996): 260-65.

_____. "China's Macroeconomy in Transition." *China Quarterly*, no. 144 (December 1995): 1083-1104.

_____. "Reforming a Planned Economy: Is China Unique?" In *From Reform to Growth: China and Other Countries in Transition in Asia and Central and Eastern Europe*, eds. Chung H. Lee and Helmut Reisen. Paris: OECD, 1994, pp. 49-74.

Nolan, Peter, and Robert F. Ash. "China's Economy on the Eve of Reform." *China Quarterly*, no. 144 (December 1995): 980-98.

Nove, Alec. *The Economics of Feasible Socialism*. London: George Allen & Unwin, 1983.

Nyers, Rezso. "Interrelations between Policy and the Economic Reform in Hungary." *Journal of Comparative Economics* 7 (1983): 211-24.

_____. "The Interaction of Political and Economic Development in Hungary." *New Hungarian Quarterly* 23, no. 85 (Spring 1982): 15-25.

_____. "The Effiency of the Intellectual Resource." *New Hungarian Quarterly* 23, no. 87 (Autumn 1982): 36-44.

_____. "Small Enterprises in Socialist Hungary." *Acta Oeconomica* 25, no. 1-2 (1980): 147-62.

_____. "Social and Political Effects of the New Economic Mechanism." *New Hungarian Quarterly* 10, no. 34 (Summer 1969): 3-24.

_____. "The Hungarian Economy in the Seventies." *New Hungarian Quarterly* 15, no. 53 (Spring 1974): 7-12.

_____. "Efficiency and Socialist Democracy." *Acta Oeconomica* 37, no. 1-2 (1986): 1-13.

_____. "The Comprehensive Reform of Managing the National Economy in Hungary." *Acta Oeconomica* 1 (1966): 19-36.

O'Brien, Kevin. *Reform without Liberalization: China's National People's Congress and the Politics of Institutional Change*. New York: Cambridge University Press, 1990.

_____. "China's National People's Congress: Reform and Its Limits." *Legislative Studies Quarterly* 13, no. 3 (August 1988): 343-74.

O'Donnell, Guillermo, and Philippe Schmitter, eds. *Transitions from Authoritarian Rule: Tentative Conclusions about Uncertain Democracies*. Baltimore: The Johns Hopkins University Press, 1986.

O'Donnell, Guillermo, Philippe Schmitter, and Laurence Whitehead, eds. *Transitions from Authoritarian Rule: Prospects for Democracy*. Baltimore: The Johns Hopkins University Press, 1986.

O'Relley, Z. Edward. "Hungarian Agricultural Performance and Policy during the NEM." *East European Economics Post-Helsinki*. Joint Economic Committee, 95th Cong., 1st sess. Washington, D.C.: U.S. Government Printing Office, 1977, pp. 356-78.

Oi, Jean C. "The Role of the Local State in China's Transitional Economy." *China Quarterly*, no. 144 (December 1995): 1132-1149.

_____. "Fiscal Reform and the Economic Foundations of Local State Corporatism in China." *World Politics* 45 (October): 99-126.

_____. *State and Peasant in Contemporary China: The Political Economy of Village Government*. Berkeley: University of California Press, 1989.

_____. "Commercializing China's Rural Cadres." *Problems of Communism* 35 (September/October 1986): 1-15.

Oksenberg, Michel. "China's 13th Party Congress." *Problems of Communism* 36 (November/December 1987): 1-17.

Oksenberg, Michel, Lawrence Sullivan, and Marc Lambert, eds. *Beijing Spring, 1989: Confrontation and Conflict*. New York: M. E. Sharpe, 1990.

Oldnam, John R., ed. *China's Legal Development*. New York: M. E. Sharpe, 1986.

O'Neil, Patrick. "Hungary's Hesitant Transition." *Current History* 95 (March 1996): 135-39.

Orleans, Leo A. *Chinese Students in America: Policies, Issues, and Numbers*. Washington, D.C.: National Academy Press, 1988.

_____, ed. *Science in Contemporary China*. Stanford, Calif.: Stanford University Press, 1980.

Packenham, Robert A. *Liberal America and the Third World: Political Development Ideas in Foreign Aid and Social Science*. Princeton, N. J.: Princeton University Press, 1973.

Parkin, Frank. *Class Inequality and Political Order*. London: Paladin, 1975.

Pei, Minxin. "Microfoundations of State-Socialism and Patterns of Economic Transformation." *Communist and Post-Communist Studies* 29, no. 2 (1996): 131-45.

Pelczynski, Z. A. "Solidarity and 'the Re-birth of Civil Society' in Poland." In *Civil Society and the State: New European Perspectives*, ed. John Keane. London: Verso, 1988, pp. 367-80.

Perkins, Dwight H. "The Prospects for China's Economic Reforms." In *Modernizing China: Post-Mao Reform and Development*, eds. A. Doak Barnett and Ralph N. Clough. Boulder: Westview Press, 1986.

Perkins, Dwight, and Shahid Yusuf. *Rural Development in China*. Baltimore: The Johns Hopkins University Press for the World Bank, 1984.

Perry, Elizabeth, and Ellen Fuller. "China's Long March to Democracy." *World Policy Journal* 8, no. 4 (Fall 1991): 663-85.

Perry, Elizabeth, and Christine Wong, eds. *The Political Economy of Reform in Post-Mao China*. Cambridge: Harvard University Press, 1985.

Pitkin, Hanna Fenichel, ed. *Representation*. New York: Atherton Press, 1969.

Pokol, Bela. "Changes in the System of Political Representation in Hungary." In *Economy and Society in Hungary*, eds. Andorka Rudolf and Laszlo Bertalan. Budapest: Karl Marx University of Economic Sciences, Department of Sociology, 1986, pp. 267-86.

Polanyi, Karl. *The Great Transformation*. New York: Rinehart, 1944.

Portes, Richard. "Hungary: Economic Performance, Policy and Prospects." *East European Economics Post Helsinki*. Joint Economic Committee, 95th Cong., 1st sess. Washington, D.C.: U.S. Government Printing Office, 1977, pp. 766-815.

————. "Economic Reforms in Hungary." *American Economic Review: Papers and Proceedings* 60 (1970): 307-313.

Poznanski, Kazimierz. "An Interpretation of Communist Decay: The Role of Evolutionary Mechanisms." *Communist and Post-Communist Studies* 26, no. 1 (March 1993): 3-24.

————. "Economic Adjustment and Political Forces: Poland Since 1979." In *Power, Purpose and Collective Choice: Economic Strategy in Socialist States*, eds. Ellen Comisso and Laura Tyson. Ithaca, N.Y.: Cornell University Press, 1986, pp. 279-312.

Pozsgay, Imre. "The Interaction of Economics and Politics." *New Hungarian Quarterly* 20, no. 76 (Winter 1979): 17-26.

————. "Socialist Society and Humanism." *New Hungarian Quarterly* 19, no. 70 (Summer 1978): 10-30.

Prybyla, Jan S. "China's Economic Experiment: Back from the Market?" *Problems of Communism* 38 (January-February 1989): 1-18.

————. "Mainland China and Hungary: To Market, To Market..." *Issues and Studies* 23, no. 1 (January 1987): 43-85.

Przeworski, Adam. *Democracy and the Market: Political and Economic Reforms in Eastern Europe and Latin America*. Cambridge: Cambridge University Press, 1991.

Pye, Lucian. *Asian Power and Politics: The Cultural Dimensions of Authority*. Cambridge, Mass.: Belknap Press, 1985.

Qi Dajun. "Binrugaohuang de fuhua" [Incurable corruption]. *Zhongguo Zhi Chun*, no. 81 (February 1990): 37-39.

Qian, Yingyi, and Chenggang Xu, "Why China's Economic Reforms Differ: The M-Form Hierarchy and Entry Expansion of the Non-State Sector." *Economics of Transformation* 1, no. 2 (1993): 135-70.

Qin Xiaoying. "Shehuizhuyi minzhu ye yinggai baokuo shaoshu yuanze" [Socialist democracy should include minority principle]. *Xinhua Wenzhai*, no. 12 (1988): 12-15.

Racz, Barnabas. *The Hungarian Parliament in Transition: Procedure and Politics*. Pittsburgh: University of Pittsburgh Center for Russian and East European Studies, 1989.

_____. "Political Participation and the Expanding Role of the Hungarian Legislature." *East European Quarterly* 22, no. 4 (January 1989): 459-93.

_____. "The Parliamentary Infrastructure and Political Reforms in Hungary." *Soviet Studies* 41, no. 1 (January 1989): 39-66.

_____. "The Socialist-Left Opposition in Post-Communist Hungary." *Europe-Asia Studies* 45, no. 4 (1993): 647-70.

Racz, Barnabas, and Istvan Kukorelli. "The 'Second-Generation' Post-Communist Elections in Hungary in 1994." *Europe-Asia Studies* 47, no. 2 (1995): 251-79.

Rakowska-Harmstone, Teresa, and Andrew Gyorgy, eds. *Communism in Eastern Europe*. Bloomington: Indiana University Press, 1979.

Ramet, Sabrina P. "Eastern Europe's Painful Transition." *Current History* 95 (March 1996): 97-102.

Ranki, Gyorgy. "The Introduction and Evolution of Planning in Hungary." In *Market Reforms in Socialist Societies: Comparing China and Hungary*, ed. Peter Van Ness. Boulder, Colo.: Lynne Rienner Publishers, 1989, pp. 31-51.

Reddaway, P. B. "Aspects of Ideological Belief in the Soviet Union." *Soviet Studies* 18, no. 2 (April 1966): 473-83.

Renyi, Peter. "Socialism and Reform." *New Hungarian Quarterly* 24, no. 91 (Autumn 1983): 43-56.

Revesz, Gabor. *Perestroika In Eastern Europe: Hungary's Economic Transformation, 1945-1988*. Boulder, Colo.: Westview Press, 1990.

Rigby, T. H., and Ferenc Feher, eds. *Political Legitimation in Communist States*. London: Macmillan, 1982.

Robert, Pierre. "Let 2,970 Flowers Blossom: The Seventh NPC." *China News Analysis*, 15 May 1988.

Robinson, William. *The Pattern of Reform in Hungary: A Political, Economic, and Cultural Analysis*. New York: Praeger, 1973.

_____. "Hegedus, His Views and His Critics." *Studies in Comparative Communism* 2, no. 2 (Autumn 1969): 121-52.

Ron Jian and Fan Henshan. "Lun suoyouzhi de kaifang" [On ownership openness]. *Xinhua Wenzhai*, no. 4 (1989): 36-39.

Rona-Tas, Akos. "The Second Economy as a Subversive Force: The Erosion of Party Power in Hungary." In *The Waning of the Communist State: Economic Origins of Political Decline in China and Hungary*, ed. Andrew Walder. Berkeley: University of California Press, 1995, pp. 61-86.

Rosen, Stanley. "Value Change Among Post-Mao Youth: The Evidence from Survey Data." In *Unofficial China: Popular Culture and Thought in the People's Republic*, eds. Perry Link et. al. Boulder, Colo.: Westview Press, 1989, pp. 193-216.

_____. "Public Opinion and Reform in the People's Republic of China." *Studies in Comparative Communism* 22, no. 2/3 (Summer/Autumn 1989): 153-70.

_____. "Prosperity, Privatization, and China's Youth." *Problems of Communism* 34 (March/April 1985): 1-28.

Rosenbaum, Arthur Lewis, ed. *State and Society in China: The Consequences of Reform*. Boulder, Colo.: Westview Press, 1992.

Ross, Lester. "The Changing Profile of Dispute Resolution in Rural China: The Case of Zouping County, Shandong." *Stanford Journal of International Law* 26, no. 1 (Fall 1989): 15-66.

Rowe, William. "The Public Sphere in Modern China." *Modern China* 16, no. 3 (July 1990): 309-329.

Rozman, Gilbert et al., eds. *Dismantling Communism: Common Causes and Regional Variations*. Baltimore: The Johns Hopkins University Press, 1992.

Rustow, Dankwart. "Transitions of Democracy: Toward a Dynamic Model." *Comparative Politics* 2, no. 3 (April 1970): 337-63.

Sabel, Charles F., and David Stark. "Planning, Politics, and Shop-Floor Power: Hidden Forms of Bargaining in Soviet-Imposed State-Socialist Societies." *Politics and Society* 11 (1982): 439-75.

Sachs, Jeffrey, and Wing Thye Woo. "Structural Factors in the Economic Reforms of China, Eastern Europe, and the Former Soviet Union." *Economic Policy* 18, no. 1 (1994): 102-145.

Saich, Tony, ed. *The Chinese People's Movement: Perspectives on Spring 1989*. New York: M. E. Sharpe, 1990.

Sampson, Steven. "The Informal Sector in Eastern Europe." *Telos* 66 (1986): 44-66.

Scarrow, Howard. "The Scope of Comparative Analysis." *Journal of Politics* 25, no. 3 (1963): 565-77.

Schell, Orville. *Discos and Democracy: China in the Throes of Reform*. New York: Pantheon Books, 1988.

Schmitter, Philippe. "Still the Century of Corporatism?" *Review of Politics* 36 (January 1974): 85-31.

Schopflin, George. "Conservatism and Hungary's Transition." *Problems of Communism* 40 (January-April 1991): 60-68.

_____. "Hungarian People's Republic." In *Marxist Governments: A World Survey*. Vol.2, ed. Bogdan Szajkowski. London: Macmillan, 1981.

_____. "Opposition and Para-Opposition: Critical Currents in Hungary, 1968-1978." In *Opposition in Eastern Europe*, ed. Rudolf L. Tokes. Baltimore: The Johns Hopkins University Press, 1979.

Schram, Stuart R. "Economics in Command? Ideology and Policy since the Third Plenum, 1978-84." *China Quarterly*, no. 99 (September 1984): 417-61.

Schurmann, Franz. *Ideology and Organization in Communist China*. Berkeley: University of California Press, 1968.

Schweitzer, I. "Ten Years of the Development of Economics in Hungary." *Acta Oeconomica* 3 (1968): 335-42.

Selucky, Radoslav. Trans. Zdenek Elias. *Economic Reform in Eastern Europe: Political Background and Economic Significance*. New York: Praeger, 1972.

Seymour, James. *The Fifth Modernization: China's Human Rights Movement, 1978-1979*. New York: Human Rights Publishing Group, 1980.

_____. *China's Satellite Parties*. New York: M. E. Sharpe, 1987.

Shen, Xiaofang. "A Decade of Direct Foreign Investment in China." *Problems of Communism* 39 (March-April 1990): 61-74.

Shi, Tianjian. "Role Culture of Deputies to the Seventh National People's Congress, 1988." Paper prepared for the annual meeting of the Association for Asian Studies. Washington, D.C., March 1989.

Shirk, Susan. *The Political Logic of Economic Reform in China*. Berkeley: University of California Press, 1993.

Shue, Vivienne. *The Reach of the State: Sketches of the Chinese Body Politic*. Stanford: Stanford University Press, 1988.

Sik, Ota. *The Third Way*. Trans. Marian Sling. London: Wildwood House, 1976.

Skocpol, Theda. "Bringing the State Back In: Strategies of Analysis in Current Research." In *Bringing the State Back In*, eds. Peter Evans, Dietrich Rueschemeyer, and Theda Skocpol. Cambridge: Cambridge University Press, 1985, pp. 3-37.

_____. *States and Social Revolution: A Comparative Analysis of France, Russia, and China*. Cambridge: Cambridge University Press, 1979.

Solinger, Dorothy. "Democracy with Chinese Characteristics." *World Policy Journal* 6, no. 4 (Fall 1989): 621-32.

_____. *Chinese Business Under Socialism: The Politics of Domestic Commerce, 1949-1980*. Berkeley: University of California Press, 1984.

Soloman, Susan G., ed. *Pluralism in the Soviet Union*. New York: St. Martin's Press, 1982.

Stark, David. "The Micropolitics of the Firm and the Macropolitics of Reform: New Forms of Workplace Bargaining in Hungarian Enterprises." In *State Versus Markets in the World-System*. Vol. 8 of *Political Economy of the World-System Annuals*, eds. Peter Evans, Dietrich Rueschemeyer, and Evelyne Huber Stephens. Beverly Hills: Sage, 1985, pp. 247-73.

Starr, Frederick. "Soviet Union: A Civil Society." *Foreign Policy* 70 (Spring 1988): 26-41.

Starr, John Bryan. "Redefining Chinese Socialism." *Current History* 83 (September 1984): 265-68, 275-76, 280-81.

_____. *Ideology and Culture: An Introduction to the Dialectic of Contemporary Chinese Politics*. New York: Harper & Row, 1973.

Stavis, Benedict. "The Political Economy of Inflation in China." *Studies in Comparative Communism* 22, no. 2/3 (Summer/Autumn 1989): 235-50.

Stepan, Alfred. "State Power and the Strength of Civil Society in the Southern Cone of Latin America." In *Bringing the State Back In*, eds. Peter Evens, Dietrich Rueschemeyer, and Theda Skocpol. Cambridge: Cambridge University Press, 1985, pp. 317-43.

Stigler, George. *The Citizen and the State: Essays on Regulation*. Chicago: University of Chicago Press, 1975.

Strand, David. "Protest in Beijing: Civil Society and Public Sphere in China." *Problems of Communism* 39 (May-June 1990): 1-17.

Su Shaozhi. *Democratization and Reform*. Nottingham, England: Spokesman, 1988.

Su Wei. "Nage chuntian de gushi" [The story of that spring]. *Zhongguo Zhi Chun*, no. 110 (July 1992): 9-12.

Sullivan, Lawrence. "The Emergence of Civil Society in China, Spring 1989." In *The Chinese People's Movement: Perspectives on Spring 1989*, ed. Tony Saich. New York: M. E. Sharpe, 1990, pp. 126-44.

Sullivan, Michael J. "The Impact of Western Political Thought in Chinese Political Discourse on Transition from Leninism, 1986-1992." *World Affairs* 157, no. 2 (Fall 1994): 79-91.

Sulyok, Bela. "First Experiences with the Economic Reform." *New Hungarian Quarterly* 12, no. 44 (Winter 1971): 49-62.

Sun, Yan. *The Chinese Reassessment of Socialism, 1976-1992*. Princeton, N.J.: Princeton University Press, 1995.

_____. "The Chinese and Soviet Reassessment of Socialism: The Theoretical Bases of Reform and Revolution in Communist Regimes." *Communist and Post-Communist Studies* 27, no. 1 (1994): 39-58.

Swain, Nigel. *Hungary: The Rise and Fall of Feasible Socialism*. London: Verso, 1992.

Szamuely, L. "The Second Wave of the Economic Mechanism Debate and the 1968 Reform in Hungary." *Acta Oeconomica* 33, no. 1-2 (1984): 43-67.

Szekely, Istvan P., and David G. Newbery, eds. *Hungary: An Economy in Transition*. New York: Cambridge University Press, 1992.

Szelenyi, Ivan. *Urban Inequalities under State Socialism*. New York: Oxford University Press, 1983.

Szelenyi, Ivan, and Robert Manchin. "Social Policy Under State Socialism: Market Redistribution and Social Inequalities in East European Socialist Societies." In *Stagnation and Renewal in Social Policy: The Rise and Fall of Policy Regimes*, eds. Martin Rein, Gosta Esping-Andersen, and Lee Rainwater. New York: M. E. Sharpe, 1987, pp. 102-139.

Szolboszlai, G. Y. *Politics and Political Science in Hungary*. Budapest: HSWP Institute for Social Sciences, 1982.

Szorcsik, Sandor. "Social Sciences, Political Science and Societal Practice." In *Politics and Political Science in Hungary*, ed. G. Y. Szoboszlai. Budapest: HSWP Institute for Social Sciences, 1982, pp. 247-63.

Sztompka, Piotr. "The Intangibles and Imponderables of the Transition to Democracy." *Studies in Comparative Communism* 24, no. 3 (1991): 295-311.

Tardos, Marton. "Economic Organizations and Ownership." *Acta Oeconomica* 40, no. 1-2 (1989): 17-37.

Tian Sansong. "Election of Deputies to a County People's Congress." *Beijing Review.* 25 February 1980, pp. 11-19.

Tismaneanu, Vladimir, ed. *In Search of Civil Society: Independent Peace Movements in the Soviet Bloc.* New York: Routledge, 1990.

To, Lee Lai. *Trade Unions in China: 1949 to the Present.* Singapore: National University of Singapore Press, 1986.

Toma, Peter A. *Socialist Authority: The Hungarian Experience.* New York: Praeger, 1988.

Toma, Peter A., and Ivan Volgyes. *Politics in Hungary.* San Francisco: W. H. Freeman and Company, 1977.

Tong Dalin. "Gufenhua shi shehuizhuyi qiye de yige xinjidian" [Stockification is a new supporting point for socialist enterprises]. *Xinhua Wenzhai*, no. 10 (1986): 63-64.

Tong, Yanqi. "State, Society, and Political Change in China and Hungary." *Comparative Politics* 26, no. 3 (April 1994): 333-53.

_____. "Mass Alienation Under State Socialism and After." *Communist and Post-Communist Studies* 28, no. 2 (1995): 215-37.

Tsou, Tang. *The Cultural Revolution and Post-Mao Reforms: A Historical Perspective.* Chicago: University of Chicago Press, 1986.

Tyson, Laura D'Andrea. "Aggregate Economic Difficulties and Workers' Welfare." In *Blue-Collar Workers in Eastern Europe*, eds. Jan Triska and Charles Gati. London: George Allen & Unwin, 1981.

Urban, Laszlo. "Hungary in Transition: The Emergence of Opposition Parties." *Telos* 79 (Spring 1989): 108-118.

Vajda, I. "Economic Science in Hungary and the 'Acta Oeconomica'." *Acta Oeconomica* 1 (1966): 3-17.

Van Ness, Peter, ed. *Market Reforms in Socialist Societies: Comparing China and Hungary.* Boulder, Colo.: Lynne Rienner Publishers, 1989.

Verba, Sidney, Norman H. Nie, and Jae-on Kim. *Participation and Political Equality.* Cambridge: Cambridge University Press, 1978.

Volgyes, Ivan, ed. *Political Socialization in Eastern Europe: A Comparative Framework.* New York: Praeger, 1975.

_____. "Dynamic Change: Rural Transformation, 1945-1975." In *Modernization of Agriculture: Rural Transformation in Hungary, 1848-1975*, ed. Joseph Held. New York: Columbia University Press, 1980, pp. 351-508.

_____. "The Impact of Modernization on Political Development." In *The Politics of Modernization in Eastern Europe*, ed. Charles Gati. New York: Praeger, 1974, pp. 328-37.

Volgyes, Ivan, and Mary Volgyes. *Czechoslovakia, Hungary, Poland: Cross-roads of Change*. New York: Thomas Nelson, 1970.

Voszka, Eva. "Spontaneous Privatization In Hungary." In *Transition to a Market Economy*, eds. John Earle, Roman Flydwarz, and Andrzej Rapaczyuski. New York: St. Martins Press, 1993, pp. 89-107.

Wakeman, Frederick. "The Price of Autonomy: Intellectuals in Ming and Ch'ing Politics." *Daedalus* 101 (Spring 1972): 35-70.

Walder, Andrew. "China's Transitional Economy: Interpreting its Significance." *China Quarterly*, no. 144 (December 1995): 963-79.

_____, ed. *The Waning of the Communist State: Economic Origins of Political Decline in China and Hungary*. Berkeley: University of California Press, 1995.

_____. "Workers, Managers and the State: The Reform Era and the Political Crisis of 1989." *China Quarterly*, no. 127 (1991): 468-70.

_____. "The Political Sociology of the Beijing Upheaval of 1989." *Problems of Communism* 38 (September-October 1989): 30-40.

_____. *Communist Neo-Traditionalism*. Berkeley: University of California Press, 1986.

Walder, Andrew, and Gong Xiaoxia. "Workers in the Tiananmen Protests: The Politics of the Beijing Workers' Autonomous Federation." *Australian Journal of Chinese Affairs*, no. 29 (January 1993): 1-29.

Wang Dingkun, and Wang Yuanjing. "Dui gongyouzhi de chongxin dingyi" [The redefinition of public ownership]. *Xinhua Wenzhai*, no. 1 (1989): 48-50.

Wang, Shaoguang. "The Rise of the Regions: Fiscal Reform and the Decline of Central State Capacity in China." In *The Waning of the Communist State: Economic Origins of Political Decline in China and Hungary*, ed. Andrew Walder. Berkeley: University of California Press, 1995, pp. 87-113.

Wang Ying et al., *Shehui Zhongjianceng: gaige yu zhongguo de shetuan zuzhi* [Middle layer of the society: reform and China's social organizations]. Beijing: China Development Press, 1993.

Wang Zhaojun. "Rongjie: zhongguo shehui de fei zhengzhihua" [Melting: the depoliticization of Chinese society]. *Zhongguo Zhi Chun*, no. 127 (March-April 1994): 59-62.

Wei Qun, and Duan Yue. "Yinmi wangguo zhong de jige wenti: zoufan zhongguo shehui diaozha sitong" [Several questions in the hidden kingdom: a visit to China's social survey system]. *Zhongguo Qingnian*, November 1987, pp. 12-14.

White, Gordon. "Prospects for Civil Society in China: A Case Study of Xiaoshan City." *Australian Journal of Chinese Affairs*, no. 29 (January 1993): 63-87.

————. "The Politics of Economic Reform in Chinese Industry: The Introduction of the Labour Contract System." *China Quarterly*, no. 111 (September 1987): 365-89.

White, Stephen. "Economic Performance and Communist Legitimacy." *World Politics* 38, no. 3 (April 1986): 462-82.

Whyte, Martin King. "Social Trends in China: The Triumph of Inequality?" In *Modernizing China: Post-Mao Reform and Development*, eds. A. Doak Barnett, and Ralph N. Clough. Boulder, Colo.: Westview Press, 1986, pp. 103-123.

————. "Urban China: A Civil Society in the Making?" In *State and Society in China: The Consequences of Reform*, ed. Arthur Lewis Rosenbaum. Boulder, Colo.: Westview Press, 1992, pp. 103-120.

————. "The Social Roots of China's Economic Development." *China Quarterly*, no. 144 (December 1995): 999-1019.

Wilson, Jeanne L. "'The Polish Lesson': China and Poland 1980-1990." *Studies in Comparative Communism* 23, no. 3/4 (Autumn/Winter 1990): 259-79.

Womack, Brantly. "The 1980 County-Level Elections in China: Experiment in Democratic Modernization." *Asian Survey* 22, no. 3 (March 1982): 261-77.

World Bank. *Hungary: Structural Reforms for Sustainable Growth*. Washington, D.C.: World Bank, 1995.

Wu Guoguang, and Gao Shan. "Cujing women shehuizhuyi minzhu zhengzhi de zhiduhua" [Promoting the Institutionalization of Our Socialist Democratic Politics]. *Hongqi*, no. 21 (1987): 43-48.

Wu Jiaxiang. "Xin quanwei zhuyi shuping" [On neo-authoritarianism]. *Shijie Jingji Daobao*, 16 January 1989.

————. "Guanyu xinquanwei zhuyi de taolun" [Discussions on neo-authoritarianism]. *Xinhua Wenzhai*, no. 4 (1989): 1-9.

Wu Jinglian. "Choice of Strategy in China's Economic Reform." Paper presented at the annual meeting of the American Economics Association. Chicago, December 1987.

Wu Xiaoming, Yu Wujin, and Zhou Yicheng. "Lun xueshu ziyou" [On academic freedom]. *Xinhua Wenzhai*, no. 3 (1985): 5-6.

Wu, Yu-Shan. "The Linkage Between Economic and Political Reform in the Socialist Countries: A Supply-Side Explanation." *ANNALS* 507 (January 1990): 91-102.

————. *Comparative Economic Transformations: Mainland China, Hungary, the Soviet Union, and Taiwan*. Stanford, Calif.: Stanford University Press, 1994.

Yan Jiaqi. "Cong feichengxu zhengzhi zouxiang chengxu zhengzhi" [From non-procedural politics to procedural politics]. *Xinhua Wenzhai*, no. 10 (1988): 1-5.

Yang, Mayfair Mei-hui. "Between State and Society: The Construction of Corporateness in a Chinese Socialist Factory." *Australian Journal of Chinese Affairs*, no. 22 (July 1989): 31-60.

Yang, Winston, and Marsha Wagner, eds. *Tiananmen: China's Struggle for Democracy, Its Prelude, Development, Aftermath, and Impact*. Baltimore: University of Maryland Press, 1990.

Yang Xiaobing. "NPC: Its Position and Role." *Beijing Review*, 30 March 1987, p. 20.

Yu, Mok Chiu, and J. Frank. Harrison. *Voices from Tiananmen Square: Beijing Spring and the Democracy Movement*. New York: Black Rose Books, 1990.

Zhang Boli, "Cong jueshi dao fushi" [Hunger strike from beginning to the end]. *Zhongguo Zhi Chun*, no. 127 (March/April 1994): 72-76; and no. 128 (May 1994): 45-48.

Zhang Shuyi. "Statism—the Root Cause of All Defects of the Old System." *Shijie Jingji Daobao*, 15 August 1988, p. 15. Text from FBIS-CHI-88-170. 1 September 1988, pp. 21-24.

Zhao Jun. "Zhongguo zhengtan zhinang xinshengdai" [New generation of think-tanks on China's political arena]. *Zhongguo Zhi Chun*, no. 75 (August 1989): 45-47.

Zhong Dong. "Lun siyouzhi he gongyouzhi de gongneng hubu" [On the function of mutual compensation of private and public ownership]. *Xinhua Wenzhai*, no. 4 (1989): 40-43.

Zhou Weimin, and Lu Zhongyuan. "Xiaolu youxian, jiangu gongping" [Efficiency first, and take justice into consideration at the same time]. *Jingji Yanjiu*, no. 2 (1986): 30-37.

Zweig, David. "Prosperity and Conflict in Post-Mao Rural China." *China Quarterly*, no. 105 (March 1986): 1-18.

————. "Opposition to Change in Rural China." *Asian Survey* 23, no. 7 (July 1983): 879-900.

INDEX

ABOUT THE AUTHOR

Yanqi Tong studied at the Department of International Politics, Peking University in China and earned a BA degree in 1982. She received her MA and Ph.D. degrees in political science from the Johns Hopkins University in 1986 and 1991. She is currently an assistant professor of political science at the University of Utah.